"Yoder's approach can be applied to many different disciplines. What's required is careful planning, hard work and patience."

—*Miami Herald*

"… excellent, profitable, and highly recommended supplemental reading for businesspeople and marketers on all scales and theaters of commerce."

—*Midwest Book Review*

"Few things can have greater impact on your personal brand and your organization's brand recognition than developing and sharing your expertise with the world. Whether you call it becoming a thought leader or a public expert, or, as marketing guru Steven Yoder's book espouses, *Get Slightly Famous*, you should do it. Trust me. I'm living proof that it works."

—**Keith Ferrazzi**, Inc.com

"*Get Slightly Famous* is the perfect recipe for any business owner who wants to stop making cold calls and start making sales."

—**C.J. Hayden**, author of *Get Hired Now!*

"… an ingenious, how-to, directional path to recognition. Yoder out-lines a tutorial track that assures elevation from the unknown to the '*slightly famous*' and beyond."

— **Dee Wood**, former diversity council member of the Conference Board

"Steven Van Yoder's book demonstrates that creating a buzz is only half the battle. He shows that success in business means staying true to your customers and your vision in order to build and sustain a strong and enduring brand."

—**Lillian Vernon**, founder and chief executive officer,
Lillian Vernon Corporation

"In this book, Steven Van Yoder reveals the step-by-step details of how to create long-lasting power—and profits—in your business."

—**Terri Lonier**, founder, workingsolo.com

"*Get Slightly Famous* is a blueprint to give you an 'unfair' advantage over your competition."

—Patricia Fripp, CSP, CPAE, past president, National Speakers
Association and author of *Make It, So You Don't Have to Fake It!*

"What a treasure chest of great ideas you can do yourself! I recommend that you buy a quantity of these books and use them as gifts for your clients."

—Dottie Walters, CSP, president and CEO, Walters International Speakers
Bureau and publisher, *Sharing Ideas* magazine

"*Get Slightly Famous* offers a refreshing approach on how to build your business and succeed in the marketplace."

—Dr. Ivan Misner, founder of BNI and co-author of
Masters of Networking

"These are powerful business-building tools, and Steven Van Yoder explains them clearly and concisely."

—Shel Horowitz, author of *Grassroots Marketing:*
Getting Noticed in a Noisy World

"Steven Van Yoder has taken all the best marketing ideas out there today and put them together into a practical, down-to-earth, must-read book."

—Susan RoAne, author of *How to Work a Room*

"If I'd read *Get Slightly Famous* before I became *slightly famous*, I might have appeared at the top of these quotes!"

—Bob Blumer, aka "The Surreal Gourmet," cookbook author and
Food Network celebrity

GET slightly FAMOUS

Become a Celebrity
in Your Field and
Attract More Business
with Less Effort

Get
Slightly
FAMOUS

2nd
Edition

by STEVEN VAN YODER

BAY TREE PUBLISHING
POINT RICHMOND, CALIFORNIA

Get Slightly Famous™ is a trademark of Steven Van Yoder, San Francisco, California.

Cover design by Bryan Bindloss
Copyediting by Linda Jay Geldens

Library of Congress Cataloging-in-Publication Data

Van Yoder, Steven.
 Get slightly famous : become a celebrity in your field and attract more business with less effort / Steven Van Yoder.—2nd ed., rev. and expanded.
     p. cm.
 Includes index.
 ISBN-13: 978-0-9720021-7-2
 ISBN-10: 0-9720021-7-0
 1. Marketing—Management. 2. Sales promotion. 3. Mass media and business. 4. Fame—Economic aspects. I. Title.

 HF5415.13.V36 2007
 658.8—dc22
                              2007020970

Contents

How to Break Out of the Anonymity Trap

If business seems ever harder and more competitive, that's because it is. Working in a global economy means the number of businesses competing for the same customers, even in a local market, has grown proportionately.

For a small business, it's no longer possible to assume a home turf advantage, and so the challenge of marketing has changed. You can now work with a travel agent, a graphic designer, or an insurance broker across the country as easily as someone across town. You can find the same products on the Internet and the corner store, and often it's more convenient to make your purchase from your desk and take delivery on your porch tomorrow.

For large companies, the battle to win new clients and customers has intensified. Companies risk becoming irrelevant, and their products treated as commodities, if they rely on traditional advertising-oriented marketing. Consumers now shun sales pitches in favor of educational marketing. They expect companies to help them make informed decisions at each stage of the buying cycle.

Against this backdrop of increased competition, every business must fight to avoid blending into a sea of look-alikes. The Internet has created empowered consumers who lend their attention and loyalty to companies that demonstrate a top down commitment to integrity and thought leadership.

If you're in business and looking for more customers or clients, you need to ask yourself these questions: Do the right people fully understand what I do? Have I targeted my most likely customers and delivered a message that speaks to their unique needs? Have I embraced the Internet to its full potential and developed a credible online presence? Do I struggle to differentiate myself from competitors? When a local paper, trade journal or prominent industry blogger does a story on my area of expertise, do they call me?

If you can't answer these questions with an unequivocal "yes," *Get Slightly Famous* will boost your marketing into a new realm of effectiveness. It is based on proven strategies that can help you get more business with less effort. Even if you're already practicing these general principles, you will find lots of specific techniques that you can add to your ongoing efforts.

This book provides a roadmap to help any business break out of the anonymity trap and effectively attract clients and customers. It's filled with practical tips and techniques, advice from leading marketing experts, and dozens of real-world success stories from *slightly famous* entrepreneurs.

Get Slightly Famous was written to be read, reread, and put into action. For additional inspiration, visit www.getslightlyfamous.com, where you will find further resources and business success stories.

Welcome to marketing in the twenty-first century!

PART I

The Center of Your Universe

1 Just a Little Fame Will Do

Some businesses seem to attract clients and customers by magic. Their marketing seems effortless. They may not have made a cold call in years, they may not spend a dime on advertising, yet somehow they're regularly featured in newspapers and magazines, and their owners or executives get invited to speak at conferences. Everyone knows their name, and they get all the business they can handle. It's almost as though they were famous.

In fact, they are, but not in the way movie stars and top athletes are famous—they're just *slightly famous*. Just famous enough to make their names come to mind when people are looking for a particular product or service, and let them reap the benefits. They get more business—not only more, but the right kind of business—and they don't have to work so hard to get it.

Want to join them and enjoy this ideal state of affairs, where customers come to you? You can, but it may require a new way of thinking and a new marketing strategy. And though it may seem effortless to the outside observer, it does require work.

The *Slightly Famous* You

In a crowded marketplace, where your potential clients and customers have lots of choices, you can stand out by being just sightly famous. This is the exact opposite of mass marketing. It's not about being all things to all people, but being a mini-celebrity to the right people. It's about targeting your market and developing a reputation as a great resource—trustworthy, knowledgeable, and close at hand. Your goal is to become the lord of a small, profitable domain of your choosing. Within that domain, you will attract more customers and clients, including those you want most.

Naturally, such results require thoughtful and consistent efforts. Underlying and guiding these efforts are seven basic principles:

1. Targeting the best prospects
2. Developing a unique market niche
3. Positioning your business as the best solution
4. Maintaining your visibility
5. Enhancing your credibility
6. Becoming a thought leader
7. Establishing your brand and reputation

By working on these principles, you get out of the anonymity trap, create a *slightly famous* you, and build a successful business. In the pages that follow, we'll look more closely at how you can act on these principles.

Targeting the Best Prospects

Market research is like sticking your toe into a lake before jumping in. If you know who you want to reach and what their needs are, you avoid wasting time and money in poorly conceived marketing programs. You can alter your products or services to fit the needs of your target market, and you can craft a message that reflects your business and your customer. Moreover, market research needn't involve expensive consultants, surveys, or focus groups—it can be as simple as asking your best customers the right questions.

For example, Larry Klein discovered his target market from the inside. A successful financial advisor, he retired from his primary job and became a marketing guru to other financial professionals. He knew they needed several kinds of marketing help, but as he talked to them and worked with them, he discovered that what they wanted most were ways to reach seniors.

Klein explains, "I'm not yet 60. So, you don't have to be a member of your ideal marketplace. But if you talk to enough people in that market group, you're going to get it. You have to be awake and aware and be listening for what it is.

"All the information you need to target and succeed in an ideal marketplace is out there waiting to be found," says Klein. "You can take the guesswork out of building a business."

Having talked to enough seniors to understand their needs, Klein refined methods for approaching them with investment opportunities. Now he offers seminars, writes articles about these strategies, and acts as a consultant to former colleagues. You and I may not have heard of him, but within his targeted sector of the financial planning community, Klein is *slightly famous*.

Developing a Unique Market Niche

Large companies aspire to total market domination. Small businesses with a *slightly famous* strategy flourish by establishing themselves within a carefully selected segment of a market; they target a market niche that they can realistically hope to dominate.

Market niches can be defined by region, by special customer needs, or by demographics, such as a particular ethnic or age group; sometimes a market niche can be generated by a product that's a variation on an established one. (Interestingly, the word niche, which comes from French, means "nest." As a small business you want to build your nest away from the hawks of big business.)

Positioning Your Business as the Best Solution

In a crowded marketplace, it may not be enough just to carve out a niche. You've narrowed your focus, but you still have competitors. This is the time to distinguish yourself as the pre-eminent source of solutions by refining your

REAL-WORLD SUCCESS STORY

Mari Gottdiener Finds a Market She Didn't Know Was There

Sometimes people find themselves thriving in a niche without planning it. Such was the case with Mari Gottdiener, who refocused her credit and consumer advocacy business from general consumers to the narrowly defined market of professional mortgage brokers.

Mari specializes in getting credit bureaus to address and correct credit-report errors. After struggling to find clients throughout the general population, she discovered that mortgage brokers were ready-made prospects. They had an ongoing need for her services on behalf of their loan applicants. She began networking with brokers at trade association meetings, and gave presentations at several mortgage offices.

"My decision to focus on the mortgage broker sector transformed my business," says Gottdiener. "The more I focused on being the person who fixes credit problems for mortgage brokers, the easier it became to define what I could do for them. Now, my name gets passed around, and I've developed a special reputation within that market that makes getting business easier than ever."

Mari's niche fame really became apparent when the California Association of Mortgage Brokers invited her to talk about credit issues at their luncheon. Since then, she's spoken to broker groups regularly, and has reached out to similar associations in other states.

"Word-of-mouth referrals built my reputation at a local level," she says. "Now I'm expanding to reach a national audience of mortgage brokers by writing articles in national mortgage broker trade publications and even doing online seminars."

expertise. You need to know more about something, or be better at something, than anyone else, and you have to let people know.

When you can honestly convey such a message, potential customers and clients see you as the obvious answer to their problems and challenges, and the logical choice when they're looking for a supplier.

Maintaining Your Visibility

When was the last time your name appeared in print? Yesterday? Last week? A month ago? Even if you remember, that doesn't mean a potential customer will.

One key to succeeding in the marketplace is to have your message out

REAL-WORLD SUCCESS STORY

Fred Phillips Finds His Special Niche

Fred Phillips, a restaurant industry veteran, landed his first job at a hamburger franchise when he was in his teens. Now, twenty years later, he is president of RestQuip, a supplier of environment-friendly restaurant equipment.

Rather than blend into the woodwork of look-alike restaurant supply houses, Phillips focused on helping restaurants reduce waste. Drawing on his knowledge of industry issues, Phillips observed what he foresaw would be a major industry problem: "a ten-fold decrease in the amount of landfill space available for dumping refuse."

Within this situation he saw the business opportunity. "As a greater emphasis was placed on waste reduction by government agencies, my clientele needed options to deal with this potentially costly problem."

RestQuip developed a number of programs that addressed these issues, and at the same time made sure that their environmental products and services got plenty of attention in the trade press. They have consistently stayed abreast of environmental issues and solutions, and take advantage of this knowledge to market themselves as the experts within their industry.

there, if not continuously, then often enough to keep your name alive in customers' minds. This is the meaning of visibility, and if you're not visible to your potential clients, you cease to exist. If you haven't done any marketing in months, you'll miss getting clients because they will forget about you, and instead call your competitor, whose name was in this morning's paper.

Visibility is a cornerstone of every *slightly famous* business strategy, and it begins by placing your core marketing message in front of as many of your target customers as possible, as often as possible.

Enhancing Your Credibility

Visibility, of course, is only a means. To produce results, visibility must be combined with credibility. This means that you need to embrace visibility strategies that display your distinction, competence, expertise, authority, and leadership—and this is where the *slightly famous* strategies in this book go beyond marketing strategies that rely on advertising.

"Exposure plus 95 cents might buy you a decent cup of coffee," says networking expert Bob Burg. "The key is to position yourself in your market as the expert, the resource, the only person your prospect would ever even think of doing business with, or referring to others."

The surest way to make a credible name for yourself is by becoming a "recognized" expert. Who counts as an expert? Experts include authors, speakers, consultants, business owners, managers, and professionals. If you have in-depth knowledge about a specific subject—and that subject can be your business—you qualify, too. The test is how much you know, and if you know a lot about something, you can leverage that knowledge into a halo of authority.

As an authority, you can write articles for trade and special interest publications (if you're too busy to write, or uncertain of your writing skills, it's easy to find help use the Web or the Yellow Pages to look for "Editing and Writing Services"). You can give talks. And you can become a news resource, providing quotes to the media on issues relating to your industry.

Theresa Iglesias-Solomon started Niños, a Spanish/English bilingual catalog business, out of her home in Michigan several years ago. Realizing that her focus on the Hispanic market made her newsworthy to business writers pursuing stories on niche markets, she regularly notified reporters and editors about new ethnic products and buying trends.

Over time she built a reputation as an expert on the Hispanic market, and this has led to frequent media mentions, including some in the *Wall Street Journal, Entrepreneur, USA Today,* and *Catalog Age.*

In addition to making the news, you can augment your marketing and your business by creating information products—booklets, e-books, classes, audiocassettes—around your area of expertise. These will cement your place as the leader in your market niche.

A business coach herself, C. J. Hayden markets to other professional business coaches, marketing consultants, and sales trainers. While her book, *Get Clients Now!,* helped to establish her credibility in this field, Hayden took the concept one step further. After writing her book, she trademarked the name and developed the "Get Clients Now! Licensee Kit," which includes a 60-page facilitator's guide, audiovisual aids, and tools for marketing the program to students. The result has been a profitable package that helps others reproduce her program.

Hayden has sold more than 200 licenses internationally, and the program has helped her land book deals in the U.S. and China, and publicity in several national magazines. This is a perfect example of visibility and credibility building on each other.

Becoming a Thought Leader

Standing out in the current din of self-promotion requires a profound shift in outlook. There's no point in trying to yell louder, but you can get noticed if you offer something different—information, insights, and ideas, for instance. This is the skill of thought leadership that positions you and your company as an industry authority and resource.

In a sense, thought leadership is a consultative approach to marketing, earning your company the role of trusted advisor by demonstrating that you know your business deeply, shape your industry, and understand and anticipate the needs of your target market.

When done authentically, and with a genuine spirit of helping others, thought leadership can serve as the touchstone of your *slightly famous* marketing strategy, helping you attract prospects and grow your business by establishing your reputation as a generous contributor to your industry.

When David Silverstein launched Breakthrough Management Group (BMG) in 2001, he sought ways to establish BMG as business performance improvement specialists in the financial services, healthcare, and manufacturing industries. He spoke at industry conferences and commented on his industry trends in his Leadership and Business blog. He coauthored *INsourcing Innovation* (Breakthrough Performance Press), a book that articulates BMG's approach to developing core business competencies that drive innovation. He offered his expertise to the media, helping BMG garner coverage in over 100

REAL-WORLD SUCCESS STORY

White Dog Café Serves Good Food and Community Education

A popular restaurant in Philadelphia's University of Pennsylvania area, the White Dog Café is well-known for its commitment to social responsibility as well as its food. Since opening in 1983, the White Dog has become a Philadelphia institution, known and valued for the social and environmental activism of Judy Wicks, its founder and owner.

The business is dedicated to environmental responsibility (it was the first business in Pennsylvania to purchase 100 percent of its electricity from wind power sources), pays a living wage to employees, and sources food from local farms where meat and poultry are raised humanely.

The café hosts educational events on social issues and organizes public service work, including a trip to New Orleans with 35 customers and staff, who provided assistance after Hurricane Katrina.

In addition to the restaurant itself, Wicks started the White Dog Café Foundation, whose mission is to help build a local living economy in the Greater Philadelphia region. The Foundation is funded by 20 percent of White Dog Café profits, grants from other foundations, and customers who like contributing to local community causes.

"I joke that I'm not really a restaurant business, but use good food to lure innocent customers into social activism," says Wicks. "By taking a stand and leading with our values, we've cultivated passionate, loyal customers and great word of mouth by people who feel emotionally connected to our business," she adds.

"I've built a very successful business, and garnered great community exposure, because I run my business for the benefit of the common good as opposed to pure profit," says Wicks. "You can, in fact, use the market as a vehicle for serving humanity."

publications, including the *Wall Street Journal, Business Finance* magazine, and *Investor's Business Daily*. He also appeared on CNN's *Squeeze Play*.

In roughly five years, thought leadership took BMG from an unknown startup to a global organization with eleven offices on five continents. "Our reputation as a thought leader helped us expand into core markets, including Asia and Latin America, where credibility and name recognition go a long way," says Silverstein. "Our reputation now helps our sales team get their foot in the door in key markets."

Regardless of a company's size or industry, thought leadership always starts at the top. Thought leadership is most effective when led by a company's top management, who develop and express new ideas that keep a company at the forefront of change.

Establishing Your Brand and Reputation

Nothing overcomes consumer skepticism more effectively than a good report from someone who's dealt with you before. When people get a recommendation about you from a friend, they approach you with positive expectations. In essence, they have an insurance policy that reduces the risk of doing business with you. If, on top of hearing about you from someone they know, they also see your name in print, the effect grows synergistically. Marketing guru Marcia Yudkin expresses this idea in an algebraic formula:

Visibility + Credibility + Word-of-Mouth = REPUTATION

Brand recognition and reputation matter when it comes to generating sales leads. In *How Clients Buy: The Benchmark Report on Professional Services Marketing and Sales from the Client Perspective,* the online publication *RainToday.com* asked 200 buyers of professional services how they find and learn more about potential service providers. After referrals, "I already knew about the service provider" (in other words, reputation or brand reach) was the top source.

"One argument seems to never go away," says Mike Schultz, publisher of *Rain Today.* "On the one side you have people who say, 'We need to increase our brand recognition in order to truly succeed with marketing.' The other side typically maintains, 'Just get out there and sell. Name recognition doesn't matter.' Yet, our research shows that when you are well known in your field, whatever lead generation tactics you employ are likely to work better."

None of this is possible, of course, if you don't provide customer satisfaction. There are a number of good books on the subject of customer service,

REAL-WORLD SUCCESS STORY

PR Newswire Brands Its Executives

PR Newswire, the global leader in news and information distribution services for professional communicators, positions its executives as thought leaders in key industry markets, offering advice and educational information in a variety of formats. PR Newswire's executive thought leadership efforts promote the company's services to corporations, government agencies, public relations (PR) professionals, investor relations (IR) staff, public affairs agencies, and non-profits.

White Papers PR Newswire executives author white papers that serve to promote the company's thought leadership and act as lead generation tools. Broadcast & Beyond: A Guide to Broadcast and Web-based Public Relations, a white paper authored by Tim Bahr, president of PR Newswire's multimedia and broadcast PR services company, generated more than 2,500 leads when downloaded from the company website. Using Media Intelligence Tools to Drive Communications Success, a white paper by Nancy Sells, generated more than 4,500 requests with one-fourth asking to be contacted directly.

Bylined Article PR Newswire executives—including the COO, Senior Vice President of Sales, Vice President of Marketing, Vice President of Public Relations, and numerous product managers—contribute articles to trade publications, including *PRWeek, PR News, Bulldog Reporter, IR Magazine, Entrepreneur.com, PR Tactics*, and others.

and you should take their advice seriously. Without visibility, you can provide excellent services and still find yourself without enough business. But if you pursue visibility and credibility marketing strategies and provide an outstanding product or service, word-of-mouth will take on a life of its own. And although you can't personally be present at every moment your prospects are about to buy, your reputation will function as a surrogate salesperson within your prospect's mind.

Roseann Sullivan, a corporate trainer and owner of San Francisco-based Sullivan Communications, has an excellent local reputation as a public speaking coach. Nevertheless, she credits the articles she has written with providing the lion's share of new clients.

Conferences PR Newswire executives regularly participate as speakers in industry conferences that reach the PR and IR fields or communications pros in targeted industries. These have included The Conference Board's programs on Communications and Technology, PRSA conferences, Bulldog Reporter's Media Relations conference, NIRI conferences, Ragan conferences, and more.

Webinars PR Newswire executives appear on webinars discussing topics that are relevant to their customers and that showcase company services. The company hosted 23 webinars in 2006, including PR Across Borders and Vital Signs: Reaching Journalists Who Cover the Business of Healthcare.

Blog Several PR Newswire executives host their own blogs. Mark Hynes, PR Newswire's Managing Director of Investor Relations Services, who is responsible for developing regulatory disclosure solutions and strategies, uses his blog to discuss global disclosure and transparency issues.

While the bulk of PR Newswire's online thought leadership efforts involve senior leaders, everyone in the organization is encouraged to get involved. Employees and managers at all levels of the company participate in the blogosphere, and executives at all levels of the company read and post comments on blogs relevant to the PR and IR fields.

By offering new insights, investing in research, and delivering advice and information directly from PR Newswire executives, the company demonstrates its commitment to driving new developments in the continually evolving PR and IR industries while positioning PR Newswire as a consultative partner.

"I've landed work from clients who hear about me through my published articles," says Sullivan, whose work has been featured in numerous professional journals and business publications, including *Apartment Owners News, Southwest Airline's Spirit,* and *The Business Journal.* "And I get calls from prospects who had already heard about me, but were then 'nudged' to call and hire me after reading one of my articles."

Big corporations spend millions to promote a brand identity because it pays. The best-known brands spread with the speed of spicy gossip, jumping from prospect to prospect, community to community. While you're probably not in a position to spend your way to success as they do, there are economical ways you can make your business an attractive, distinguished, and distinguishable microbrand that represents your values and expertise.

Your brand will integrate all your marketing around a core idea and vision. It will actually make knowing what to do to successfully market yourself easier. Because you have a unique identity, you will have less to fear from competitors, thereby opening the door for mutually beneficial partnerships with other businesses.

The Sonoma County Woodworkers Association (SCWA) emerged when a handful of independent furniture retailers in Northern California banded together to survive the recession of the early 1990s through cross-promotion and buying strength. Together, the group bought advertising at local radio stations and newspapers, and developed combined events where customers were eligible to win prizes. They even printed a joint brochure that included a map to their locations, along with a headline that read, "People You Can Trust." Because each retailer had a distinctive identity, they were able to work together to survive rough times.

Your *slightly famous* brand identity will become the guiding star of your entire business. It will ensure that all your marketing efforts pull in the same direction. You'll waste less time, and make fewer marketing mistakes, because you have a long-term strategy of investing in your *slightly famous* reputation.

EXECUTIVE BRANDING

Thomas Nies Articulates His Legacy

Thomas M. Nies, CEO of Cincom Systems, Inc., founded Cincom in 1968 with just $600, a card table, and the dream of selling software separately from computer hardware. His idea took hold and revolutionized the way computers and their components are sold. Today, Cincom is a leading software company, serving thousands of clients on six continents, including BMW, Citibank, Boeing, Northwestern Mutual, Federal Express, Ericsson, Siemens, Rockwell Automation, and Trane.

Despite being profiled by the Smithsonian Institution as one of the "pioneers of the software industry," Nies remained virtually unknown, although he had led Cincom for more than four decades. As he neared retirement, wanting to set the stage for his eventual departure from the company, Nies undertook a campaign to articulate his company legacy.

To showcase Nies's entrepreneurial spirit and leadership philosophy, Cincom pursued an executive branding program that sought to feature their CEO's stature and accomplishments while positioning him as a thought leader and elder statesman within the software industry.

Utilizing print, broadcast, the Internet, and speaking opportunities, Nies talked about leading Cincom through numerous economic cycles, his rationale for keeping Cincom a private company, and his management style, encouraging employee initiative and innovation. His prime audience consisted of those at the centers of influence in the software industry and business world, including editors, analysts, and columnists.

In just one year, this concentrated executive branding campaign generated considerable exposure and recognition for Nies' outlook, expertise, and accomplishments. Articles by Nies appeared in *American Executive, Financial Executive,* and other business magazines, and he secured high-profile speaking engagements, including Red Herring's London Venture Market Conference CEO Roundtable.

A major element of this campaign was the desire to identify Nies as an advocate of entrepreneurship. The vehicle for this initiative was the Cincom Encouraging Entrepreneurship (CEE) Program, which joined forces with educational institutions and other non-profit organizations to support and encourage entrepreneurial activity. This consortium donated software, services, and resources to assist aspiring entrepreneurs, and also sponsored University MBA Plan Competitions, in which students enrolled in MBA programs could compete to win cash prizes.

2 Aim for a Target

Harry Shepherd started his bookkeeping service with the same concerns facing most start-ups. He needed clients right away. But because he was in competition with dozens of other bookkeepers selling essentially the same thing, he knew he needed to find a way to differentiate his company.

After asking around, Harry discovered that many businesses had recently taken to doing their own bookkeeping with accounting software. He also learned they were having a hard time because they lacked basic accounting knowledge—and here Harry saw his opportunity.

He quickly mastered *QuickBooks*, a popular accounting program, and started marketing himself as a "*QuickBooks* Software Training Consultant." Immediately, Shepherd went from blending into a sea of look-alike competitors to occupying a unique market niche.

Word spread fast. He introduced himself to accountants as a resource, and they gladly referred him to their clients. In addition, other bookkeepers, who were formerly his competitors, became his clients as he trained them to use accounting software. Harry's new niche meant that his services were in hot demand. He charged higher fees, and he did not have to work as hard to get new clients.

This chapter examines the process Harry pursued in targeting a market and establishing a profitable market niche—the process you will be going through as well. You must first develop a keen understanding of your market by doing research. With this knowledge you can position your business as a *slightly famous* provider of choice that understands the needs, desires, and challenges of your target market.

To Find a Niche: Focus!

Many entrepreneurs think that selling to the widest possible market is the likeliest path to success. They are afraid to pursue a market niche because they fear they'll lose business by turning away customers. But this "take all comers" approach is not very effective. It's hard to stand out when you market your business without a distinctive set of prospects in mind.

Occupying a niche means you won't be competing with a lot of similar businesses solely on price. And because you will be selling products and services that are customized to the specific needs and predispositions of a select group of people, you can often charge more. Your products and services serve a market that can't easily find alternatives.

To determine if a particular niche is right for you, ask these questions:

- Do I have an identifiable target population with similar interests and needs?
- Is the market large enough to support my business?
- Can I tailor my products, services, and business identity to address that market's particular needs?
- Is my target market currently underserved?
- Can I reach my potential customers in a cost-effective manner?

Your niche will give your marketing efforts a natural, sharp focus. The more you specialize, the more your market will see the value of your services because you speak directly to their unique situation. Assuming your niche is large enough, you can do quite well by becoming a provider of products and services that can't be found anywhere else.

Dan Poynter is a successful self-publisher who started writing books about parachuting and hang-gliding over thirty years ago. Though it might sound as if his audience would be too small to generate significant sales, he knew his market and where to find them. Best of all, he had the market all to himself.

Rather than try to fight for attention in general bookstores, he sold books to skydiving clubs, parachute dealers, and the U.S. Parachute Association. He developed a reputation in skydiving circles, and has enjoyed steady sales of his books for more than three decades. Because Poynter's topic was tailored to a group of people he could easily target, and because he provided useful information where little was to be found, he found greater success than if he had pursued a more general audience.

For small businesses, niches are, above all, manageable. You can get your mind (and pocketbook) around them well enough to design a marketing strategy that speaks in personal terms to real prospects. Conversely, you can avoid wasting time and money broadcasting your message to a general population that isn't particularly interested in what you have to offer.

Tony Roeder learned this when he launched RedWagons.com, a specialized retailer of Red Flyer toy wagons on the Internet. Roeder knew that there was no way he could compete with the likes of Amazon.com and eToys.com, which all carry Red Flyer wagons in their huge toy inventory. Instead, he decided to deal in Red Flyer wagons exclusively, and offer their entire product line. Now, while Roeder's big competitors carry only a few models, he has the entire Red Flyer collection, and is the first resort of any avid Red Flyer wagon enthusiast.

The key is identifying your ideal customers—and the communities they belong to. By targeting the best, most favorably inclined prospects within a niche, you can become your target market's vendor of choice, and sell more with much less effort. Having done this, you've mastered your market—and if that market is large enough, you're a success.

As you identify possible market niches, consider how to specialize your products and services to the unmet needs of the most qualified prospects in them. By developing inside knowledge of this group, and giving them exactly what they want, you will inspire the loyalty that people give those who understand them.

This is what Tom Williams, of WestMark Realtors in Lubbock, Texas, accomplished when he began his career in real estate. Looking for ways to differentiate himself, he soon noticed that the majority of his colleagues gravitated to older, repeat clients who were comfortable with the home-buying process.

Because conventional wisdom says that first-time homebuyers are too much trouble and not worth the small commissions, Williams realized he could have this potentially lucrative market to himself. He threw himself into his newly discovered niche with great success, and his clients found his dedication, advice, and upbeat attitude refreshing.

Niche by Design

Although many discover their niches by accident, the most rewarding market niches are usually identified through deliberate effort. Choosing a market niche is a strategic process that matches your desires and resources to opportunities in the outside world. You can define your niche to include all existing customers, just a subset of them, or a wholly new population. First identify those customers you most want to serve within market niches large enough to sustain you, but not dominated by competitors. Then, steer your research in that direction.

Identify your niche category or the overall industry or consumer segment you wish to serve, and try to find what members of your prospective niche have in common. Additional factors may include:

Your Niche: A Special Region Your niche might comprise prospects in a particular neighborhood, city, county, or state. You might work with veterinarians in Chicago, restaurants in San Francisco, or lobster fishermen in

REAL-WORLD SUCCESS STORY

Dean of Beans Reaches Coffee Shops Worldwide

Although you've probably never heard of Alex Fisenko, in the world of coffee he's known as "the Dean of Beans." The 60-something coffee expert started his first espresso shop in Berkeley, California, in the 1960s. Since then he's owned 16 coffee shops and now sells his expertise on launching a successful coffee business to aspiring entrepreneurs.

"Espresso is my life," says Fisenko. "I started this business back when there were only a few coffee houses across the country, and they served mainly as 'beatnik' hangouts. Coffee was incidental to the whole setting. It's my personal expertise that makes my niche so successful."

Alex is a coffee guru who conducts coffee shop seminars and also sells a training course called "Espresso Business Success." He brought his niche onto the Internet. His website, www.espressobusiness.com, generates thousands of dollars a month in product sales and consulting engagements in the United States, Thailand, South Korea, Belgium, Saudi Arabia, and Barbados.

While Alex's target market of aspiring coffee shop owners is narrow, his business of selling them how-to information is so focused that he easily stands out and finds all the business he can handle.

"My Website gets close to 18,000 visits a month because my niche is so narrowly defined," says Fisenko. "By narrowing my market niche to aspiring coffee shop owners, I now make more money through book sales and consultations than when I ran coffee shops."

Cape Cod. Or you could consider ethnic and linguistic boundaries, or a particular age cohort of those that reside in your community.

First-time author Amit Gilboa, author of *Off the Rails in Phnom Penh*, stumbled across his market niche during a visit to Cambodia in 1995, just as the country was opening its doors to outside travelers. The result was a best-selling book, based on his travels in Cambodia, that caused a stir in Southeast Asia.

Gilboa's success is due to the fact that he essentially had the Cambodian travel niche all to himself, and his book continues to sell well throughout Asia. "I'm world famous in Southeast Asia" is the way Gilboa puts it. "My publisher is too small to cram the book down the throat of Barnes & Noble, but I still do very well, even though for every person on this planet who has read or even heard of my book, there are millions who haven't."

Your Niche: Meeting Unmet Needs Are there groups with needs you can serve that are not currently being met by other businesses? If so, you have the basis for a successful niche.

Your Niche: Offering Industry-Specific Specialties A business can easily focus on a particular industry niche. A chiropractor, instead of seeking as patients "everyone with a back," could target trucking companies, offering treatment and safety seminars to their employees.

Your Niche: How and When You Work Do you specialize in fast turnaround? Are you open seven days a week, twenty-four hours a day? If so, you may be able to capitalize on your schedule to develop your niche.

Your Niche: The Group You Serve Sometimes, if you are the only business that specializes in working with narrow categories of customers, such as seniors, children, or Hispanic-owned small businesses, you can use your knowledge of that special population as the basis for building an identity.

Next, narrow down your chosen category to a more focused subgroup. If your category is health care, for example, your subgroup might be nursing, gynecology, hospital administration, or surgical suppliers. Consider other attributes of your niche that will help you focus as specifically as possible on groups of people with common needs.

The more you narrow your focus, the more likely you are to find a profitable niche market. Terry McVey realized this when he started a medical insurance seminar business. Terry teaches doctors' offices how to collect fees from insurance carriers. Because he targets specific medical specialists, such as orthopedic surgeons, his seminars have a higher perceived value than his generalist competitors.

Knowledge Is Power

Once you have a working idea of the market you'd like to serve, you need to dig deeper to test your assumptions. The process starts with market research: analyze your best potential customers, your competitors, your market's predisposition toward your products and services, and your ability to serve these people so well as to make you their vendor of choice.

Market research can provide relevant information for establishing a solid foundation under any business. Even if you have been in business for years, it's a good idea to stay up-to-date with market research that might help you understand where your market niche is going.

Market research can, among other things, help you understand your potential customers, the likelihood that they'll buy your products and services, why they'll buy them, and how much they'll pay. Market research can also help you evaluate your competitors' strengths and weaknesses, thereby providing one of the keys to dominating your niche.

There is no rule to tell you where exactly you will find the information you need to qualify your market niche, or just how much market research is necessary, but you can assume that your research will involve analyzing the market, the market's response to your product or service, and how you will effectively market to your niche audience

You begin by looking at primary data. This is data that you generate from direct personal experience or from within your own business. It can come from customers, clients, vendors, existing contacts, or business associations to which you belong. You can gather primary data by talking to people, performing surveys, holding focus groups, or bouncing ideas off prospects on the Internet.

At a more abstract level, secondary data is information and research that has been compiled by others. This can include census reports, articles in trade and consumer publications, and surveys by business associations. All secondary data comes from sources outside your business, and can contain valuable insight into your potential market niche and those already involved with it.

Effective market search combines primary and secondary research to arrive at an adequate understanding of your market niche. By exploring as many secondary sources as possible, combined with a commitment to "get out there" and connect with people who can help you better understand your target market, you'll find the information you need to make intelligent, informed decisions about the viability of your market niche.

A trip to the library can be worthwhile, too. You can look at business directories (several are listed in the appendix) that can provide specific information about your target group, search periodical databases for articles related to your business, and research industry associations and professional organizations (many of which publish their own reports).

Librarians can help you locate lots of free material, including listings for:

- local, state, and national chambers of commerce
- industry associations
- trade journals
- periodicals
- vendors and suppliers
- government agencies and departments

The Internet is another great market research tool. You can do a tremendous amount—from reading articles about your niche and visiting trade and business organization websites, to actually chatting with potential prospects in online chat rooms—all from the comfort of your office or study.

Finally, of course, it's important to get out and talk to people. Visit local offices of trade and business associations. Find people on the inside willing to help, and invite them to lunch for a brainstorming session. Approach industry insiders, and tap their knowledge. They are the ones who can best help you refine your niche marketing strategy, because they understand your market better than anyone else. These are people who can point you to specific information about your prospects, and tell you whether your products and services are in demand.

Competitive Intelligence

Before you expand your business, you'd better know what you're up against. You'll need to thoroughly investigate your competitors to understand their products and services, and how they are being received by your prospects.

Approach competitive businesses as though you were a customer. Visit their business sites if possible. At a competitor's location, watch the customers and their interactions with the employees. Do they seem happy? Are they buying anything? Do you see things that could be improved? This is a time when being critical and nosy is essential.

Request your competitors' marketing materials. Make frequent searches to see if they are appearing in the news. Study their websites. Talk to their vendors and past customers. Do everything you can to understand your competitors and how they are received.

Consider both direct competitors and indirect competitors. Determine how many competitors you have, and their size. If your intended market niche lies in a specific geographic location, start your search with the phone book. There are a few good online telephone search directories, such as Switchboard.com, that allow you to search by industry category and zip code.

Study competitors through the North American Industry Classification System (NAICS) codes. The Census Bureau uses these codes to report on businesses, including such information as payroll size. You can access the census data yourself at the U.S. Census Bureau website. Most public libraries also carry business directories that can help you determine business classifications.

Trade shows are great places to get information, not only about the market, but also about your competition. At a trade show you can get copies of your competitors' literature and samples of their products, see demonstrations, experience their sales pitches, listen to what their prospects are asking them, and even interview attendees. With a little detective work, you can come away from a trade show with a gold mine of market research.

Getting Close

As you refine your market niche, you need to develop an insider's understanding of your prospects. This means personally experiencing the world your clients and customers live and work in, so that you really understand their daily concerns.

You need to know how your customers live, work, and spend their time, on and off the job. You need to know the key players within the niche, and understand the structure and dynamics of your market. This requires that you get involved enough to see through the eyes of your prospects.

Identify points of entry, such as associations, related businesses, and the people who contribute to the world of your niche market. Your list should include:

- Organizations they belong to
- Places they network
- Conferences or workshops they attend
- Competitors and other businesses already serving them
- Magazines or publications they read
- Websites they frequent
- People they use as guides or mentors

Read every magazine that targets your niche, and contact editors at these publications. Subscribe to news clipping services, or do periodical Web searches on key words related to your niche. Visit trade associations representing your niche audience, and learn everything you can from their websites and newsletters, or call and ask to speak with a representative. Always be on the lookout for information relevant to your niche.

Talk to members of your niche about your business. Talk to businesses that already serve your niche. They can often help you understand not just where your niche is today, but also where it's been and where it may be going.

Develop a questionnaire about your prospective products and services and distribute it to several prospective customers. You'll find that most people are willing to help. Their answers will help you fine-tune your offerings, and tailor your services and marketing messages.

What's Your Position?

Positioning communicates, in no uncertain terms, the benefits your brand delivers to your target market. It is a statement of value. Defining your market position is about articulating the clear customer benefits you offer, relative to competitors who serve the same market niche.

You do this for two reasons. First, it helps you develop a clear public image for your own business, so that potential customers know why they should do business with you rather than with someone else. And second, by defining for yourself precisely who your customers are, you can choose appropriate sales and marketing techniques and messages.

A deliberate positioning strategy addresses the fact that people no longer respond to one-size-fits-all marketing. It does this by clearly expressing the Ultimate Benefit of your business, answering the question "What's in it for me?" while cutting through the clutter and confusion of the marketplace.

Positioning emphasizes your strengths, and differentiates you from competitors. In turn, prospects cultivate a mental image of your company that lives and thrives in their minds.

Big companies know this well, and work hard to identify some key attribute of their company and its product, something that focuses customers' minds on a benefit offered by their products that's not offered by competing products. For example, 7-UP is the "uncola" for people who want to drink something different, and Apple computers are for those who "think different."

Small businesses that embrace positioning understand that the marketplace is competitive and cluttered. They know they will be ignored or forgotten by prospects attempting to wade through a barrage of information and marketing noise unless they distinguish themselves somehow.

Positioning means you'll never be confused with thousands of other businesses selling essentially the same thing. This is because you won't allow yourself to be just another "graphic designer," a mere "management consultant," or a humble "wedding photographer." You will use the power of positioning to make your business distinct, meaningful, and indispensable, with the result that your potential customers pick you out.

Standing Apart from the Crowd

In today's ultra-competitive business world, you need to find ways to really stand out. You must develop a strategy that makes your business distinct from your competitors by communicating the value you deliver in a way that is all your own.

Bruce Smith refuses to be seen as just another travel agent. After considering ways to distinguish himself from thousands of other general travel agents, he had a fortunate accident. His wife asked him where they would celebrate their first wedding anniversary. When he gave her a blank look, she set about planning a trip—but wouldn't tell him what she was planning.

Because he enjoyed the mystery leading up to the trip, and the hints his wife gave him, he repackaged his travel service as The Veiled Voyage, selling "destination unknown" vacations to couples and others. The idea was a hit. It radically repositioned his business in a very competitive industry, and developed a memorable brand.

Like Bruce Smith, begin by developing a positioning strategy that distinguishes your brand with a simple message that communicates value to the needs of your target market. If you don't determine your place in the market, the marketplace will simply think of you as one undistinguished business among many.

Your market position evolves from the characteristics of your product. Elements that contribute to your unique position include:

What Benefits Do You Offer? What do your customers get when they work with you? Increased business? More physical comfort? Financial well-being? Use this as the keystone in your positioning strategy together.

Does Your Price Point Differentiate You? Is your product a luxury item, somewhere in the middle, or cheap? Pricing can be used effectively to differentiate you from competitors.

Is Your Quality Better? Is your product particularly well produced? What quality controls are in place to assure consistency? What national or international standards do you meet? Do you back your quality claims with customer-friendly guarantees, warranties, and return policies?

Do You Offer Special Services? Customers expect good service—but do you offer something better or different? Do you offer the added value of Web-based or 800-number telephone support? Do you have a guarantee? Is your product customized or personalized? Do you offer quick turnaround or around-the-clock service?

If you are surrounded by businesses offering similar services or products, you must combine a number of features valuable to your target market in order to develop a strong positioning statement.

Start by doing research to understand your current practices, the practices of your competitors, and, most importantly, the practices you will need to adopt to achieve the position you want.

- Do you save people time or money?
- Do you make money for people?
- Do you offer a larger selection?
- Are you more conveniently located?
- Do you offer free installation, inspection, or other services?
- Are you more expensive, less expansive?
- Do you offer better or faster service?
- Do you guarantee the lowest price?
- Do you match the lowest price your customers can find?
- Do you honor your competitors' special discounts?
- Do you offer a stronger guarantee?
- Do you use technology to respond faster to a customer's needs?

You don't need to be completely original in your positioning statement, as long as it offers something significantly different from and superior to that of your competitors.

In the crowded marketplace of boutique winemakers, for instance, Guy Davis stands out because he combines a passion for what he does with a sense of how to get noticed. He embraced a simple positioning strategy—hand-crafted wines from carefully selected vineyards—which he implemented by searching out wine grapes grown in places most conducive to their style. In addition to his vineyards in California's Sonoma County, he traveled to other countries, including Argentina and New Zealand, in search of vineyards to pursue his craft in the best way possible.

Soon he was working two harvests a year (the southern hemisphere harvests grapes in March and April) and this translated into his personal positioning statement, "a winemaker for all seasons." The phrase stuck, pleasing his loyal customers and getting the attention of wine writers.

Positioning is power. It creates a strong link in prospects' minds between you and the product or service you've made your own. Then, every time they need your products or services, your company will be the first name that pops into their mind—or even better, the only one. The most important thing to remember is that positioning is not what you do to a product or a service; it's what you do to the minds of your prospects.

Develop a Positioning Statement

Your positioning statement is a succinct promise to the target market that you will provide them with the benefits they care about the most. The trick is capturing that promise in a very short space and in a very compelling way that engages the reader.

Imagine you're in an elevator with a potential customer, and you have 30 seconds to answer his question, "What business are you in?" A positioning statement answers that question in a couple of sentences, clearly stating the benefits you provide, and why customers should choose you over the competition. A positioning statement defines what's important and appealing about your business.

Here are some examples:

- We are an accounting firm specializing in nonprofits in Houston.
- We are an all-organic grocery delivery service.
- We help professional service firms attract more clients.
- Our design firm specializes in refurbishing Victorian homes.

Keep your statement short, focused, and easy to remember. If you can't make a statement in one sentence, you'll have a hard time getting your fellow-rider in the elevator to remember you after you've reached the lobby.

EXECUTIVE BRANDING

Partners Rise above Tainted Industry

In 2002, two former investment bankers, Brad Stroh and Andrew Housser, went looking for start-up opportunities and discovered the credit counseling business. Though the industry had earned a reputation for exploiting consumers desperate for relief from personal debt, the two saw the opportunity for providing an honest service in debt relief.

Today, they are co-CEOs of Bills.com (formerly Freedom Financial), a California firm that manages $200 million in consumer debt for more than 5,000 clients. Their profits are derived by taking a share of the savings they achieve for their clients.

Within a few years, Stroh and Housser differentiated their firm by establishing a good reputation in an industry generally regarded as shady.

Contrasting their "blue chip" backgrounds (Ivy League educations and experience at top-level financial, consulting, and technology companies) with the seedy reputation credit counseling agencies had developed, the partners developed a three-pronged branding strategy based on providing financial literacy education to American consumers.

1. Consumer Education — A common charge leveled at credit counselors is that they fail to educate their customers, since it is not in their narrow interest to do so. In contrast, Stroh wrote a detailed consumer education guide, "Budgeting

Evolving Your Niche

In the ever-changing marketplace, if you don't want to be left behind, you need to stay plugged in, be aware of current conditions and anticipate trends.

Approach market research with an open mind and a willingness to change and Financial Education Tools for Today's Consumer." The document provides budgeting tools, worksheets, and general advice to help consumers avoid or escape debt. All Bills.com customers get a copy, along with a monthly newsletter offering practical advice.

2. Media Outreach — Stroh and Housser aggressively court the news media with their message and their personal stories, much of it around branding themselves as experts on consumer debt. In the midst of an IRS crackdown on credit counseling firms, Bills.com issued a press release offering Stroh and Housser as experts to comment on the issue, an offer only a company with a clean reputation could pull off. Since the beginning of 2005, Stroh and Housser have been featured in more than 150 publications reaching a total circulation of 16.5 million. These publications include *Fortune,* the *Los Angeles Times,* the *Christian Science Monitor* and the *San Jose Mercury News.*

3. Contributed Articles — Bills.com builds its credibility by authoring bylined articles on personal finance issues. Housser is a regular contributor to WorldNow's Local Media Network, a service that syndicates editorial content to more than 170 local television station websites. His articles have appeared on major TV station websites, including KRON in San Francisco, KMOV in St. Louis, and WABC in New York.

Stroh and Housser's efforts to set themselves apart, both through their business practices and their media relations, have proven effective. In May 2006, the Internal Revenue Service revoked the tax-exempt status of forty-one credit-counseling agencies audited during a crackdown on the credit-counseling industry. Bills.com stayed above the fray. The company has tripled its revenue every year since it opened, and expects to double its employees over the next year.

direction if necessary. It can show you that a seemingly great niche is not predisposed to buy your services, or is already served by a number of competitors. The hardest thing about market research isn't finding or understanding the data, it's that market research can burst bubbles.

REAL-WORLD SUCCESS STORY

Ed Lyon Uses Humor to Stand Out from the Pack

Like most people, Cincinnati-based tax specialist Ed Lyon is commonly asked what he does for a living. But rather than reply, "I do taxes," he says, "I'm the funniest tax guy in America." It's an immediate attention-getter that has helped Lyon get noticed, and remembered, in his competitive field.

Lyon came into his moniker after compiling top ten lists of humorous tax deductions to promote his book, *The 60-Minute Tax Planner.* His efforts resulted in an appearance on The Roseanne Show in April 1999, where the television hostess dubbed him "the funniest tax guy in America." This led to appearances on CNN, CNBC, MSNBC, and Fox News Network.

The name stuck because Lyon made it stick. "I've used it in all of my marketing. It starts a conversation," says Lyon. "When somebody asks me what I do for a living and I say, 'I do taxes,' it does nothing to distinguish me from all the other CPAs and tax preparers. When I tell them, 'I'm the funniest tax guy in America,' it always starts a conversation, even if they say, 'Well, you don't have much competition.'"

"If you had told me when I was sitting in Federal Income Taxation class that I would someday appear on CNN—discussing boob jobs for strippers—I would have told you that something was about to go terribly wrong!" says Lyons. "But my yearly lists of celebrity tax deductions result in media coverage that lends me tons of credibility and a lot of new clients."

REAL-WORLD SUCCESS STORY

Dr. Robert E. Balon Meets Change Head-On

Dr. Robert E. Balon enjoyed a strong, comfortable niche for many years performing market research for the broadcast radio stations. Then there came the day when he had to recognize that all his expertise couldn't reverse the fact that radio markets were consolidating, and the demand by radio stations for that expertise would be sharply diminished.

"We thought, okay, our business is going to drop by 60 percent in the next two years. Where do we go from here?"

Balon contacted a local Texas restaurant association, and pitched the idea of a column on market research for their newsletter. After that, he organized a trend-analysis conference targeted to the central Texas food and hospitality industry.

Not having the money to totally bankroll the event he envisioned, Balon sought out potential industry partners who could lend funding and credibility to his conference. "I wanted to be the one that the trade press was excited about. I looked at where we're going to present it, how we're going to present it, and how we're going to position it."

Balon partnered with a large, upscale hotel chain and Block Distributing, the largest southwest wine distributor, and got them to underwrite part of the seminar. "It was a win-win proposition: the Four Seasons liked having top local CEOs visiting their space, and the distributor appreciated the opportunity to network with a lot of his clients who had been invited to the free-of-charge conference."

The conference helped the Benchmark Company refocus its target market, and become established as a market research firm that works with the Texas restaurant industry.

3 The Brand Is You

M artha Stewart, Michael Jordan, Emeril Lagasse, and Dr. Ruth Westheimer—all are examples of the power of personal branding. And though you may not aspire to their level of brand stardom, there's nothing preventing you from doing the same for your small business on a smaller scale.

Today, brands distinguish products and services from many competing choices. That's why all kinds of products and services—from accounting firms to sneaker makers to restaurants—are figuring out how to transcend the anonymity of mere category membership, and attain a unique brand identity.

But isn't branding the domain of soap, tires, and toothpaste? Think again. In "The Brand Called You," an article written for *Fast Company* magazine in 1997, management guru Tom Peters describes how brand equity has emerged over the past few years as a key strategic asset, not just for products, but also for business people and companies of all sizes.

"Charles Schwab was just a broker toiling on Wall Street until he turned his name into a winning brand," says Peter Montoya, publisher of *Personal Branding* magazine and author of *The Personal Branding Phenomenon*. "He made his self-named brokerage service a brand by saturating the media with his name, face, and company identity. Now, millions of Americans recognize in the Charles Schwab name perhaps the best known brand in finance."

Brands have a number of strategic functions, enabling you to:

- Differentiate yourself from your competition
- Position your focused message in the hearts and minds of customers
- Persist and be consistent in your marketing efforts
- Customize your services to reflect your personal brand
- Deliver your message clearly and quickly
- Project credibility
- Strike an emotional chord
- Create strong user loyalty

For small businesses, branding is not about slick advertisements. Small-business branding is about getting your target market to see you as the preferred choice. Building a *slightly famous* brand is not just about what you do; it's about what you do differently from everyone else.

"Branding is about getting prospects to see you as the only solution to their problems," says branding guru Rob Frankel, author of *The Revenge of Brand X*. "You want them to see your competition, and then run your way bellowing, 'Nobody understands me the way you do!' That's what gets them in the door—and keeps them coming back for more."

The Soul of Your Company

Your brand holds your entire *slightly famous* marketing strategy together. Once created, your brand will be the central theme that connects your business, both rationally and emotionally, to your market. It will convey personality, mystique, and drama. It will become the total aura around your business that cannot be duplicated by anyone else.

Branding is the total integration of everything your company does—including public relations, customer service, networking, newsletters, and word-of-mouth—that reflects on your company's reputation for quality of products and services within your target market.

Effective brands send a deliberate message that encompasses all aspects of a product or service, including a distinctive logo that appears on stationery, business cards, signage, packaging, advertising, website, and place of business. It also ties into prices, customer service, and guarantees.

"When most people think of a brand, they visualize a slogan, a logo, a campaign, a promise, or a product. A brand is much more," says Karl Speak, co-author of *Be Your Own Brand*. "Your company's brand is a powerful relationship fueled by a loyal belief system and knotted to the principle of providing exceptional value."

Whether positive, negative, or indifferent, every company has a brand. Your brand "describes the total experience of doing business with you, or consuming your products or service," according to Speak. Every business needs to evaluate its brand identity against the following criteria:

Relevance to the Market A brand must stand for something that is meaningful to members of a target market. Your brand encompasses the total experience of doing business with you.

Consistency of Behavior Customers must be able to depend on the brand to deliver the same experience every time. Because your market experiences your values through your brand, the only way they will truly become loyal to your brand is through your dedication and consistency.

Relationship-Building A brand is not a logo or an advertising strategy. "The strength of any brand is in the relationship it has between a company and its customers," says Speak. "The stronger the relationship, the more business they will do, and the more likely it is that customers will refer them to their friends and business associates."

Loyalty to the Customer Is Returned The test of a brand is, in fact, the strength of loyalty it generates. If you have a strong relationship with your target audience, then you have a strong brand and a strong business.

EXECUTIVE BRANDING

Lillian Vernon Puts a Human Face on Her Business

When a company is named after a person, it puts a human face on an anonymous corporate entity. This marketing strategy has obviously worked for Lillian Vernon, a woman who created a very successful personal brand from her kitchen table five decades ago.

Lillian Vernon is one of America's most accomplished and well-known leaders in the catalog industry. According to an Opinion Research poll, more than 39 million Americans are familiar with the Lillian Vernon name.

"When I first launched the company in 1951, my marketing plan was simple. I wanted to establish a memorable face behind my company to add a personal touch to our business," says Vernon. "I wanted my customers to feel that I am their personal shopper. My persona is the key to maintaining our loyal customer base."

Reputation Is Priceless The only way to be successful in business is by establishing a good reputation, and a brand can help you do that. Your reputation works as your strongest marketer by communicating the relationship you have with people who've done business with you, and your target market.

The following pages focus on two critical elements that communicate a brand identity: personality and expertise.

Personality Branding

Personality branding is a strategy that showcases your personality and equates it with your business to produce an emotional bond with your prospects. In other words, you put a human face on your business by bringing your personality to the forefront of your marketing and business identity. It's also an opportunity to express your entrepreneurial passion—to show how your background and interests inform the soul of your business.

REAL-WORLD SUCCESS STORY

Dave Hirschkop Proves That a Little Insanity Goes a Long Way

When you meet Dave Hirschkop at a trade show, don't expect to shake his hand, because he'll be wearing a straitjacket and standing before a simulated insane asylum to promote his popular line of "Insanity" hot sauces.

Hirschkop has become a living testament to the power of personal branding. His company, Dave's Gourmet, Inc., steps to the front of the crowded hot sauce category, while his brand identity has resulted in fiercely loyal customers and great media exposure.

"When people eventually meet me, they expect to find a wild man who wants to burn everything in sight," Dave says, "but I'm just a normal guy with a sense of humor who went into my business and created my brand by accident. It was sort of a joke."

Dave's "Insanity" sauces came into existence when he owned a small Mexican restaurant near the University of Maryland. Late at night, a number of his patrons became drunk and troublesome. "I discovered that when I'd feed drunks my hot sauce, they either left or became extremely quiet. The hotter the sauce, the faster drunk patrons left."

After her catalogs grew in popularity, she created a bond with customers by including a personal letter and photograph in each catalog. Lillian's letters became such an inspiration that Hillary Rodham Clinton once told a group of leading businesswomen that she felt that she knew Lillian Vernon by reading her letters long before they actually met at the White House.

Because customers responded with true curiosity about Vernon's life, she wrote about her dog, which then gained a role in making the Lillian Vernon brand. "Mopsey gets fan mail, has appeared on the front cover of our catalog and even has her own page on our website," says Vernon. "Our customers like knowing that I'm a happy pet owner."

In 1995, when Lillian Vernon went online, the Internet turned out to be a

This gave Dave the idea that he could become a standout maker of hot sauces in a crowded market by making the hottest sauce possible, even hotter than people really liked! Instead of promising sensual pleasure, he promised pain, even danger—but pain that came with bragging rights. It took a while to realize that he had to be really extreme. "At first, nobody wanted the sauce, and we got no respect. We decided we'd really need to hammer people."

When Dave introduced his Insanity Sauce at the National Fiery Foods Show in New Mexico, he made attendees sign a release form before tasting from a bottle that came in a coffin-like box wrapped with yellow police tape.

His Insanity Reserve hot sauce is still the brand leader, so fiery that he doesn't recommend it for human consumption. His best publicity coup happened when a show promoter had a minor respiratory problem after tasting his sauce, and banned him from the show. "That really had a part in our growing popularity," says Dave. "Although you'd have to be insane to eat some of my products, they get people talking."

"I think personal branding works because America wants entrepreneurs to succeed," says Dave. "There are a lot of competitors in hot sauce. We outsell them because they can identify us. We have a certain cachet in our brand."

The more he personalizes his business, the more people gravitate to his products. "People feel like they know me," says Dave. "We get calls at 3:00 a.m. saying, 'Dave, man, you burned me!' I think my all-American name helps, but it's really because we use our smallness and specialty in ways that corporate giants can't touch."

natural vehicle for selling her products and promoting her brand. "The website helped us further promote the brand and reach new people," says Vernon. "Our website includes a page called 'Lillian's Corner,' devoted exclusively to my life, complete with a baby picture and the first ad in Seventeen Magazine that launched our company."

Lillian Vernon has become a household name, an icon featured on numerous television programs including *David Letterman, Conan O'Brien, Jeopardy!, Saturday Night Live, The Daily Show, Northern Exposure*, and *Roseanne*. Her management team spreads her branding philosophy throughout the company to ensure that everyone from customer service representatives to forklift operators are trained to represent the company image.

T. Scott Gross Offers Ten Steps to-Create a MicroBrand

Branding means owning a tiny corner in the mind of someone you want to influence. T. Scott Gross, author of *MicroBranding*, believes the most powerful brands are those with a personal or local identity, implemented through clever promotions, innovative targeted marketing, and strategic networking.

"MicroBrands are efficient, local, and often rely on individual personality," says Gross. "But it's important not to confuse image with brand. A brand rests solely in the mind of the consumer, and it evokes a whole range of information and emotions. An image can evoke a brand but, by itself, a clever logo does not a brand make."

Gross suggests ten specific steps for you to take in creating your "microbrand," as he calls a brand designed to win you a niche market:.

Step One: *Start with Your Own Values*
List your personal values as you perceive them, creating an itemized list that might include such general concepts as integrity, teamwork, and profitability. In twenty-five words or less, describe what it is like working for you from the viewpoint of your employees.

Step Two: *Define the Mission*
The mission statement answers the question, "What is the point of pursuing this line of business?" Good mission statements are meaningful, and short enough to remember easily.

Step Three: *Capture the Vision*
A vision statement answers the question, "How will you know when you have done what you said you would do in your mission statement?" The most important thing about vision is to have one.

Step Four: *Take a Snapshot*
Look at where you are right now. In twenty-five words or less, describe your business in terms of where you are in reaching your vision. Address the issue of awareness and market penetration. What percentage of the market is aware of your brand? What percentage of the market do you currently own?

Step Five: *Identify the Market*

Define your market. Here's an example of the kind of statement you are after: "The ABC market consists of medium-sized companies in the healthcare industry. They have high customer contact and have shown a dedication to customer service. They have a history of investing in training. Fun and creativity are characteristics of their operations and marketing."

Step Six: *Create a Persona*

You need a position statement that defines the mental real estate you want to own. How do you want the market to think of you? A good tag line should start the positioning process.

Step Seven: *Give Yourself a Name*

A name has to capture every aspect of what a company does. It is the most important part of the process. Great names are not generic. Generic names encourage generic business.

Step Eight: *Establish Your Logo*

A great logo will immediately create brand recall, while being a positive, accurate representation of the brand promise. Evaluate it in terms of these two points; then list opportunities for getting your logo seen.

Step Nine: *Enter Your New World*

MicroBranding emphasizes strategic networking. You must recognize the network you already have, and use it to define and grow your brand. List the influential people you already know, and then list the important networking events that you need to attend.

Step Ten: *Command Attention*

MicroBranders get others talking about them. Who are the most influential people in your industry? Who do you already know that could you get an introduction? Who might make a good co-marketing partner? This could even be a competitor!

"It's obviously gratifying to be in the limelight, but our real reward comes from the four million customer orders we receive each year," says Vernon. "Our company works hard to project a unified brand in our eight catalog titles and two websites, and these orders are the payoff."

To Brand Is to Promise

In the information age, brand marketing, which creates an emotional connection between a product and its audience and sets itself apart from the crowd, is more important than ever. Your brand should be your best defense against a cynical world.

Simply put, a brand is a promise. Today's busy consumers don't have time to investigate everything and don't want to be taken. There is more competition than ever. We've seen it all. We've heard every outrageous claim imaginable. And before we are willing to spend our money, we need reassurance.

Against this backdrop, merely doing good work or selling good products is no longer enough. By identifying and authenticating a product or service, branding delivers a pledge of satisfaction and quality. A brand promises value. It gives people something to trust and identify with in a complex world where it's increasingly hard to know what's real and what's not. A brand provides a reassuring aura that not only shows prospects you understand their needs, but that you will deliver value to them time and again.

"A brand is a promise you are willing to keep, to yourself and the clients you serve," says Debra Valle of Marketing U, a virtual university and coaching company for small business owners. "It's doing something consistently and authentically that represents the work you present to the world. This is a formula that is very fulfilling for the small business owner and very attractive to their customers."

Valle, who has been a brand strategist and marketer for Fortune 500 companies, finds that many small businesses believe they're too small to create the kind of distinctive message of a powerful brand. "It doesn't take a Madison Avenue to create distinction in the marketplace; what it takes is a simple willingness to think like a major brand—and a determined effort," says Valle.

"Most small businesses present themselves to the world as a list of facts and services without heart or passion," she explains. "They are unfocused at best, bland at worst, because they fail to connect their brands to who they are or those they serve." Most professionals spend little or no time crafting their brand identity. She believes it is imperative that we intentionally craft our brand, or central message, around our unique passions, skills, and values.

"Your brand must be central to who you are," says Valle. "It must be authentic to you and exclusive to your target market. When you define and live your brand, you live the life you want. You attract the right kind of clients because your brand resonates with desirable clientele. Brands draw from your passions."

Another mistake is to fail to include clients as central players in brand identity. Crafting a brand means finding the overlap between your "gifts" and your customers' "ultimate desires." The territory where the two intersect provides fertile ground for a brilliant marketing campaign, and the key to great brand identity.

"When you are focused with the help of your brand identity, you contribute in a way that's genuine and useful," says Valle. "Your brand helps you know where you're going and how you want to be seen. When businesses make a stand and get behind their brands, business seems to find them."

Trust Opens the Door

If you establish a place of trust and relevance in prospects' minds, you're already in the door. The more people believe in your brand, the more it will spread throughout your niche market without your pushing. If your brand is clear, distinctive, and easily understood, and expresses a compelling benefit that people believe in, it will bring you all the business you can handle.

Brand Extension: Building on What You've Established

When your brand is established, you can use it to grow your business in new directions. Called brand extension, this strategy is employed by businesses that recognize the possibility of taking a brand name that is well-established

TIPS FROM THE GURU

Terri Lonier Briefs Novice Entrepreneurs

Terri Lonier's first business in 1978 was a pottery studio in New York. In selling her own work, Lonier found that she had a natural marketing flair. Soon she was giving workshops to artists on how to market their work. When they started bringing their friends—owners of other small businesses—Terri realized that she could expand to provide business information to the growing ranks of solo entrepreneurs.

Lonier is now the author of five books, including the classic entrepreneurial startup guide, *Working Solo*. Her book was named the #1 choice for solo entrepreneurs by *Inc.* magazine and "the free agent's bible" by *Fast Company* magazine. As the president of Working Solo, Inc., Terri is a recognized authority on the small office and home office (SOHO) market.

As a SOHO professional herself for more than 20 years, Terri knows SOHO from the inside out. "My market niche and resulting brand grew from the fact that I identified an area where I didn't have too many competitors, and I built a brand around it," says Lonier. "When I conceived *Working Solo*, I knew it would be more than just a book. I knew I could develop seminars, tapes, consulting, and eventually an online component around my brand."

An important consideration in brand extension is realizing that markets change, and it is important to analyze your current and future business opportunities periodically. "My interests, like my brand, are always evolving," says Lonier. "Each year I consider my biggest pains and design the coming year to focus on the most promising opportunities."

When *Working Solo* came out, for example, there were a limited number of small business marketing books, and competition was not as fierce. But now, there are many books in her market niche, and Lonier has decided to carve out a new niche, showing the corporate market how to better market to SOHO entrepreneurs.

Terri still works with SOHO businesses, but she also delivers her knowledge on what she calls a "small business revolution" to major corporations through conferences, the media, and her books and seminars. Terri's insights are regularly featured in such publications as the *New York Times, Wall Street Journal, USA Today, Fortune,* and *Business Week*, and on CNBC, CNN, the BBC, and radio programs nationwide.

"Small businesses must be keenly aware of changes in their marketplace," says Lonier. "I initially drew from my core life pursuits, which all involved working solo, to give birth to my brand. Through my ability to adapt to both the challenges and opportunities of my marketplace, I've been able to use 'working solo' as the core idea and unifying center for everything in my evolving empire."

within a particular niche, and cultivating new customers in neighboring niches. Alternatively, a business can capitalize on brand loyalty to provide new services and products to existing customers.

Barbara Hemphill, for instance, started her organizing business in 1978 by placing a $7 ad in a New York City newspaper. Since then, she's developed a multi-pronged branding strategy that targets both individuals and businesses, offering organizing skills designed to reduce stress and increase productivity.

Her *Taming the Paper Tiger* book series established her reputation as a pioneer in the field of professional organizing. This led to the development of Kiplinger's *Taming the Paper Tiger* software, an endorsement by Pendaflex, and the founding of the Hemphill Productivity Institute, a company employing more than 70 Paper Tiger Authorized Consultants in the U.S. and Canada.

The *Slightly Famous* Executive

Branding starts at the top. A CEO, company executive, or solo entrepreneur is a company's most persuasive brand champion. The people in charge set the tone, define the style, and become the company's public face.

A notable executive distinguishes a company from its competitors, infuses character and values into the company's brand, and delivers value in the marketplace and among employees. When products and services are increasingly viewed as commodities, executive branding helps a company differentiate itself.

A study by global communications consultancy Burson-Marsteller indicates that a CEO's reputation is responsible for approximately fifty percent of the company's reputation, directly helping to achieve key business objectives and increase sales. Based on the reputation of the CEO, of those surveyed:

95 percent decide whether to invest in a company

94 percent will believe in a company under pressure from the media

93 percent would recommend a company as a good alliance/merger partner

92 percent maintain confidence in a company

88 percent recommend the company as a good place to work

The survey concluded that establishing the credibility and authenticity of a CEO was the most effective way to drive the reputation of a company.

Executive Branding: A Team Effort

Executive branding must be central to a company's overall strategic plan. A survey by Grant Thornton LLP, a business advisory organization, notes that company leaders must see themselves as the voices of the brand and convey its meaning in words and actions, either individually or as part of a senior leadership team.

"Executive branding sets a company apart from the crowd," says Gregg Feistman, sequence head for public relations at Temple University. "Other things being equal, executive branding helps companies stand out in their industries. When executives get personally involved in the branding process, they position their companies as having a vision for their key markets and a strong commitment to their clients and customers."

"Companies have vision and mission statements, which is all well and good," says Feistman, "but the real question is, 'Okay, how are we going to translate this into real action?'"

According to the Grant Thornton study, keeping the brand promise stays at the top. The CEO is the principal representative of the brand, and brand validity can only be fully achieved if the CEO embodies the brand and its values.

"A company's top executives must live and breathe the company brand," observes Feistman. "A CEO can't say, 'Okay, guys, I want you all to get out there,' unless he or she is also willing to get out there. When a company's top people walk the talk, the rest of the company perceives, 'Wow! This must be serious. They really mean it. It's central to the culture of our organization.'"

Internal Branding: Create a Common Mission

Executive branding not only influences external audiences, it reinforces a company's internal brand, creating a cultural climate within an organization that is consistent with its public message. Employees at all levels of the organization need to reflect the brand promise.

The Grant Thornton study notes that executive branding inspires employees to become brand champions. While the CEO is the chief champion of the brand, he or she cannot promote the brand alone. Branding is a process in

Leslie Gaines-Ross on Building CEO Capital

Leslie Gaines-Ross, author of *CEO Capital: A Guide to Building CEO Reputation and Company Success*, spearheaded the first comprehensive research on CEO reputation and its impact on corporate reputation and performance. Her message is simple: CEOs and corporate reputation are inextricably linked and have a proven impact on the bottom line, influencing whether people choose a company's products, buy its stock, visit its website, or take its side in a crisis.

"Consumers now care more than ever about the authenticity of the corporate brand, and CEO reputation is a critical ingredient. CEO capital transcends 'image' and is based on credibility," says Gaines-Ross. "Are a CEO's actions consistent with his words? Does he contribute to his industry and communicate new ideas that keep his company at the forefront of change? Does he demonstrate thought leadership that distinguishes his company from competitors?"

"CEO capital must be built and maintained, just like any other wealth-creating asset," she continues. "CEOs need to articulate their overall corporate brand promise to customers, how their company is differentiated from competitors, and how its products and services are innovative and high-quality. It needs to be in invested in, managed, and leveraged over the long term to reap enduring benefits."

which CEOs should inspire every employee to share. By rallying employees around the brand, they become brand champions themselves and can promote the brand both within and outside of the workplace.

Executive Branding In Action

Reputation is built over time, and authenticity comes from consistently doing the right thing over a long period of time. Executives must maintain a strong, long-term commitment to executive branding. They should avoid the "big bang" approach, where heavy concentrations of effort around branding initiatives are followed by periods of relative inactivity.

TIPS FROM THE GURU

Jim Jenkins Shows the Key to Strong Internal Brands

"Executive branding is most effective when it achieves buy-in throughout the entire company," says Jim Jenkins, a management consultant and creator of the Renaissance Leadership Program. "This happens when employees experience a direct connection between daily tasks and the organization's brand as it is communicated by company leadership. When executive branding includes an internal branding focus, the benefits of executive branding come full circle. Executive branding creates a credible, emotional connection between employees and the company brand that translates into better customer service, employee loyalty, and a company culture that moves in one direction." He offers the following advice.

Synchronize Your Brand and Corporate Culture Unless executive branding aligns with a company's internal culture, there will be a disconnect between the public message and employees' perceptions about how the company is actually run.

"If a company's brand promise revolves around innovation and the CEO is resistant to change, the brand becomes meaningless," says Jenkins. "A company can't claim to be family-friendly and demand that employees regularly work weekends to meet deadlines. A lack of consistency between what executives say and how employees live company realities can reduce morale, increase turnover, and erode customer service."

Brand from the Inside Out An effective internal branding plan should include:

- Company-wide town hall meetings, making use of multimedia such as video conferencing or telephone bridge lines
- Two-way communication using a Woblog on a company intranet site, allowing opportunities for employees' feedback
- A robust internal branding communications program, including employee handbooks, e-mail, podcasts
- A "from the desk of" executive column in the company newsletter
- Brand celebration events to mark the introduction of, and achievements in, your executive branding strategy
- Company training that reinforces the brand message

Engage in Two-Way Feedback Ensure that employees understand how the external brand relates to their job functions. Keep a pulse on how employees feel about being part of the company, while allowing them to influence how you evolve your external brand.

At JetBlue Airlines, executives solicit employee feedback through town hall meetings at the airline's major hubs. JetBlue executives maintain congruency between the company's external brand message and its internal climate. Once a week, JetBlue's CEO boards a flight and assumes the duties of an airline attendant to personally greet each customer. "The CEO later takes the crew to dinner for an open discussion about the company, making him one of the most accessible executives in business," Jenkins comments.

4 Thought Leadership

Marketing used to be about finding prospects, delivering your pitch, and selling them your products and services. Today, consumers are dismissive of self-promotional marketing because they see it for what it is—a biased message lacking both objectivity and credibility.

In addition, consumers are harder to reach and actively impose barriers against marketers. They prefer to initiate contact on their own terms. With the help of the Internet, consumers are better informed and possess a much greater ability to investigate purchasing decisions. They want to be educated, not sold.

The answer is to offer the information prospects are seeking, making your business a partner in your prospects' research and evaluation process. Instead of marketing at prospects, you become a "thought leader," providing useful, honest information at each stage of the buying cycle that will help consumers make informed buying decisions.

REAL-WORLD SUCCESS STORY

Beryl Chooses Educational Marketing over Self-Promotion

A provider of outsourced customer service to the healthcare industry, The Beryl Companies recently created The Beryl Institute, a research and education arm for developing white papers, webinars, and benchmarking statistics that are disseminated free to healthcare providers nationwide.

"The richness of the information we have at our fingertips provides great insight into the behaviors, needs, and demographics of healthcare consumers across the U.S.," says Paul Spiegelman, founder and CEO of Beryl. "The Beryl Institute provides value to our target market and positions our firm as a thought leader by disseminating this valuable data."

The Beryl white paper "Understanding the Importance of Accountability for Hospital Marketing Investments," for example, helps hospital executives measure the return on investment of their marketing expenditures. Beryl's educational seminars and webinars about the value of customer relationship management are offered to directors and executives at client and prospect companies.

Beryl's educational efforts have helped a relatively small, privately held company develop a national reputation. "Our thought leadership initiatives give customers comparative data and case studies that improve their businesses," says Spiegelman. "Thought leadership positions us as a partner who puts our customer's needs first, rather than a vendor eager to sell more products and services. We've earned a reputation as a company that actively shapes our industry."

Thought leadership marketing depends on your developing new concepts and solutions, and then sharing that information with your prospective clients and customers.

Thought leaders earn trust by delivering valuable information with no strings attached. Instead of creating sales resistance by pushing your products and services, you establish yourself as a business with integrity.

New Rules for Selling to Big Companies

Corporate executives wield tremendous buying clout. According to the 2006 U.S. Business Elite Survey by Ipsos Media, senior executives make or influence more than $1.2 trillion a year in spending decisions. These executives have purchasing responsibility for information technology, telecommunications, office and industrial equipment, financial and insurance services, automobiles, and business services.

Yet, over the past decade, selling to corporate clients has become more difficult. Corporate buyers are facing pressure to accomplish more with fewer resources. Many companies have consolidated, making it difficult to locate the appropriate internal decision makers. Voicemail is the new gatekeeper, making it harder—if not impossible—to reach the very people within large companies who are critical to begin the selling process.

With filters intercepting e-mail and telephone solicitations, sellers must reengineer their strategies. "Corporate decision makers have no time for self-serving salespeople," says Jill Konrath, author of *Selling to Big Companies.* "They want to work with people who possess keen insights into issues and trends that impact their companies."

Konrath asserts that effective corporate sales strategies must shun traditional self-promotion in favor of approaches based on improving a prospect's business, solving problems, and creating value through unique ideas and insights. She offers three rules:

1. Focus on making a difference, not getting a sale.
Successful sellers understand that corporate buyers work with vendors who provide value through their knowledge and expertise, not well-honed sales pitches or elevator speeches.

"Thought leadership appeals to the corporate decision makers' need for relevant, useful information. It helps you stand out from a crowd of cold callers," says Konrath. "Thought leaders strive to make a difference by delivering value to prospects. They position themselves as visible, credible, prospect-focused resources."

As products and services become more commoditized, successful sellers articulate their value by providing relevant information that helps prospects see why change is imperative and why their business is part of the answer.

"Selling must combine your offering with your expertise and depth of knowledge," Konrath remarks. "Instead of sending self-promotional brochures, you can publish articles about business issues and send them to prospects. You can create blog entries and podcasts that discuss issues facing their best prospects. This approach positions you as a business improvement specialist; prospects will view interactions as valuable consultations rather than as sales meetings."

2. Understand the role of the Internet.

The Internet creates new opportunities for sellers. It also empowers corporate buyers with easy access to information about products and services. "Corporate buyers perform online research to avoid meetings with salespeople whenever possible," says Konrath. "This effectively eliminates the traditional role of the salesperson as a provider of basic facts and features about their products and services."

People expect to find basic information about your company at the click of a mouse. Those who continue to rely on traditional selling techniques risk becoming obsolete. To make the Internet an effective part of your selling strategy, you must focus on showing your value, demonstrating your worth, and making a difference. A credible web presence delivers value. Your website should provide fresh, educational content that helps corporate prospects see your business as a solution.

"Corporate buyers visit and read vendor websites throughout the sales cycle," says Konrath. "Your website must scream credibility. Show prospects that you contribute to your industry by including articles, case studies, and success stories. If your website is only an online brochure, they'll disregard it as biased and self-promotional."

3. Seek outside validation.

Thought leaders are recognized by their industry and peers. Strive to obtain third-party endorsements from trusted resources. Publish articles and offer quotes to trade magazines. Contribute to respected industry websites and blogs. Give talks and take part in panel discussions at conferences and professional association meetings.

According to a recent KnowledgeStorm/CMO Council study, "Define What's Valued Online," buyers access independent, third-party content to make more informed buying decisions. The top six most trusted sources were industry associations, analysts, journalists, independent product reviews, peer forums, and online discussion groups.

"Buyers go to trusted sources for tactical tips, for higher-level strategic insights, and to stay on top of emerging industry trends," says Heather Foster, director of marketing at KnowledgeStorm. "These buyers want to know what other people—especially experts—think about solutions and information in your industry."

Konrath adds, "Your expert knowledge may seem like common sense, but it's exactly what corporate prospects want and need. When you give away your knowledge and expertise, it comes back to you in greater abundance. Ultimately, if you keep up these strategies, clients and prospects will say, 'I see your name everywhere.'"

Reach Prospects Regardless of Their Readiness to Buy

Ongoing lead generation is a pressing concern for most marketers. But if you only plan for those sales prospects who have an immediate need, you leave behind the majority, all the people who could benefit from your service at some point in the future. Prospects may come across your business months, even years, before they need your services. It can happen in a Web browser when someone looks you up, or within an e-mail newsletter that mentions your name.

Marketing through thought leadership expands the possibility of what constitutes a sales prospect, positioning your business in the minds of your prospects early in the buying cycle. It establishes your business as a familiar, trusted entity, ensuring that your company comes to mind when the need arises. People evaluate companies and products on the Internet, and 'selling' takes place even when a salesperson isn't present.

Moreover, your information can reach all who influence the buying process. This includes corporate assistants who are instructed to research potential vendors in your industry, or a company representative who searches for you online after hearing you speak at a conference. Information they find now may help them remember your company later, when they are making buying decisions.

REAL-WORLD SUCCESS STORY

Spencer, Fane, Britt & Browne Provides Information to a Defined Market

Spencer, Fane, Britt & Browne is a Kansas City law firm that specializes in working with professional building contractors. In 2005, they committed to positioning their firm as thought leaders to Midwest construction industries and created Midwest Construction Law, a comprehensive online resource.

Midwest Construction Law has articles, educational teleseminars, a blog, and a free e-booklet called *How to Use Your Law Firm to Get the Most from Your Construction Business*.

"It's given us credibility and lent us notoriety in our target market. Twenty-five to eighty participants regularly take part in our teleseminars, and some become clients. Prospects contact us from the website and say, 'I see you do succession planning. Can I talk to you about it?' The site has generated two or three speaking opportunities because it's created a buzz within the Midwest construction industries, as more and more people turn to it as a resource," says David Seitter, a principal at the firm.

Perhaps the most profound benefit is that Midwest Construction Law helps prospects during the purchase research phase and demonstrates a credible commitment to the construction industries. "When I hand my card to a prospect that includes the tagline, 'If you want more information about the construction industry, visit www.midwestconstructionlaw.com,' it really piques their interest, because they see that we are committed to the construction industry."

Expertise: You Have It, So Flaunt It

Branding your business around your expertise means using your knowledge to communicate competence and industry leadership to your target market. Achieving an expert's reputation transforms you from being just another vendor vying for your customers' limited funds, to being a trusted advisor with intimate knowledge of their situation. In a world where product characteristics are easily copied, or are perceived to be minimal, your expertise communicates your individuality—something that nobody can duplicate.

Not so long ago, expertise was equated with the number of years you were in business, or the college diploma that hung on your wall. That has changed

TIPS FROM THE GURU

Brian Carroll on the Art of Nurturing Leads

"Lead nurturing is about consistent and meaningful communication, regardless of prospects' timing to buy," says Brian Carroll, author of *Lead Generation for the Complex Sale*. "It's not calling up every few months to find out if a prospect is ready to buy yet. Lead nurturing is about building solid relationships with prospects from their first interaction with your company, through the sales process, until the sale closes."

According to Carroll, lead nurturing is not a single marketing tactic or event, but a series of steps that establish a relationship between a business and a potential customer. It starts with a conversation that keeps going. "The true value of lead nurturing comes from staying in touch with prospects and providing them with useful information as they move through the exploration, evaluation, and buying process," says Carroll.

An effective lead nurturing program can include a series of letters, e-mails, voicemails, case studies, success stories, articles, events, white papers, and webcasts that educate prospects.

"Lead nurturing addresses questions and concerns, and shows prospects the benefits of working with you," says Carroll. "It delivers value and establishes trust by giving prospects meaningful information in bite-sized chunks. People say, 'How you sell me is how you will serve me.' When you are a trusted advisor, you're in a better position to get the sale, because you've delivered insights and solutions rather than sales pitches."

---

as people have become more interested in results. If you can deliver, people will be interested in you, no matter how brief your business experience or how bare your walls.

Experts are sought-after. They get more business with less effort, and command higher fees. Journalists come to them for information. They are asked to speak at conferences. They out-position their competitors because they know more and are recognized for knowing more.

Marketing guru Dan Kennedy stated, "You don't need someone else's permission to become successful." By the same token, you don't have to be appointed by anyone other than yourself to become an expert in your field.

Becoming an expert takes work, but it's within your reach. You don't need a special degree, but you do need a willingness to learn.

Commit to Lifelong Learning

To become an expert, you need a deliberate strategy to help you understand everything you can about your market niche. You don't need to know everything, which is impossible, but you need to be considerably better informed than most. Staying in this position is a process that never ends.

Your future is directly related to how much you develop yourself. You may have the fanciest brochures or an impressive client list, but if you don't continue to invest in your own development, you won't remain competitive. Look for the gaps in your knowledge, and find ways to fill them.

Experts know their fields are always changing. They constantly update their knowledge and look for ways to stay knowledgeable.

Eric Mower and Associates (EMA) is a six-office marketing communications firm that makes thought leadership central to its organizational mission. Mower encourages employees to spend five hours a week learning about their clients' businesses, anticipating problems and seizing opportunities, and pursuing opportunities to broadcast their thought leadership efforts to their market niche.

EMA principals speak at conferences, participate in expert panels and take a leadership role in the Business Marketing Association. The company conducts proprietary research on topics that affect client industries and recently published an eight-part article series called Brand Aids, which provides new insights on business-to-business marketing.

"Our employees spend at least five hours a week on thought leadership activities, including reading client industry trade journals, attending new media seminars, and perusing clients' and competitors' corporate websites," says John Favalo, managing partner and director of EMA's business-to-business practice. "It's how we demonstrate that we stay on top of our client's total business situation and illustrate our commitment to providing smart ideas to our clients."

Fred M. Tibbitts, Jr. Will Drink to That!

Frederick M. Tibbitts, Jr. founded Fred Tibbitts & Associates in 1992 to help food and beverage companies reach global markets. Since then, he's strategically cultivated a reputation in his industry as one of the most well-connected and knowledgeable global beverage-marketing experts.

Tibbitts has become *slightly famous* within the beverage world by becoming fluent in all the details of his business. He monitors global beverage trends on a daily basis while staying in contact with global account managers at hotels and restaurants. He also hosts a series of special events, "Fred Tibbitts Spring & Autumn Dinners with Special Friends," in key markets. Guest lists at these events read like a Who's Who of the beverage world.

"I'm as much a global beverage strategist as anything else," says Tibbitts. "I constantly update my knowledge of world news and events, and I read everything about the beverage world. I try to see the relationships between seemingly distinct things to see what the future holds. And I maintain a vast human network that adds value to my clients."

His commitment to understanding his niche, which means a total dedication to learning everything about his clients' condition and what may affect it, has made him the foremost expert within his industry, virtually eliminating competition.

Tibbitts also attracts media attention. He contributes a wine column to *Hospitality International Magazine* in London six times a year, and numerous industry publications have published articles about his company.

"I'm fond of the Buddhist saying, 'When you open your heart to the world, the world opens its heart to you,'" says Tibbitts. "When you know your stuff and put others first, it's a formula for becoming dominant in your target market. I'm living proof."

Establish and Articulate a Viewpoint

It's not enough just to be an expert. You need to use your knowledge to deliberately distinguish yourself from your competitors. This means fitting your expertise in your positioning and branding strategy. Assess what others are doing, saying, and writing about your industry. Your goal is not just to be fully informed, but to develop connections between your industry and the larger world.

Jump into the ongoing industry discussions. These discussions often can be found in trade publications, industry websites, newsletters, Internet chat rooms, and at trade association meetings and events. Your goal is to plug yourself into every possible outlet that influences your niche.

When you become a thought leader, your company is acknowledged as the authentic leader of the thinking in your industry. Thought leaders do not seek controversy for its own sake, but they are willing to challenge the prevailing wisdom in their industry when it can have a positive impact on their target market.

Experts know that they must actively seek out new evidence that impacts their theories and assumptions. Keep on the lookout for statistics, case studies, and research that either substantiates or refutes your thinking. You don't need an ultimate truth, but you do need to articulate your position clearly and have the relevant facts close at hand.

Read Everything You Can

Subscribe to e-mail newsletters, news services, and specialized publications. These sources enable you to take the pulse of your industry. Trade magazines cover all the issues that affect your niche, while providing up-to-the-minute information you won't find anywhere else. If you can't afford all the magazines, you might be able to find them in a library or read back issues on websites.

Don't just study the contents of the articles; note who wrote them. Because writers often specialize in an industry, you will see their names again and again. These people can become valuable sources of information and potential messengers for your business. Set aside dedicated times to read these publications and clip articles of interest.

Make frequent trips to a business bookstore for books that address your industry, niche, and type of work. Develop a reference collection you can turn to for dependable information. Read and act on what you learn. Allocate a budget for resources that advance your expertise-seeking agenda.

You Are the Resource

Becoming a resource in your target market starts with sharing your knowledge. You can give away free information—booklets, helpful reports, valuable website content—to attract interest without sales pressure. The more you become a source of expert information, the more potential customers trust you. You become part of their world, a center of influence; since people like to do business with people they know, or know of, you will be their first choice.

Thought leaders position themselves as centers of influence. They are always "present" within their target markets. Visibility is part of their formula, so they cultivate opportunities to be seen, read, and heard by the people who matter most. They make sure their prospects hear from them on a regular basis. Most importantly, they "walk the walk" as well as "talk the talk." Their credibility skyrockets because they are confident and consistent in the messages they send.

Thought Leadership in Action

As a central component of any marketing plan, thought leadership seeks to influence not just prospects and end users, but all the editors, analysts, columnists, trade associations, and relevant stakeholders that influence buying decisions. The potential is great, as the illustration shows.

This concept serves as a gateway to the *get slightly famous* marketing strategies discussed in Parts II and III of this book. Each expresses a different aspect of thought leadership.

"Thought leadership starts by taking a good look at your target market and identifying the point on the horizon where you want to take your organization," says Antony Bell, Managing Partner of The Bell Group and author of *Great Leadership: What It Is and What It Takes In a Complex World*. "Thought leaders determine opportunities to position themselves within their target market based on their key competitive advantages."

Thought leadership begins with a top-down initiative that welcomes participation. For large organizations, thought leadership marketing succeeds when CEOs and executives create the conditions that foster thought leader-

EXECUTIVE BRANDING

John Chambers Leads a Total Company Commitment to Thought Leadership

Computer networking equipment maker Cisco Systems demonstrates thought leadership marketing at the highest levels of the company. Led by CEO John Chambers, Cisco's entire senior management team promotes Cisco as a leader in the technology field, actively evangelizing business concepts that connect Cisco to its broader marketplace through speeches, articles, webcasts, and countless direct engagements with all those in the technology industry "ecosystem."

"When we practice thought leadership, we focus on several criteria. It must be visionary. It must anticipate and comment on future trends. It must be provocative, and it must put our customer's needs first," says Mark Peshoff, senior director of Cisco's Executive Thought Leadership.

Many CEOs articulate visions for their own organizations. Cisco stresses the goal of articulating a future vision for Cisco's customers. In one example, Chambers recently exhorted the telecommunications industry about the need to transition from voice to data as a key opportunity.

Chambers demands that every Cisco executive establish and nurture his or her own reputation for thought leadership, through blogging, public speaking, and writing articles. Cisco's website has an area devoted to executive thought leadership, with links to research reports, papers, podcasts, interviews, and other con-

ship at all levels of a company. "Without widespread ownership, there is little likelihood that companies will not generate the internal momentum critical to thought leadership in the marketplace," says Bell.

tent, much of it from Cisco executives.

The company publishes a newsletter, *Executive Thought Leadership Quarterly*, to which Chambers is a leading contributor. It also hosts an online resource called ExecNet that offers videos featuring Cisco senior executives discussing how Internet technologies and solutions impact all aspects of business. Recent videos include "How Can Companies Grow Profits in Today's Competitive World?," featuring Gary Bridge, senior vice president of Cisco's Internet Business Solutions Group, and "Interactions: The Next Productivity Horizon," with John Chambers.

Cisco also hosts thought leadership events, including a series of executive summits that bring together representatives from academia with Cisco executives to address very specific topics related to business and technology. These summits have addressed such diverse issues as technology challenges facing small businesses in China, and the linkages between information technology and business strategy.

Cisco produces a series of podcasts, available through the Cisco website, that feature company executives discussing issues of the day. Recently Paul Mountford, president of the Emerging Markets Theatre, discussed "Net Impact: Latin America."

Once a company has established a reputation as a thought leader, the rest of the industry, the media, academia, government policymakers, and the broader business community turn to that company for ideas and for insights. According to Cisco, that is where their thought leadership efforts pay off. "The credibility we gain through thought leadership contributes to a sustainable market leadership position," says Peshoff. "Cisco's status in the technology field and the business world, and its dedication to thought leadership are inseparable."

Thought leadership is a long-term, ongoing process. Thought leaders maintain their commitment to lead, influence, and communicate within their industries for the duration of their careers.

TIPS FROM THE GURU

Robert Middleton Offers Solutions and Information

Robert Middleton of Action Plan Marketing promotes and practices a strategy called "InfoGuru Marketing," based on his observation that giving away your expertise is an effective way to gain trust, attract prospects, and become a center of influence.

"All my successful marketing strategies are based on solutions and information," says Middleton. "For an Internet Service Provider, we created a booklet that promised to untangle the Internet. For the executive recruiter, it was a unique search process that guaranteed client satisfaction. For me, it was giving talks with a focus on attracting new clients. In every case we were offering ideas and information that promised a desired solution."

Middleton now urges his clients to give away solution-based information to leverage their credibility. The more you give away, he contends, the more you are perceived as a partner that clients want to do business with.

"This works because you're providing valuable information and resources and spend virtually no time talking about what you do or what you know," says Middleton. "Instead, you learn what prospects need and determine where they want to go. Then, instead of pushing people away because you are trying too hard to sell them, they are attracted because you have something they want."

PART II

Media Strategies

5 Media Strategies That Work

When you read about a business in the newspaper or hear about it on the radio, chances are you immediately elevate that business above its competitors. It has solidity and credibility. This is precisely why media relations (usually referred to as "public relations" or simply "PR") is the ultimate s*lightly famous* marketing strategy. No other marketing method delivers so much impact for so little investment of time and money.

The public values the media, and so should you. In one way or another, the media reach and influence everyone with a direct impact on your business. Thus, when properly pursued, media strategies will help establish your reputation and build your brand, reaching far more prospects than you could in person.

Getting media attention requires knowledge and effort on your part, but it's not magic. The strategies discussed in the following chapters are designed

REAL-WORLD SUCCESS STORY

Bart Baggett Pursues the Media and Wins

Handwriting analysis expert Bart Baggett has always had a knack for self-promotion. He began studying handwriting analysis when he was fifteen. Soon he was marketing a line of flash cards for personality assessment based on handwriting analysis, first to fellow high school students, then to fellow college students.

But when Baggett decided to make handwriting analysis his adult career, he realized that he needed to do something special to stand out in a profession comprising 30,000 other handwriting experts. He was young and unknown, and he needed an edge. Baggett turned to the media to help him establish his credibility as a handwriting expert and become a mini-celebrity in his market niche.

"I knew then that my young age was against me and that I needed third-party validation as a handwriting expert to succeed. Because I saw that successful people pursued the media, I knew that if I could convince reporters and producers of my abilities, those who read about me or saw me would believe in me too."

Baggett studied newspapers, magazines, and radio and television programs to find out what types of guests were in demand. He then looked for ways to tie his professional abilities to specific media needs.

At the height of the O.J. Simpson trial, he sent out a news release about Simpson's handwriting that resulted in several timely media interviews. He later appeared on Court TV to discuss Timothy McVeigh's handwriting, and was recommended by the director of that program to CNN. Over the years, Baggett has appeared on hundreds of programs, including Howard Stern and Montel Williams. A feature in *Biography* magazine led to stories in the *London Times,* the *Dallas Morning News,* and others.

Baggett attributed his success to his reputation for being an available, articulate, entertaining, and easy-to-work-with media guest. "I prominently display evidence of my previous media appearances on my website," says Baggett. "Now, editors and producers call me because they see my track record and tons of media experience."

specifically for small businesses, and they are within the reach of anyone with a basic understanding of how the media works. For those who take the time to understand and follow the guidelines that will be offered, the results can be spectacular.

The Rewards of Media Exposure

Media Relations, or PR, is first and foremost about obtaining favorable media exposure for your business—but unlike advertising, it's free. And though usually the result of a lot of work, it's hard to find a more cost-effective way to reach potential customers or clients. The rewards are very real. Here are the kinds of results you can look for.

Increased Sales Although PR is often seen as merely an image-building tool, it can directly bring in new clients and customers. When your phone number appears in a magazine article, for example, you generate inquiries and orders.

Instant Credibility The *slightly famous* approach to embracing the media is built on the understanding that everyone is swamped with marketing messages, and with so many alternatives clamoring for our attention, it's hard to know who is authentic.

Advertisers and marketers agree that the more often someone sees your name, the more predisposed they are to buy from you—an effect that grows when your name appears in contexts that imply you are competent. PR works because it associates your name with the authority of the media.

Enhanced Status As a businessperson, you undoubtedly possess special knowledge. But what good is that expertise if nobody knows about it? When your name appears in print or on the air, you acquire an aura of expertise that will get you more business with less effort.

Expanded Reach No matter how much you network or attend meetings, you can only go so far on your own. Public relations can quickly take you to a larger audience, sometimes focusing national attention on a small, local operation.

Continuing Benefits Any media coverage you obtain can be effectively utilized long afterward. Reprints of articles you've written or been quoted in, and copies of audios or videos of media appearances, make excellent marketing materials that are less expensive, and more convincing, than anything you create yourself. Article reprints can easily replace expensive brochures, mailers, and newsletters. You can send out cassettes of a radio appearance to prospective clients, or, if you are quoted in a magazine or newspaper, you can photocopy the article and send it to prospects as a no-pressure means of keeping in touch.

PR Versus Advertising

While the terms advertising and PR are sometimes used interchangeably, they really refer to quite distinct marketing tools. With advertising, you are purchasing space or airtime in the media. Public relations is the art of getting the media to give you free coverage.

While there are, of course, expenses involved in getting the "free" coverage of PR, especially if you hire an agency or professional to handle the job, for small businesses the relative cost-effectiveness of PR as a marketing tool can be a tremendous advantage.

As important as the cost savings involved in PR is the credibility that it carries. Advertising is, after all, what you say about yourself, and therefore always suspect. In contrast, PR has others talking about you, and because praise from others is far more credible than praise from yourself, a favorable mention in the media of you or your business is much more effective than even the most powerful advertisement. It's an independent validation of your worth.

Why then do so many businesses rely on advertising to market themselves? Because it's something over which they have complete control. When you buy an ad, you choose the publication, select the size of your ad, and determine what it says and when it appears. PR campaigns come with no such control. In particular, you have no say in the message as it actually appears in the media, or even if it will appear.

Even if you attract a reporter's attention and find yourself guiding an interview, in the end reporters print what they think makes for a good story. This does not diminish PR's place as an important investment in your *slightly famous* marketing strategy, but you do have to understand that results are

TIPS FROM THE GURU

Anthony Mora Discusses the Primacy of Public Relations

Most small businesses don't make media relations part of their marketing strategy because they don't fully understand it. In doing so they lose a lot, because PR is the only form of marketing that produces both public awareness and the implied endorsement that comes with appearing in the media as a news story.

"PR is often considered the poor step-sister of advertising—a non-essential activity that's nice to pursue but not a basic business priority," says Anthony Mora of Anthony Mora Communications. "But because media exposure carries a lot of weight with potential clients and customers, it can become the foundation for all of your success. The financial aspect of PR is very appealing — where else can you get that kind of exposure and endorsement without paying for the coverage?"

Mora believes that most businesses don't understand they are worthy of media attention — yet all businesses have a story to tell. "Smaller businesses might think they're too small for national media. That's not true," says Mora. "The golden rule of PR is that you need to think about how you can be helpful to reporters first. In other words, if you do enough favors, and help a reporter on deadline write a really good story, you will become a media darling, and PR will come to you without too much effort.

"To get the media interested in your business, you have to see the value of your expertise, or tell a story that makes readers interested. Stand back from your business and determine what makes you unique. It's a matter of determining what's distinctive about what you do or what you know, and approaching the media with a carefully crafted pitch or introduction."

The secret, says Mora, is presenting yourself as a "resource." This means adopting a long-term strategy of getting yourself seen as an indispensable part of your industry — so much so that when anyone pursues a topic related to your industry, they are doing themselves a disservice by not talking to you.

Because developing this type of media reputation takes time, businesses should not expect too much too fast, and give up on PR too soon. Like any other marketing strategy, PR is an on-going process. You have to do more than get one article in one magazine to make your name a household word in the households that count.

"Don't take rejection personally," says Mora. "Remember that when the media says 'no' to one of your suggestions, they're only saying 'no' to that specific idea, not to your business. They are only saying that what you are presenting to them is not the right fit at that time. The key is persistence. The more PR you pursue, the more you get your name in front of the media, the easier it becomes."

inconsistent. Experienced practitioners who master PR may get better percentages, but they never achieve 100 percent.

The Media Need You

The world is a big place. Because the scope of news is so vast, no media outlet could possibly know about every topic worth covering. They rely on public relations efforts from all kinds of sources to help them spot interesting news stories. People just like you help shape the news because editors and reporters need tips, specialized knowledge, and unique story ideas from small businesses.

Although many of the stories you read in the papers have been generated by reporters through investigation and research, many others are generated by PR practitioners who have pitched their story to the media.

In the book *Targeted Public Relations*, Robert W. Bly cites a study conducted by the *Columbia Journalism Review* that analyzed a single issue of the *Wall Street Journal* to determine the influence of public relations on the stories that got published. The survey found 111 stories were taken from press releases, and in only 30 percent of the stories did reporters put in additional facts not contained in the original press release.

Here are some of the many ways for your small business to get coverage:
- alert the media to story ideas within your industry
- position yourself as an industry expert or commentator
- organize and promote a public event
- tie your business to current issues
- write articles for trade publications
- showcase an unusual aspect of your business

A story of genuine interest, even one limited to a small number of readers or viewers, is newsworthy.

Partnering with the Media

Although PR is free, it is not "free advertising." Reporters are loyal to accurate reporting and genuinely good stories. The secret to success is positioning your business as a media partner. If you make your expertise and experience available where it's needed, you can help the media do its job while getting valuable exposure for your business.

Part of developing an ongoing relationship with the media involves being at their disposal. Because they have daily deadlines, reporters and editors are almost always in a hurry. They expect you to know this and adjust your schedule accordingly. You will be expected to make time for reporters who, at the last minute, want to interview you for a story due that day. Or you may have to make yourself available weekends or early mornings in order to get interviewed on a radio station.

Finally, there are no guarantees in the world of media relations. The media are not obligated to use your articles, interviews, or pitches in stories. This means that even though you spend time helping a journalist, you may not appear in the final story. You may write an article for a trade journal, only to have it pulled at the last minute due to space constraints. You might promote a charitable event with commitments from local television stations, only to have coverage pre-empted by a breaking news story.

These setbacks will happen, and there's nothing you can do about it. But editors, program directors, and journalists will remember your helpfulness. The media need you, their industry news source, because you help make their jobs possible. By being useful and putting a reporter's needs above your own, you will over time enjoy ongoing media exposure and the benefits it provides.

Establishing and benefiting from a media partnership requires a new way of thinking. It's not enough to have good information; you must give the media a reason to pay attention. You must become adept at turning your business or industry expertise into focused stories with built-in media appeal. With a little knowledge and the right attitude, this is a skill you can develop.

The *Slightly Famous* Media Plan

Slightly famous PR strategies are about developing a systematic approach to marketing that embraces the media on its own terms in ways that will directly

EXECUTIVE BRANDING

Marty Pichinson: The Grim Reaper of Silicon Valley

Sherwood Partners is a liquidator of defunct technology companies. In the aftermath of the dot-com bust of the early 2000s, venture capital firms handed over at-risk or failing operations to Sherwood to salvage what it could. This grim line of work earned Pichinson the moniker "the grim reaper" among industry insiders. When he showed up at your door, the game was usually over.

Though Sherwood is among a small number of restructuring outfits in Northern California, CEO Marty Pichinson understands the value of media exposure. His willingness to work hard to pursue media opportunities helped him position Sherwood as the go-to firm for start-ups running out of time.

"Sherwood Partners isn't the only business gravedigger in Silicon Valley," says Pichinson, "but by aggressively raising my personal profile through media appearances, I separated our firm from the rest of the pack." Pichinson became a regular on Canada's ROBtv all-business news station, and has been featured in Fast Company, National Public Radio, Economist.com, the *San Jose Mercury News, USA Today, Fortune,* the *New York Times*, the *Wall Street Journal*, the *Washington Post*, the *Boston Globe*, the *Los Angeles Times* and *The Deal.com*, among others.

Despite a busy schedule running his business, Pichinson never passes up an opportunity for media coverage. "I take media coverage very seriously," he explains. "My total commitment to generating media coverage has helped me land feature stories about my company in major publications. I've flown, at my own expense, to journalists' offices in New York when I thought it would result in a better story."

Moreover, the results have shown up on the bottom line. "There are many companies that do great work, but do you know who they are? By branding myself as a CEO thought leader in my industry, it has enabled us to demand a premium fee."

Pichinson suggests that executives should make media coverage a personal priority. "There is a major benefit for executives who get personally and intimately involved in the branding process. After all, it's your company, and you know the heart and soul of what makes your company tick. Who better to make a case to the media than you?"

benefit your business. You need to craft a plan, consistent with your business and industry, that appeals to your market niche and supports your overall branding strategy.

If you've followed the advice of previous chapters, you've established a foundation from which to launch your *slightly famous* PR campaign. Now you need to work on becoming a mini-celebrity.

Strategic Placement

PR can be-labor intensive, so it's important to fashion a media strategy that emphasizes the media outlets that regularly reach your target market. Look for the centers of influence for your niche, such as trade associations or professional groups that regularly address your audience. Are your potential customers more likely to respond if they read about you in the *Daily Bugle,* a trade publication such as *Management Review*, or a chamber of commerce newsletter?

Sometimes a humble trade publication is the ideal spot to reach your best prospects. A highly specialized consulting firm might seek and get lots of coverage in its local paper, but if its customers are distributed throughout the country, and can be reached only through a trade publication, the effort is wasted. *Slightly famous* marketers are never seduced by media coverage for its own sake. They do not measure success in column inches, but rather by how much their reputation is spread and enhanced among the right people. Effective use of the media means reaching the right people with the right message.

A Continuous Effort

Because it is central to your *slightly famous* marketing plan, media relations need to be integrated into your everyday business. Media strategies connect not just to your marketing strategy, but also to the place your business has in the life of your clients, customers, and everyone in contact with your business.

Integrating media relations into your business requires that you:

- Read everything that affects your industry
- Keep your website up-to-date with relevant information

REAL-WORLD SUCCESS STORY

Anthony Lemme Puts New Wine in Old Bottles

Anthony Lemme, the exclusive U.S. licensee for Vacu-Vin, a $20 pump resealer of wine bottles, knew the traditional way to publicize his company would be to send press releases to the media. Instead, he pursued a strategy to get people talking about his product to such an extent that press coverage would follow. His goal was to create an irresistible buzz around his business among groups of the most likely prospects.

He planned his grassroots marketing strategy before he signed his license agreement. He organized a luncheon and wine tasting for New York City's top 20 sommeliers and wine writers. The idea was to let wine industry professionals sample wines first uncorked, then resealed with the Vacu-Vin. Lemme also started a Vacu-Vin newsletter, which he sent to all of his 175 distributors, that contained tips for success, honors for top performers, and a welcome to new members.

Lemme's efforts were a success. The most influential people in the wine world loved his product, and began spreading the word among New York's biggest wine buyers. This word of mouth made Vacu-Vin the number-one gift item in Bloomingdale's. Within the first year, Lemme had 25 manufacturers' reps, 150 distributors, and sales of around $5 million.

At that point the press was clamoring to find out about his product. Stories in *The Wine Spectator* and *Wine & Spirits* were followed by write-ups in *Good Housekeeping, Playboy*, and *USA Today*. "All of a sudden I was a celebrity," Lemme marveled. "It's amazing—I've got banks calling me. Believe me, banks don't usually call asking for your business."

- Keep an eye on competitors' marketing and PR efforts
- Talk to those in your market niche, and use their feedback
- Attend trade shows, seminars, and other related events

By continually immersing yourself in the world of your customers, you can develop a sixth sense regarding PR and how it can help you maintain your reputation in your market. The more you develop a PR mindset, the more you'll see PR opportunities in your customer and client interactions,

TIPS FROM THE GURU

Stephanie Kane Gives Five Steps to Telling Your Own Story

"Great narrative technique can help companies get past the increasing resistance to marketing messages and create a genuine dialogue with members of your target market," says Stephanie Kane, an award-winning novelist and communications consultant. "Narratives establish a level of trust that encourages customers to tell you their story—what they really need."

Whatever your business's ultimate goal, good stories share the same ingredients. Kane offers five elements that form the basis for communicating a story-based message that emotionally engages the listener.

1. Character: Who Is the Story About?

Great stories have a central character or protagonist. Is it you? Your company or team? Maybe it's a customer or client. Once you decide whom your story is about, anticipate how others will relate to your protagonist.

Be honest: don't be afraid to reveal all-too-human motivations and flaws. Nobody relates to perfection. People connect to a character's normalcy, because great storytelling teaches us something about our own lives. We learn the most from people who turn weakness into strength or snatch victory from defeat.

2. Conflict: What Stood in Your Way?

The emotional heart of a story is conflict, which can involve a collision with another person or with events beyond your control. Conflicts that resonate with others reveal how you confront life's hard knocks and emerge as a stronger person or organization.

As you construct personal or organizational narratives, consider formative experiences. What did you do at a crucial moment in time? What stood in your

---

in day-to-day news and events, and in your dealings with vendors and others who affect your business.

Slightly famous marketers do not see PR as an on-again, off-again activity, nor do they expect miracles after writing an article or being quoted in a newspaper. Media strategies are dedicated not just to creating but also maintaining a visible, credible brand and reputation. This means pursuing PR with the same regularity as paying your rent.

way? How did you face trials or tests? How did you rebound, and what new direction did you take? By showing how you stood up to a challenging situation, you communicate not only that you've been there, but how others can get through it, too.

3. Context: When and Where Did It Happen?

Context is the entire cultural and psychological framework in which your central character acts. Decisions are never made in a vacuum, but by human beings responding individually or collectively to specific pressures.

How has life shaped you or your company? How are you a creature of your unique time and place? Why do your setting and upbringing compel you to react in certain ways? In the corporate world, culture is context, and context makes actions meaningful. It elevates when and where to how and why.

4. Causation: How Did You Act and React Under Pressure?

A cause-and-effect, action-and-reaction sequence of events propels your story from beginning to end. The beginning sets the stage by describing a situation that is more or less in balance, which is followed by a sequence of events that climaxes in an absolute change.

When demonstrating how your company helped a client, your narrative might explore: What crisis brought the client to you? What did the client do in response? How did the client solve a problem and rebound through your help? Were there benefits no one could anticipate, such as enabling the client to open up a whole new market?

5. Coherence: What Does it All Mean?

Great stories have a satisfying conclusion. What universal insight does your story provide? How can others learn from it to improve their own conditions?

PR is about investing for long-term results. In the same way that you shouldn't expect a small monetary investment to yield a lifetime of wealth, you should not expect a couple of media appearances to turn your business into a success overnight.

Although initial dividends may look small at first, each media appearance will add to your advantage, growing your reputation and increasing your reach.

REAL-WORLD SUCCESS STORY

Three Dogs, Two Guys, and One Big Media Break Catapult a Small Company to Stardom

Dan Dye and Mark Beckloff didn't know it at the time, but they were sitting on a media gold mine. It started when they became troubled by all the many additives and chemical ingredients in commercially available dog treats — most of them with names you couldn't even pronounce. So they set out to change the world, at least as dogs know it, when they opened the first Three Dog Bakery in 1989.

Their mission was simple: fresh-bake the world's best dog biscuits (with catchy names like PupCakes, Great Danish, and Snickerpoodles), and thereby give dog lovers everywhere healthy, all-natural treats to give their favorite four-legged friends.

Although Three Dog Bakery started as a humble operation, they learned the power of PR one fateful day in 1994 when a Wall Street Journal reporter stumbled upon their showroom full of doggie delights. The reporter was so impressed with the business that he wrote a major story featuring the company.

Little did they know that when the story broke a few days later, their lives would change forever. "We unlocked our bakery door that day and the phone was ringing off the hook," says partner Dan Dye. "At one point, the sheer volume of calls caused the line to go dead for a while. People were calling from all over the country, requesting biscuits, flyers, information, anything we could shove into a box and ship to them."

By the end of the first day, Three Dog was six weeks backlogged on mail orders. They were besieged with calls for almost two weeks, and soon were receiving requests for interviews from *People, Entrepreneur,* The Oprah Winfrey Show, *USA Today, The New York Times Magazine*, National Public Radio, and The Tonight Show.

Next thing they knew, the press was clawing at the chance to be the next to interview the young, self-proclaimed "entredogneurs." Naturally, when Oprah Winfrey called, the Three Dog crew jumped in excitement over the possibility of 40 million viewers getting a glimpse of their new creations.

Since then, Dan and Mark have been featured in articles in hundreds of other publications. They've also appeared on The Today Show, Late Night with Conan O'Brien, CNN, the BBC, NPR, PBS, and 18 thirty-minute specials aired on the Food Network.

Tell Your Story

Sometimes the most interesting business story—and the one of most interest to the media—is contained in who you are or how you conduct your business.

"You are the news!" says Jill Lublin, co-author of Guerrilla Publicity. "In public relations, your job is to define and communicate your business in a way that has built-in media appeal. Many times, that can be as simple as presenting your business in light of what you do or how you got there."

Lublin tells about a client with a lackluster job title. "He was an industrial designer — a label that wasn't very exciting," says Lublin, "but it turned out that he ran a very successful company as a virtual corporation. So we presented him to the media as an expert on virtual corporations. This angle proved to be interesting from a media perspective, and caught the attention of several national and local newspapers, and radio and television stations."

You can also gain amazing results by using a personal narrative to humanize your business. Did you overcome challenges that can be directly related to the success of your company? Are you on a personal mission to make the world a better place using your business as a tool? You see stories of this kind in the papers every day, but they always draw readers because they contain a human element.

Build Media Appeal

Don't underestimate the value of building media appeal into your business early on. As a *slightly famous* marketer, you've developed a business and brand that stands apart from others, and you've created an atmosphere of excitement, personality, and distinction for your business. Use your distinction to your advantage, attracting both prospective customers and the media, which is always in search of stories with built-in audience appeal.

Set Realistic Goals

When developing your media strategy, it's important to set appropriate goals. Though sometimes you can hit it big on the first try—and Three Dog Bakery

EXECUTIVE BRANDING

Steve Mariotti Demonstrates the Power of a Personal Narrative

Two decades ago, Steve Mariotti was on top of the world. He'd received his M.B.A. from the University of Michigan School of Business, completed a successful stint at the Ford Motor Company, and moved to New York City, where he was soon running a successful import-export business.

Then, in 1981, he was mugged by three teenagers in New York's Lower East Side. The event dramatically altered his life.

"The mugging caught me emotionally off-guard," he remembers. "In the months that followed, I suffered painful flashbacks. And, being an entrepreneur, I thought, 'Why would these kids rob me for a few dollars when they could make much more money running a business together?'"

Deciding to confront the worst of inner-city life, he became a teacher. At first his students directed their energies to challenging his authority; their attitudes changed when he taught them how to start their own businesses. Suddenly they had an incentive to learn. Their skills and behavior improved, as did their grades.

Mariotti left the classroom in 1987 to found The National Foundation for Teaching Entrepreneurship (NFTE, pronounced "nifty"). He used his personal experiences to promote NFTE and to recruit others to the cause of teaching entrepreneurship to at-risk youths. NTFE's product is a business-literate young entrepreneur with experience in the marketplace who can keep accurate financial records.

NFTE programs are now established throughout the country, and the program to date has worked with over 40,000 low-income young people. Mariotti's inspiring story has played a hand in getting NFTE a lot of media coverage; both he and NFTE have been featured in dozens of major newspaper stories and television programs that have advanced his organization's agenda.

For Mariotti, NFTE is a banner that can be carried by all who are concerned with the issues facing today's youth. His personal narrative inspires his book, *The Young Entrepreneur's Guide to Starting and Running a Business*.

"My personal narrative serves as an example and brand identity for the entire program," says Mariotti. "I came out of corporate America to do some good, and hope my story inspires others like me to do the same. If I can convince enough people to mentor kids through a NFTE-sponsored program, I'm sure we could experience an economic renaissance of amazing proportions—and possibly fix a few of society's problems at the same time."

REAL-WORLD SUCCESS STORY

Alfred J. Lautenslager Asks, Will Your PR Hit a Home Run?

Many people see marketing as a panacea to all their business woes. Some people implement marketing efforts and expect immediate results. They are misinformed, because marketing is a long-term, persistent, and consistent activity. Others try for a PR home run—that one story, event, or customer touch that will bring a bonanza of business.

The problem with these expectations, says marketing and PR consultant Alfred Lautenslager, is that home runs aren't what usually win baseball games; it's usually a collection of singles and doubles that make for the winning score. "The same applies in business, marketing, and PR. It's the little things that make for the success of a business," says Lautenslager "Sure, you may hit a home run occasionally, but you can't go into the game expecting to win that way."

Lautenslager insists that the world of PR and marketing is mainly a game of singles. A press release here, a news conference and a feature article there—these all add up to effective communication of a company's message or brand—not any one event or one communication.

"Marketing is made up of many things. They all support one another," says Lautenslager. "They all work toward getting the job done, just like in a baseball game. Sure, there's a chance every now and then to hit that home run, but looking for it all the time is futile."

Communicating with the media often proceeds slowly as you get the word out about your company, product, or service. This starts the process of awareness among editors and producers of the media.

Jay Conrad Levinson of "guerrilla marketing" fame speaks often about how many times a customer or prospect must be touched before he or she takes action. All these touches represent baby steps (or singles, in the baseball metaphor). Marketing is made up of many small things, and so is public relations.

"Think of all the topics you can write a press release about. Get one or two published, and you'll hear prospects and customers saying things like, 'I see you in all the papers,' or 'Every time I turn around, I see your name in print,'" says Lautenslager. "In actuality, this is only one or two publications that are working on the minds of the reader in synergistic fashion. Remember, synergy means adding the small to the small until suddenly, you have something bigger than even their sum—hitting singles to win the game, and taking baby steps to make great strides. PR and marketing work the same way."

Reprinted with permission from Entrepreneur Media, Inc., www. entrepreneur.com did it without even trying—you probably shouldn't expect to make your first media splash in one of the country's top publications. These tend to be the hardest to pitch, as they receive hundreds of queries a day, many more than they could ever use. Moreover, since your goal is to reach a targeted audience as frequently as possible, you can seek out smaller media outlets, and thereby avoid competing against billion-dollar firms and highly paid PR practitioners.

6 Attracting Media Attention

While your *slightly famous* media strategy needs to be customized to suit your business and circumstances, certain techniques underlie every effort. This chapter focuses on ways to create media opportunities that are based on knowing how the media work. As with any task, when you know how to approach the job, you're going to get better results.

Building a Media File

The first step in any media campaign is to identify the media outlets, and the key people within those organizations, that reach your target market. The goal is to build a list of newspapers, magazines, newsletters, and radio and television programs where you want coverage.

Your research can begin by asking your clients and customers what they read, watch, and listen to, and where they get news related to your industry.

Follow up with a visit to your public library, and familiarize yourself with the media resources available there. The business reference section in large urban libraries will often have media directories that include information on thousands of media outlets. These directories are usually organized by industry, so you can quickly find the media that address your customers. There are also directories that include industry-specific newsletters, professional organizations, and trade associations. You can, of course, purchase any of these directories, but they are expensive.

A few of the most comprehensive directories that should meet most of your publicity needs:

Bacon's Media Source *Bacon's* is the bible of the PR industry, providing detailed information on more than 450,000 editorial contacts at nearly 70,000 print, broadcast, and Internet media outlets in the U.S., Canada, Mexico, and the Caribbean.

This multi-volume set provides listings of newspapers, magazines, newsletters, and radio and television outlets, organized by geographic region and industry focus.

Burrelle's Burrelle's is another popular multi-volume media directory that provides a comprehensive list of print and broadcast media in this country. Although it overlaps with *Bacon's*, *Burrelle's* includes many smaller publications that can be useful for your media campaign. Each of the entries for the 300,000 media contacts and 60,000 media outlets listed includes addresses, telephone and fax numbers, e-mail addresses, and Website URLs where available. Individual volumes within the set include *Daily Newspapers; Non-Daily Newspapers; Radio, Television and Cable; Magazines;* and *Newsletters*.

Writer's Market This book contains listings for 8,000 magazines that accept freelance article submissions. Available in most bookstores and at www.writersdigest.com, this media directory is valuable for targeting publications that accept (and usually pay for) articles written by outside contributors.

Encyclopedia of Associations Most businesses should include associations and their newsletters in their media list. The *Encyclopedia of Associations* lists over 81,000 nonprofit, professional, and trade organizations worldwide. Entries contain complete contact information and detailed data on their membership, budgets, purposes, activities, services, organizational structure, affiliates, publications, and convention/meeting activities.

As you do your research, you'll probably be amazed at the number of tightly focused publications that cater to specialized business categories and interests. Get to know your reference librarian, one of the most under-appreciated information resources in the world, and ask him or her to help you locate resources.

Even if you serve only a local market, don't limit yourself to local media. Include publications with a national audience on your media list, and look for opportunities to be quoted in national publications. Even though such media exposure may not lead to direct sales, it can help establish your credibility.

Study the Markets

Once you've compiled the names of potential media outlets, get to know at least a few of the most promising first-hand. If they're available locally, buy a few on newsstands, or you can call the editorial offices and request a sample copy and an editorial calendar, which lists the themes of upcoming issues. Create a file area for publications and related media materials, and keep it up-to-date.

Once you've identified the media outlets that seem appropriate for your business, get the names of key people at each. These are the people on the editorial/news side of the media, the reporters, editors, producers, and writers, not the advertising sales reps or publishers who deal with the business side of a media organization. Look up articles written in the past year or so by their top reporters to learn the specific subject areas they cover, and to better understand their interests and special angles. Pay special attention to those that cover your industry on a regular basis.

Familiarize yourself with broadcast radio and television programs on your list. Listen to programs relevant to your industry to understand their format, and to pinpoint particular programs or segments where your business story might fit. Having studied the media, you will have a better idea about whom to approach with what kind of story.

Press Kits and Media Materials

Before approaching the media for any kind of story, you should assemble an introductory package about your business—in other words, a press kit.

Depending on your business and the image you want to convey, the kit can be as elaborate as a folder with expensive color materials or a simple sheaf of materials paper clipped together. In any case, it should include the following:

- company background information
- news releases with current information about your business
- biographies of company principals
- a simple, one-page summary "fact sheet" about the business
- a sheet of FAQS—sample questions and answers to a mock interview
- photos of you or your business
- articles that you have written, if any
- customer references and testimonials
- a list of past media coverage with samples

A good rule is to keep press kits simple, including just enough information to introduce the media to you and your business, provide necessary background, and make a good impression. Keep in mind that you'll be sending your press kit only on request; a kit sent to a reporter or editor whose interest hasn't already been aroused will probably wind up in the wastebasket.

With the Internet becoming just about universally available, online press kits are becoming more and more popular. An online kit contains the same items you'd find in a traditional press kit, but comes in browsable form, in an area of your website called an online pressroom.

Because journalists have the freedom to help themselves in an online press room at their own pace, you should include all kinds of additional material: articles about your company that have run in the media; white papers;

company position papers and statements to the press; industry statistics; a company directory with contact information. It's common practice to make many of the extra materials available in an easily printable format, such as Adobe's popular PDF.

Position Yourself as an Expert Resource

Journalists rely on good quotes from experts to make their stories lively and interesting. Quotes lend authority to their discussion, and provide a real-world connection to audiences. Being quoted in one story increases the chances that other reporters will recognize your expertise and call you for similar stories. Quotes beget more quotes. Once a reporter is convinced that you have knowledge that can help him write a better story, your name will come up whenever he's looking for a certain kind of information.

Shel Horowitz, a PR consultant, speaker, and author of *Grassroots Marketing*, has been quoted in hundreds of news articles in publications including *Fortune, Small Business, Woman's Day,* and *Entrepreneur.*

"The more you develop a reputation as a great interview source, the more journalists will seek you out," says Horowitz. "The more you get your name out there, the more you begin to establish a reputation within the press as a subject-area expert. Because journalists are under severe time restrictions, they value great interview sources, and will seek you out when you prove that you are one of those people."

"One thing people need to know is that the power of publicity doesn't always lie in the *New York Times*. Some of the best publicity is in local weeklies and trade publications, which are easy to break into, and then set the stage for bigger opportunities," says Horowitz. "For me, ongoing publicity has served as a credibility builder. When I say to clients that I've been interviewed in the *Los Angeles Times*, or the *Christian Science Monitor*, or the *Boston Globe*, it lets them know that I'm a serious contributor to my industry."

It's not difficult to achieve this position. Here are some helpful ways to tell the media that you are available as an authority on a particular subject.

Introduce Yourself

Writers, reporters, and producers cultivate relationships with outside experts. You can become one of these experts by letting the right people know that you exist and making a compelling case for your expertise.

The process begins with you identifying the media professionals most likely to need your expertise—for instance, journalists who regularly write about your industry, or consumer action reporters who might want information on products like yours. Introduce yourself and your qualifications as an expert, and offer to be of help when they write articles in your subject area. You can mention that you'd like to alert them from time to time to potential news stories about your industry.

Approach them as you would a new client, conveying the message, "I am here to solve one of your problems; your readers need this specific kind of information, and I have it." Send that message repeatedly.

Above all, editors and reporters must find you credible. If a reporter is receptive, send a press kit that shows you have the knowledge you say you do, and that you have a reputation for doing outstanding work.

How to Give a Great Interview

You've been asked to give an interview for a story related to your industry. Great! But to be effective, you must take a little time to prepare.

Have—and Stick to—an Agenda

Don't go into any media opportunity without a clear plan for what you want to get out of it. Although you must help the media do its job, don't ever forget that your main goal in your media appearances is to make them work to your advantage. Outline the messages you want to convey. Make sure your interview positions your business in a way consistent with your brand identity, while providing the information likely to get you included in the article.

Although a journalist will set the pace of the interview, you can assume a measure of control by being prepared with the information that you want to convey. Create an outline you can refer to as the interview takes place. Thorough pre-interview preparation will help you stay on track and remember the points you want to get across.

Background Research

Find out as much as you can about the media outlet, the reporter, and the particular story before you give your interview. Have they covered your business and its issues before? Who else will they be talking to for this story? How long will the interview be? Ask to receive a list of sample questions to help you better prepare for the interview.

Ask the reporter ahead of time to describe the nature of the interview. Offer a list of questions to the reporter that you think should be covered; a brief e-mail will do. Then prepare your answers, and have your notes in writing before you when the reporter calls.

Speak Quotably

It's not enough to have information; you must also learn to speak in a way that makes you worth mentioning. You must be able to express yourself succinctly and memorably. Practice condensing your key points into brief, clear sentences. A good quote ensures that you get mentioned in the final story. The better you become at speaking quotably, the more journalists will want to call you.

In addition, the better prepared you are prior to the interview, the easier it is to speak quotably. Anticipate questions and practice your responses. Reporters tend to look for clear, direct statements; they don't have room to print fully developed or carefully modified arguments. Speak in positive statements. Take a stand.

At the same time, don't feel obliged to fill "dead air." Pause to think before you answer. Be conversational and avoid professional jargon. Keep your message simple. Speak in terms that even somebody not familiar with your industry can understand. Most important, unleash your enthusiasm. If you don't seem to care about what you're saying, no one else will either.

EXECUTIVE BRANDING

Media Coverage Pays Off for Atherton Trust

Atherton Trust Company, a Redwood City, California-based real estate management and investment firm, competes with large financial institutions like Bank of America, Wells Fargo, and Citibank. While it can't afford to spend millions of dollars for advertising like its larger competitors, Atherton builds its brand through consistent media exposure and positioning company executives as experts who frequently comment on finance-related topics.

"Media relations is a cornerstone of our growth strategy," says Kraig Kast, Atherton Trust CEO. "We compete against established companies, so we have to raise our profile to reach prospects and establish our credibility. Our systematic efforts to gain media coverage around our core areas of expertise support the 300 people scattered across 25 major metropolitan areas of the United States who serve our high net worth clients."

"I position myself as the company spokesperson in regular media interviews," says Kast. "I make it a priority to understand how the media work and how to help reporters do their jobs effectively. The media rewards executives who approach reporters on their own terms, which means being responsive to journalists' deadlines, being well-prepared, articulate, and succinct, and communicating your company's value without being overtly self-promotional."

Kast's efforts have paid off in good press relations and hundreds of thousands of dollars of free press exposure. He has been quoted or featured in a host of top-tier publications in recent years, including the *Economist,* the *Wall Street Journal,* and the *Financial Times,* as well as smaller but more specialized investment and real estate newsletters and trade publications. He has been quoted on

Don't Pretend to Know Something You Don't

Always stick to your area of expertise. Don't feel obliged to answer questions if you're not qualified. If you don't know the answer, you can offer to find out and get back to the reporter before his deadline. If you know someone else with the information, or where the answer is to be found, say so.

a range of topics from real estate investment trusts to high-tech investing to the importance of a well-crafted will.

His goal is to give at least two press interviews a week, and he spends at least two hours a week researching interview topics. "I stay informed about what my competition is doing, where my industry is going, and keep abreast of trends that affect my clients. I make sure I can interpret current events related to my industry and articulate timely, relevant information to the media. I see this as a central part of my job," states Kast.

Atherton's media coverage increases the firm's credibility among affluent investors, such as when Kast was featured in an article in *Multifamily Executive,* a trade magazine reaching owners of large apartment buildings. "The story profiled our innovative use of office technology to service our clients," says Kast. "We circulate reprints of the article to our salespeople for use in their sales materials. For one salesperson in discussions with the owner of a 3,000-unit complex, this reprint in a prime real estate magazine will carry a lot of weight."

Moreover, prospects find and are influenced by past media coverage as they consider doing business with Atherton. "I vividly remember visiting a new client in Southern Calfornia," says Kast. "I walked into his office, and saw an article I had written for *Affluent Investor* sitting on his desk. This was a six-figure client who learned about us after reading my article, and who chose our firm over larger competitors."

Kast believes executives benefit most when they get personally involved in the company's media coverage. During annual compensation reviews, he considers team members' support of his role as company spokesperson.

"Executives should not delegate media relations entirely to the communications department," says Kast. "Many executives believe the press is there to attack them and take them down. The truth is that the media will happily give executives positive, free media exposure when they offer valuable insights and knowledge."

Pitch Your Story

Editors are gatekeepers charged with allowing only newsworthy stories of interest to their readers to pass through the gate. They hate public relations efforts that simply seek to promote companies and have no inherent news value. On the other hand, if you can offer reader-centered information and a unique story angle, your public relations efforts will be successful.

In sum, pitching stories to the media begins by seeing your business from the media's perspective. Only when you align your business interests with the media's interests—typically, by coming up with a new angle on your subject—will the media want to consult you, quote you, and write about your business.

There are plenty of ways to prove to the media that your business deserves their coverage, but all of them begin by answering the simple question, "What makes this news?"

Announcements

Open houses, tours, award ceremonies, accomplishments, anniversaries, rallies, and debates all can warrant news coverage if they capture the interest of some important segment of readers or viewers. The test of whether an announcement deserves media coverage is its relevance to the specific outlet. *USA Today* may not care about events at your local accounting firm, but a local newspaper business editor may be interested in an announcement that your firm is hosting a free tax-preparation seminar for local businesses.

Controversy

The media love controversy. An effective way to get media coverage is to challenge the status quo by taking a stand contrary to prevailing wisdom.

Lee Hull, a financial advisor, challenged an industry status quo when he wrote an article entitled, "Where Are All the Customers' Yachts?" Repeating the advice he gave his clients, the article, which drew a tremendous amount of attention, suggested that investors work only with financial advisors who charge on a pay-for-performance basis, rather than getting a commission on sales, as is common in the financial services industry.

Events

In the 1920s, long before smoking was linked to health concerns, the American tobacco industry realized the social taboo against women smoking in public was costing them half their potential business. They turned to Edward Bernays, sometimes known as "the father of modern public relations," for help.

In what is regarded as the first publicity stunt, Bernays arranged for women's rights marchers to parade down a New York City avenue smoking Lucky Strike cigarettes. The event was a media sensation. Dubbed the "torches of freedom contingent," the sight of hundreds of women openly smoking their symbolic "Torches of Freedom" was viewed as a victory for women's rights. Within months, women were smoking openly, and sales of Lucky Strikes soared.

Publicity events, or stunts such as grand openings and the like, can be used effectively to generate media coverage. You can make your event newsworthy by tying it to a current event or holiday, by involving local celebrities, or, as in the case of Lucky Strikes, by connecting it to a burning social issue.

Studies, Surveys, and Statistics

The media love stories supported by studies, surveys, and statistics. If you can provide this kind of information about your industry, you can easily get attention.

The American Association of Advertising Agencies, for example, in a report called "Advertising in a Recession," cited a number of studies that show a strong correlation between sustained spending on advertising, even in a recession, and increased market share. The report was cited widely in newspaper, magazine, and online articles.

Similarly, Biz Rate, an Internet e-commerce rating service, conducts surveys on various Internet retailing issues throughout the year. They announce their findings in press releases, offer statistics and background findings for free, and make themselves available to the media to answer questions about e-commerce trends.

A very different kind of business using the same strategy, PGT Industries, a manufacturer of custom-built patio rooms, conducted a national survey and found that 64 percent of all homeowners wished they could add a sunroom. They also found that nearly 70 percent of homeowners who currently

REAL-WORLD SUCCESS STORY

B.L. Ochman on How to Write Effective Pitch Letters

I've been a publicist for the past 20 years and I'm going to share a trade secret with you. I haven't sent out a traditional press release in the last 10 years, but I have placed stories about my clients in the *Wall St. Journal, New York Times, ABC News, The Today Show, Good Morning America,* and just about every major media outlet on the planet.

Editors surely don't need me or any other publicist to write their stories. They need me to point them in the direction of a good story, succinctly give them the facts and sources, and then get out of the way so they can write their own stories. I do those things by writing pitch letters, damn good ones. Here are some guidelines I recommend.

Say Why You Are Writing Begin with your reason for writing; for example, "I am writing to suggest a story about . . ." or "I'd like to recommend an interview with . . ." Too many times the reason for the letter is hidden several paragraphs into the letter. Editors are busy. If you don't give them an immediate reason to keep reading, you've lost them.

Explain Your Premise in No More Than Two Sentences Explain what makes your idea newsworthy. Why is this a good person to interview or a good story to cover? Describe your idea's relevance to current events—its connection to an existing trend, or a coming one—or the likelihood that it will interest a broad cross section of the audience.

Explain Your Story Idea in One or Two Paragraphs Explain how the story would work, what it involves, what role you will play in assisting the reporter.

A journalist friend who told me he gets a three-foot stack of snail mail and

have sunrooms consider them "extremely important" living spaces. Here's the core of a news story that could easily find its way into the real estate or family living section of a newspaper.

As a source of reliable statistics, you are a quotable media source. Out-placement firm Challenger, Gray & Christmas exploits this opportunity thoroughly by regularly performing studies on employment in the United States, and sharing their findings with the media. As a result, company spokespeople over 150 e-mails a day shared this story with me. "Let me tell you about a letter that typifies the ones we journalists never finish reading. I got one the other day that started off by saying 'I've been on the Joe Franklin Show, this show, that show, been talked about by so and so. I've also done this and that.' The next line was 'I'm not a status-oriented person.' There were about eight more pages, but I didn't bother to read them. I just laughed, showed the letter around, and threw it away."

Timing Can Be Everything Timing is incredibly important. Your chances improve when you can say, "This is a hot topic, and I have a great source." Let's say you're an ophthalmologist and the President is going to have eye surgery. You stand a good chance of getting a phone call for your opinion if your e-mail arrives when the reporter is looking for a resource. At other times your pitch will become a story only if it is an attention grabber. I think of it as the "hey, Martha" factor; editors look for stories that would make someone say, "hey, Martha, look at this!"

List Topics Your Spokesperson Can Address If you're pitching an expert interview source, list in bullet form topics he or she can address.

Get It All into 350 Words or Less Mark Twain said, "If I'd had more time, I would have written less." Edit. Then, edit again. Once you get reporters interested, they will ask you for more information. And then you can give them mountains of background you've researched, because another thing my reporter friend shared with me is this: most reporters hate to do research. If your website features a company fact sheet, management bios, relevant photos, and other articles about your company, be sure to include a URL.

are frequently asked by major newspapers and magazines to comment on employment trends.

Timely Tie-Ins

Relating your business to breaking news or current issues can be especially effective. In the summer of 2001, media attention was on California's then-critical energy crisis. Solardyne, a Portland-based company that sells solar and wind power equipment, seized the moment by sending out a news release with the heading, "Energy-Strapped Consumers Take Another Look at Solar, Wind Alternatives."

Parenting expert Caron Goode, author of *Nurture Your Child's Gift*, wrote a short article called "What Harry Potter Can Teach Parents About Kids" shortly after the movie *Harry Potter and the Sorcerer's Stone* was released. The article was picked up by a number of media outlets because of the timely tie-in and clever angle.

The more you look for connections, the more you'll see them. Make a habit of looking at current events and asking, "How can I hook onto that?"

The Pitch Letter

Whether you're looking for a story on a particular topic, hoping to be interviewed, or suggesting coverage of an industry issue or trend, editors, reporters, and producers will expect you to present your ideas in writing in the form of a pitch letter. Like a sales letter, a good pitch letter will reduce a story to its bare-bones essentials, demonstrate the topic's inherent news value, and inspire a reader to ask for more.

Rules for the Pitch Letter

A pitch should be brief—no more than a page—conversational, upbeat, and confident. It should also include the basic information reporters need to follow up: how to set up an interview, for example, or request a sample product. It should also communicate how the proposed story will appeal to the media's audience.

Following are important elements of a good pitch letter. (PR professional B.L . Ochman provides more details in her Tips from the Guru.)

A Strong Hook Make the first sentences of your pitch letter so interesting, and so relevant to the needs of the media outlet, that a busy editor will give your letter his full attention and read it from beginning to end. Start with your strongest material, and make it irresistible.

A Clear Statement of Purpose Say exactly what you're offering. Are you pitching yourself as an expert interview source? Proposing a feature story about your business, products, or services? Don't make the reader guess why you're writing to him; state the purpose of your pitch letter in the first few sentences.

Relevance After presenting your strongest material in your opening sentences, your pitch letter must go on to explain why your idea is of interest to the publication's or program's audience. Highlight broader themes that relate to your story idea. A pitch letter must make a convincing case that your idea "matters" and has relevance to the media outlet in question.

The Closer State clearly how and when you'll follow up. Following up within a week or two can improve your chances. Even if you don't get a positive response, a follow-up call can elicit valuable feedback that may help the next time you pitch a story.

The Press Release

A press release is a formal announcement of something new and newsworthy —a company launch, new or enhanced products or services, or a customer milestone.

Editors have a love-hate relationship with press releases. Press releases can serve as valuable sources for story ideas. A good press release can be a lifesaver when it arrives at the right time.

On the downside, press releases are often poorly written or useless. Editors complain about having to slog through piles of misdirected press releases that have nothing to do with their publications. They also complain about press releases that arrive en masse, having been sent to thousands of media outlets in one swoop, or that are blatantly promotional pieces with no obvious news value.

"Too many businesses write poorly thought-out releases about non-news events, and wonder why editors never give them a second look," says Darryl Roberts, publisher and editor of *Wine X*. "I get so many media people that

TIPS FROM THE GURU

Bill Stoller on Smashing the Myth of the Press Release

Bill Stoller is the founder and publisher of *Free Publicity, The Newsletter for PR Hungry Businesses*. A twenty-year public relations veteran, Bill teaches entrepreneurs and small businesses how to achieve maximum publicity with minimal investment. The following comes from Stoller's article, "Smashing the Myth of the Press Release."

The press release has taken on a magical reputation as the alpha and omega of publicity. Wanna become rich? Send out a press release. Wanna become famous? Press release. Wanna get on the cover of *Newsweek*? Press release.

Publicity "gurus" are springing up all over the Internet touting the press release as the answer to all marketing ills. Just knock out a release, mass e-mail it to journalists, sit back and wait for Oprah to call.

It's a cruel joke.

If you don't have a story to tell, your press release is utterly worthless. I'm not knocking the press release — it's an important tool. But it's just that: a tool. It's not the first thing you need to think about when it comes time to seek publicity. In fact, it's one of the last. And it's not even absolutely necessary. (I've gotten plenty of publicity with just a pitch letter, a quick e-mail, or a phone call.)

If you worship at the shrine of the press release, it's time to rearrange your priorities. Here, then, are the things that are essential for a press release in generating publicity:

1. A Newsworthy Story It's the very basis for your publicity efforts. Without it, your press release means nothing. To learn about how to develop a newsworthy story, ask yourself, "Is my company/website/life really newsworthy?"

2. Learning to Think Like an Editor Oh, what an edge you'll have in scoring publicity over all those press-release worshippers once you learn how to get inside the head of an editor. Give an editor what he wants in the way he wants it, and you'll do great.

3. Relevance Tie in with a news event, make yourself part of a trend, piggyback on a larger competitor's story, but, by all means, make your story part of a picture that's bigger than just your company. Stories that exist in a vacuum quickly run out of oxygen.

4. Persistence Sending out a press release and waiting for results is lazy and ineffective. If you really believe in your story, and you believe that it's right for a particular media outlet, you need to fight to make it happen. Call or e-mail the editor to pitch your story before sending the release. If one editor says no, try somebody else. If they all say no, come back at them with a different story angle.

approach me with a press release without having taken the time to look at my magazine. They send completely inappropriate materials that do not in any way appeal to our readership. Then, they wonder why I don't give them any coverage."

Editors get hundreds of press releases each week. They have one job, and it isn't to please everyone sending in a release—it's to please their readership. Knowing this, you should ask the same question of your press release that editors ask, "Will it interest our readers?"

Formatting Your Release

A press release is a mini feature story that should resemble in style and structure actual stories or articles that appear in the publications you are approaching. There are eight basic elements that every press release should contain.

The Release Statement The words "FOR IMMEDIATE RELEASE" should appear in all caps on the upper left of the sheet or computer screen. This lets the media know your story is current. If you have upcoming news, but want to send the release earlier, note the exact date on which it is acceptable to release the information.

Contact Information A line or two after the release statement, list the name, title, e-mail address, and telephone and fax numbers of the person you want editors and reporters to contact if they need more information. Provide home and cell phone numbers, since reporters on deadline sometimes call after business hours.

The Headline The headline is one of the most important parts of the release, and often the most difficult to write. Because it is competing with dozens of other releases, your headline must be compelling. Keep headlines short and tight. Spend some time studying the headlines in a few newspapers. The headline should appear two lines after the contact information, in boldface type.

The Dateline A dateline conveys the geographical origin of the release, and the date you make your information available to the press, for instance:

"Oakland, CA, January 15, 2003." The dateline appears as the first sentence of your first paragraph.

The Lead The first paragraph of your release does a lot of work. It must provide essential information—who, what, where, when, why, and how—and present the essence of your story. A good lead anchors everything that follows, and clearly shows how your proposed story relates to its audience. A "summary lead," the most common and usually most effective technique, relates the news and how it affects people.

B.L. Ochman proposes the following helpful formula. "The lead paragraph of a release should try to state its point in 40 words or less. Of those 40 words, no more than six words should be used to describe what the company does."

Another effective lead style imitates a magazine or newspaper feature story, as in the following example.

Three-Part Series Examines Miners' Courage,
Lack of Progress on Safety

CHICAGO, Sept. 20 /PRNewswire/—In the shadow of September 11, word on Sept. 23, 2001, of the most catastrophic mining disaster in the U.S. since 1984 went all but unnoticed. One year later, with coal mining back in the news following the successful rescue in July of nine Pennsylvania miners, the *Chicago Tribune* revisits the events that cost 13 men their lives—and the state of an industry that remains plagued by accidents and safety violations.

Body Copy You only have room for a couple of short paragraphs to develop the material introduced in your lead, so keep the body of your release short and relevant. Keep paragraphs short, no more than four sentences, and use subheads or bullets so that your release can be read at a glance. Use quotes from company executives if they add something essential to the story.

The Ending Let editors know where your release ends with either the word "end" or the symbol ###.

Honing Your Style

Well-written press materials get better results than those that are awkward, confusing, or overly complicated. Here are some additional guidelines that will improve your chances of eliciting a positive response.

Get to the Point Don't waste time clearing your throat at the beginning of your release. Skip the company introduction, and go straight to the news that makes your press release relevant. Assuming that editors will not read past the first paragraph unless it's a grabber, put your strongest material first.

One way to achieve this kind of tight writing is to practice "speaking" your main point until you can get it down to one or two clear sentences. Once you have it on paper, build your release around it.

Provide Some Flair You can give your releases a more journalistic feel—making them more like stories than advertisements—by including anecdotes, human-interest elements, and sensory images. Put a face on the facts by telling about someone who's benefited from your product or expertise.

Size Counts Against You Keep press releases to no more than one page. Write concisely, including only the most essential details. Cut out every excess word and be sparing of unnecessary adjectives. If you can't include everything on one page, attach a fact sheet. When sending press releases by e-mail, keep them no more than one screen long, eliminating the need to scroll.

Sending Your Release

Sending news releases en masse is akin to dropping leaflets out of an airplane. Although you might hit an editorial target if you throw enough press releases into the editorial wind, you waste a lot of energy and good will. Editors expect your pitch to address their needs.

If you're targeting several publications, take time to customize different versions, one for trade journals, another for business publications, another for online media, and so on. Wherever possible, craft each news release or pitch letter to the style and needs of the individual outlet you are sending it to.

Before you send anything, contact the publication to determine who is responsible for reading press releases like yours. Also, ask how they prefer to receive press releases—whether by mail, e-mail, or fax. This is not the time to pitch your story. Rather, just get basic contact information to ensure that your release reaches the right person in their preferred format.

While your press release may provide all the information you want to present, you can't assume that editors will read it thoroughly. This is especially true in busy newsrooms that receive hundreds of press releases every day. That's why it's important to include the kind of pitch letter discussed above. Your pitch letter is a summary of your story. When editors or journalists like what they read in your pitch letter, they can continue reading the accompanying release for a more complete treatment of your subject.

Know the Editor's Deadlines Allow enough time between when you send the release and the time you want it to appear. Publications have lead times. For newspapers and broadcast media, this can range from several days to a week. Magazine lead times are longer, anywhere from one to several months.

Keep Your Website Up-to-Date Before sending your release, make sure a journalist or editor can find further information about you and your subject on your website. If you are pitching a new product, update that section of your site. If the product is not important enough to be covered in detail on your own site, why should anyone write about it?

Think of Yourself as a Journalist's Assistant Access to sources, updated facts and figures, accurate and detailed contact information, points of view in opposition to yours—these are all things a journalist needs for a story. Links to such information on your website can score you big bonus points.

Following Up

Most PR professionals agree that following up after sending pitch letters and press releases betters your chances of getting coverage. Sometimes, sending a brief note offering to answer questions or provide missing information not contained in the original release is sufficient, but many times a phone call to

REAL-WORLD SUCCESS STORY

King, Brown & Partners Makes the News It Wants You to Read

King, Brown & Partners (KB&P) saw an opportunity to demonstrate their talents and gain free media exposure. As a market research firm specializing in online surveys, KB&P orchestrated a media survey of consumer online purchasing behaviors before and after the 2000 holiday shopping season to gauge.

The campaign and the information it generated got the media's attention. Over 30 media outlets published references to the survey findings, many times running the following press release in its entirety without changing a word.

FOR IMMEDIATE RELEASE

Brand Familiarity Vital to Online Purchasing

SAN FRANCISCO, CA, February 4. An online survey by market research firm King, Brown & Partners (KB&P) revealed that online shoppers were strongly influenced by Old Economy factors last holiday season. Findings among 1,178 respondents revealed that brand familiarity and paper catalogs—mainstays of Old Economy marketing—still strongly impact online purchasing decisions.

Shoppers are willing to purchase from unfamiliar sites as long as they have a familiar brand name. A full 71% of respondents bought at sites they had never purchased from before. However, the same proportion (71%) were already familiar with the brand name and almost two-thirds (64%) felt that knowing the brand name beforehand was "very" or "somewhat" important.

Paper catalogs are an important part of the online purchasing process. A full 79% who purchased online this holiday season received a catalog in the mail from an online retailer, and 72% said paper catalogs were "very" or "somewhat" useful when making online purchasing decisions. Nearly two-thirds (62%) who received a catalog bought from the company who sent the catalog. Of those, 89% went to the site to purchase.

To obtain the complete 2000 Online Holiday E-tailing Study, visit www.kingbrown.com/pressframe.htm

the person who received your materials is the best bet.

Be warned, many reporters and editors, under constant deadline, do not welcome follow-up calls and may be gruff or annoyed when you reach them by phone. "Nothing sets a writer or editor's teeth on edge more than an eager

TIPS FROM THE GURU

An Interview with Marc Harty on the Role of Online Press Releases

Marc Harty is CEO of MainTopic Media, Inc., an information publishing and strategic marketing company. Marc's work has won over 300 awards, including several Clios as well as Best of Show at the Dallas Tops Awards.

How has the Internet changed traditional PR?

The Internet has changed the rules of PR, especially the media's traditional "gatekeeper" role in getting media coverage. Online PR can help you reach not just the traditional media, but provides a means to directly reach prospects, customers, industry influencers, and organizations that impact your business.

Online PR has tremendous reach. You can submit one press release and reach thousands of media outlets and news-oriented websites, as well as Web 2.0 channels like podcasts, blogs, social bookmarking, RSS feeds, photo search, and online video.

What is an online press release and how is it different from a traditional one?

Online PR appeals to both humans and search engines. Releases are "optimized" with keywords people use to find your company, product, or service. Those keywords appear in certain places in the release to make it "search engine friendly."

Another difference? Staying power. Online releases are easily found via search engines, continuously generating exposure for weeks, months, even years.

How are online press releases distributed?

Your release is sent via RSS-syndicated news feeds to tens of thousands of media outlets. Numerous distribution service providers are available; larger

voice saying, 'I'm calling to see if you got the press release we sent,'" says Esther Schindler in her article, "The Care and Feeding of the Media." "When we're in the middle of a tight deadline, the last thing we want is a phone call that contains no new or useful information whatsoever."

When you make follow-up calls, know exactly what you're going to say before you telephone the reporter. Have it written down in front of you. When you reach an editor or journalist, quickly get to the point. Ask them whether companies prefer PRnewswire.com because of its extensive reach, while smaller businesses on a budget like PRweb.com.

Bottom line, if you can cut and paste into a Web form and follow some simple instructions, you can do online PR. There's no software to master, and the process is very user-friendly. Just open an account with a service provider, then choose the appropriate categories. For example, for a diet or exercise product, a category such as "health" makes sense.

Are there any stylistic elements for a well-written online press release?

Use a benefit-oriented headline. Have a real message and story. Include relevant facts, a quote or two, plus a call to action. Offer something of value, such as a white paper, special report, or free consulting.

Overall, the most compelling online releases read more like articles. This boosts the viral marketing potential of being shared among individuals and online communities.

Can you give an example of an online press release delivering these benefits?

A Canadian therapist wanted to position himself as an expert on Attention Deficit Hyperactive Disorder (ADHD). Rather than talk about himself, his online press release piggybacked on the FDA's recent approval of the Ritalin Patch (a medication for ADHD).

The release got significant search engine traffic and was picked up in Google News Alerts, which are monitored by many businesses and journalists. This generated exposure related to other ADHD news stories and elevated the therapist's visibility and expertise within the ADHD community. The exposure prompted by the release led to a pharmaceutical firm hiring the therapist as an expert spokesperson for its ADHD product.

they are on deadline, and if they can spare a moment. Use your instincts. If the reporter sounds rushed, ask when you should call back.

When you reach the right person, remind them who you are and what you sent, and offer to answer any questions they may have. If a reporter rejects your story idea, ask if he or she can recommend someone else who might be interested. When you receive a positive response, send a thank-you note.

Going It Alone Versus Hiring Outside Help

If you're a small business owner single-handedly dealing with all facets of your operation, you might want to consider outsourcing some or all of your PR work. One advantage of working with an outside PR firm or professional writer is that you can put together a publicity plan for your business and know that it will actually get carried out.

Professional PR firms often work on a monthly retainer that covers a certain level of service, such as a preset number of press releases to be sent on your behalf. But full-service PR firms can be costly, and their results, and the degree of personal attention your small business can expect from them, are sometimes questionable.

Between the extremes of doing everything yourself and hiring a large, expensive firm, it is possible to find independent professionals and small firms willing to work on a project basis. There are also plenty of freelance writers and publicity consultants who can be hired for less money than a full-service firm.

7 Getting an Article into Print

Early in my career, I wrote an article about how to publish articles as a marketing strategy for small businesses. It took only a few hours because I knew the subject intimately, and the results were incredible.

Almost immediately after it was published, I landed a new client, was invited to submit two proposals, and added dozens of names to my mailing list. I reprinted the article as a newsletter, made copies for my marketing kit, and posted it on related websites. I later republished the article with minor revisions in other publications, including *SPAN* (a newsletter for book publishers), *Dynamic Business* (a Pennsylvania business journal), *Opportunity World* (a business opportunity magazine), and several others.

Years later, the benefits continue to roll in as prospects read my article on the Internet, recommend it to associates, and hire my firm because I'm an "expert" in targeted public relations strategies. In one instance, a reader who later became a client requested a proposal from my company, even though her company had almost finalized a decision to hire a competitor. "We came across your article, and it made all the difference," they said. "We knew from your article that you could help us."

Not every article you publish will hit the jackpot, but once you start getting your name in print on a regular basis, you'll reap many benefits. An article published in your name gives you instant credibility because it's editorial matter—not advertising—and hence carries the endorsement of the publication in which it appears. Articles help you get taken seriously and attract prospects, sometimes—as in the incident I described above—delivering them right to your door. Also, article reprints make excellent marketing materials.

You don't have to be a professional writer or seasoned journalist to get your name in print. Whether you're a management consultant or a masseuse, publishing articles under your byline can do wonders for your business. With more than 10,000 publications in print today, your opportunities are virtually unlimited. You can do it.

Publications Need You

From fillers to features, most magazines you see on newsstands every day rely on freelance writers for some of their content. No, you don't have to have a cousin in the publishing world to see your name in print. You just have to follow the same rules as journalists, and one day editors will be calling you.

This chapter provides a step-by-step tour of how to get your work in publications that reach your target market. Once you learn the ropes, you'll find that placing articles in publications relevant to your business is a powerful and effective way to market your services. There are thousands of business, trade, and Internet publications covering every imaginable industry and audience, and many are fairly easy to break into, even for beginners.

Your Road to Becoming a Published Expert

Bylined, contributed articles are a mainstay in many business publications. Often written for a small fee—or given freely in exchange for an author bio or byline designed to elicit business—these articles show off the expertise of the businessperson or consultant who authored it.

TIPS FROM THE GURU

Kimberly Stanséll Describes Her Marketing Mix

Kimberly Stanséll is president of Research Done Write!, a Los Angeles-based consulting and training firm that offers workshops and seminars for entrepreneurs, especially for professional women. Stanséll has written two books, articles, and a syndicated column, "Bootstrappers' Success Secrets." Since 1992 she has been a noted expert on entrepreneurship, largely because of these publications.

Stanséll has written for dozens of publications, including *Home Office Computing*, *Entrepreneurial Edge*, and *Self-Employed Professional*. "I write articles based on information from my books, workshops, and networking experiences. As a bonus, I often get paid top dollar to write them," she says. "I've found that having three to six pieces in circulation at any time gives me consistent coverage."

Stanséll credits these articles with expanding her name recognition and promoting her book. "At conferences, people tell me that they read about my book in *Black Enterprise*, or that they recognized it at Kinko's and bought it. I get invitations to participate in events from people who've read my columns and articles. I also get credibility. People automatically assume I'm expensive, which raises my fee even before I open my mouth."

How much of her current business comes from her articles? "It's hard for me to measure, because my publishing affects my business in different ways. The name recognition my column has given me is tremendous."

Stanséll advises that you treat your writing efforts as part of your overall marketing strategy. "Publishing articles is just one cylinder in my marketing engine," she explains. "My business is to teach, speak, research, and write about issues that are important to entrepreneurs. The articles I write complement my other efforts to create recognition for my books, and attract teaching and speaking engagements."

Start Small

When you begin approaching publications as a potential expert contributor, be realistic. Too often, new writers expect to publish their first article in top publications like *Inc., Business Week,* or *Fast Company.* That's being as unrealistic as a baseball player who expects to bypass the minor leagues and go straight to the World Series. Many of these publications are entirely staff-written, and do not accept contributed articles.

On the other hand, there are thousands of trade, business, and special interest publications with names like *Marketing News, Pharmaceutical Executive, Bay Area Parent,* and *New Jersey Outdoors.* If your business serves the readers of these magazines, these publications want to hear from you. Editors at trade publications are more accessible to you than those at general interest publications, and because trade periodicals provide information that is critical to their readers' businesses, they are often read with intense interest.

Coming Up with Ideas

Coming up with interesting article ideas is often a struggle, but there is no reason to strain your imagination or look for something completely novel. Study your chosen publications, and determine the types of stories each of them seems to favor—then use them as starting points for your own ideas. Look for patterns, trends, and points of discussion.

Save relevant news stories as launching points and ready-made research for your articles. Gather publications that serve your target market, and look for ideas that relate to your business. Look to your own experiences and those of your colleagues and clients—there's plenty of good material all around you. Few story ideas are truly original. A new slant, an interesting angle, timeliness, and focus—these are enough to make a story publishable.

The Difference between a Topic and a Story Idea

"I'd like to write a story about marketing" is unlikely to attract an editor because the idea is too vague. To turn your idea into a workable story, you need to narrow your topic and slant it to a particular audience. Though it may be connected to larger issues, you need to address a sufficiently narrow range of applications so that you can offer the kind of detail that will be of value to your readers.

"Employee references" is a topic; "Should Employers Be So Tight-Lipped About Former Employees?" is a story idea. To turn a topic into a magazine article requires focus. A 500-word article, for example, requires a laser-sharp

TIPS FROM THE GURU

Gordon Burgett on How to Look at a Publication

Gordon Burgett, author of *Sell & Resell Your Magazine Articles,* offers the following advice on how to study publications and approach them with saleable ideas.

Read closely each article in recent issues of the publication you are targeting. As you read the articles, study how they address the basic working questions of who, what, why, where, when, and how. Put yourself in the writer's shoes. How did the writer slant the subject to appeal to the magazine's readers?

Study how the writer carries the main theme through the article. Study the writer's use of facts, quotes, and anecdotes. List every source used, including direct references and quotations. Ask yourself where the writer might have found the facts, opinions, and quotes that are not clearly identified by source in the article.

Concentrate on the lead. How long is it, in words or sentences? Does it grab your interest? Does it make you want to read more? Why? How does it compare with other leads in that issue? Look throughout the article at the transitional words and sentences, and see how the overall article structure ties the treatment together. Is the subject treated chronologically, developmentally, by alternating examples, or just point by point?

How does the article end? Does it tie back to the lead? Does it repeat an opening phrase or idea? The conclusion should reinforce and strengthen the direction that the article has taken. Does it? How? Finally, look at the title. How well does it describe the article that follows? What technique does it use to make the reader want to read the article?

focus on one tiny aspect of a subject. A 2,000-word article could have a somewhat wider focus, but still needs to be specific.

Take an imaginary walk around your subject the way you would walk around a building. Look at it from a variety of angles and perspectives, and think about how you can slant it according to the demands of different audiences and publications. Editors evaluate an idea by deciding how well it fits their particular publication. No matter how strong your idea or how well you write about it, if it doesn't meet an editor's needs, he or she won't buy it.

TIPS FROM THE GURU

Financial Executive Editor Jeffrey Marshall Discusses the Role of Expert Contributors

Jeffrey Marshall is the editor-in-chief of *Financial Executive* magazine, the flagship publication of Financial Executives International (FEI). The magazine provides senior financial executives with financial, business, and management news, and with trends and strategies that help them work better, faster, and smarter. Marshall regularly has businesspeople contributing articles to his publication. His advice should be helpful to anyone who wants to work with a trade journal or magazine.

Can you discuss the role of expert contributors at *Financial Executive*?

Experts play a larger role at *Financial Executive* than at many business publications for one obvious reason: they will write articles for free, a major consideration for a publication with a small budget that simply cannot afford to pay freelancers to fill the magazine. Additionally, business experts bring specific expertise that is targeted and often very useful, especially for complex areas of accounting, tax, and corporate finance.

In your experience, what value do expert contributors bring to the table?

Expert contributors bring depth of field, focus, and, yes, expertise. Ideally, they are current on the latest nuances in their field, and also bring a historic perspective—often knowing what was happening five years ago or 15 years ago. Also, they know the hot buttons in their subject area better than anyone outside it.

What are some things that expert contributors do, in general, that needs improvement?

Most of the time, expert contributors don't have the sophisticated style of full-time writers or the ability to craft a thesis that draws readers into their article. Their phrasing is often formal or clunky, and the organization of their material may be weak. As a result, some articles run considerably longer than they should. The bottom line is that expert contributors should work on being decent writers, or get help.

Also, company experts need to steer clear of talking about their company and how well they do things. Business magazines don't want commercial sales pitches disguised as editorial matter.

How to Study a Publication

Do your homework before you start pitching ideas to editors. Contact magazines and request a sample issue. This is not the time to pitch your ideas! Ask for their writer's guidelines (policies for contributing writers), an editorial calendar (a schedule of editorial topics for upcoming issues), and an index of previously published articles.

Look at a few copies of the publications you've targeted. Study their style to better focus and slant your ideas. Armed with this information, you should be able to get a good sense of the magazine's style and content. This will put you in a much better position to develop and pitch appropriate story ideas. Remember, the quickest way to turn off editors is to pitch an idea that has nothing to do with their magazine.

Selling to Editors

As a rule, professional writers try to sell an idea before they do the writing; they don't develop an article and send it scattershot to all the magazines they think might be interested. Why not? Because editors want to have input that will help shape the stories they assign. A query letter starts a dialogue between you and the editor that will hopefully land you an assignment, a request for an article of a certain kind and length on a specified topic with a particular slant.

As a matter of policy most magazines do not accept and will not read completed manuscripts because they just don't have the time to look at materials submitted outside their regular ways of working. A query letter saves everyone time. An editor will not have to read a lengthy manuscript that might not be right for the magazine, and you don't spend hours researching and writing an article that may never see the light of day.

The Query Letter

You need to sell to editors just as you would to any client. You do this with a query letter—a mini-proposal that sells your article idea before you write the article. It also sells you, the writer, as someone qualified to deliver on your

TIPS FROM THE GURU

An Interview with Lisa Tomaszewski, Magazine Editor

Lisa Tomaszewski is the assistant editor of *Physician's Money Digest*. She regularly works with expert contributors, and values their contributions. She also offers advice on how best to work with publications like hers.

Why are expert contributors important to you?

They are an invaluable resource to our readers and a cost-effective way for us to continue providing quality editorial. Many readers even take the next step and contact our contributors for more information or to employ their services.

Are there things that contributors could improve upon?

They need to write helpful articles that provide a lot of useful information, not advertisements for their company. While I understand that expert contributors are motivated by getting a free "plug" in our publication, there's nothing more frustrating than receiving articles that are mere advertisements for the writer's firm, and leave out crucial information to "tease" readers into contacting them.

I once had an estate planning article submitted that said, "You can be hit with an 80 percent estate tax ... if you want to know how, please contact our firm." Statements like this get cut, or we pull the article from the publication entirely.

Furthermore, an article that provides incomplete information can do more harm than good to our readers. Novice investors may read the "80 percent estate tax" article and take drastic, and potentially illegal, steps to protect themselves. Authors who leave out information are not only a detriment to our readers, but also themselves. No one is going to pursue advice or service from someone whose only concern is their own profit.

What constitutes a good approach to writing contributed articles?

---

promise. In some ways like cold calls, they are, nevertheless, the best way to solicit writing assignments from editors who don't know you.

On any sales call, the first moments are the most important. Your query letter is all an editor knows about you. Many good article ideas get rejected because an editor sees nothing in the presentation that says the writer is up to the job. You need to put your best writing into your query letter.

A good query letter presents the facts in a conversational tone with just a

There are several qualities that "ideal" writers possess. They first take the time to understand the magazine's style and audience. Are they experienced? Will you need to explain concepts to them? For example, you shouldn't use terms like P/E ratio or FICO Score if the magazine's audience doesn't know what they are. My magazine is a finance magazine written for doctors, so the content has to be explanatory, just as a medical article written for brokers would have to be written in "layman's terms."

Good writers also turn in copy that is clear, concise, grammatically correct, and conforms to the style of the magazine. They're willing to crack open that grammar book. Don't count on editors to catch your mistakes; if you do, it will not reflect well on your abilities. If you feel that your writing skills aren't up to scratch, but you still want to submit your ideas, either take a writing course at a local college or hire a PR firm to do the writing for you.

Ideal writers also need to be independent; that is, they don't need to have their hand held throughout the submission process. There's nothing more infuriating than a writer calling me ten times asking me pointless questions about their 500-word article. I edit over 50 articles per issue, twice a month; I don't need every author calling me about irrelevant details. In sum, an ideal contributor will follow instructions and submit a clean, proofread copy on time.

Finally, focus on the reader's opportunity to learn from you, rather than the opportunity for you to sneak in an advertisement. I can't stress this enough. Readers can tell when you are trying to sell them something; this strategy always backfires (not to mention the fact that editors will cut your advertising efforts and you may not be asked to submit again). When your article is published it will reach many eager readers, and you want to appear to be a teacher, not a salesperson.

hint of formality. Pretend you are telling your story idea to a friend who is slightly senior to you. Avoid exaggeration, but if you have special knowledge of the topic, mention it. If you have a perspective other writers might not have, say so.

The Lead The first step for writing a letter that will sell you and your idea is to create a lead. In journalism, a "lead" is a short summary that introduces a news story or magazine article. Also known as an opening, introduction, or hook, the lead is a paragraph or series of paragraphs that have been carefully constructed to capture and hold reader interest. The lead anchors the central theme, thesis, or organizing principle of an article. A lead must:

- answer the questions who, what, why, when, where, and how
- introduce the article's topic, focus, and slant
- arouse interest, making an editor want to read on
- present your strongest material at the beginning

Your lead needs to be good enough to distract editors from their daily concerns and make them give their full attention to your idea. You want them to finish the letter and think, "Yes, here's an article that would work for us, and a writer we can trust to write it appropriately."

Write the lead in the same style as the article you're proposing. It can, in fact, double as the first paragraph of the article when you get the assignment. A lead is a stage setter, conveying the tone, style, and voice of the article. Your lead will resonate throughout your query, and eventually your article, as the central principle that holds everything together.

An "anecdotal lead" opens with a short account of an incident or situation that supports, illustrates, or embodies the main point of the article topic you are proposing. Highly popular because they engage our feelings as readers, anecdotal leads are built around a miniature story—for example:

As Joe Smith watched a tow truck pull his minivan from the driveway of his suburban home, he was speechless, unable to explain to his daughter how he would take her to school. He had lost everything— house, car, and self-respect. Joe is one of thousands of people each year forced into bankruptcy after overextending themselves in a culture of easy credit.

"Hard fact leads" are packed with statistics, information. They get a reader's attention by revealing a hidden opportunity or danger. Because it is grounded in fact, this kind of lead feels substantial and compelling. When done correctly, readers feel the relevance of the information, and keep reading to find out what they need to do about it. Here's a fact-based lead:

Did you ever wonder where your tax dollars go? As a small business owner, you should want to see some of them coming back to you. Each year the government sets aside $210 billion in contracts for goods and services, resulting in many millions in procurements daily——all of it up for bid by America's businesses. Federal, state, and local governments need businesses of all types and sizes to provide the goods and services necessary to run the country. Why can't your business be one of them?

A "news peg" is another way to start a query or an article. This is simply some interesting news item on which you can hang the story. Even if you have a story idea that would tie into a topic with a longer shelf life, such as an ongoing political saga or crisis, you might be able to tap into current events in a way that improves its chances of getting accepted.

Alternatively, you can jump right into your subject matter with a "strong statement lead." This can work well if your topic is something your reader is already familiar with. Here's a sample:

> Let's face it—politics is about money. Whoever gives the most gains the most. The average American may give a few bucks here and there to his favorite candidates, but that's small potatoes compared to how much the average corporation shells out every election cycle, both directly and indirectly.

This "point/counterpoint" lead presents a statement of fact, then contradicts it with an opposing fact. The state of tension established between the two then becomes the subject of the article.

> In the 1990s, the home became a hotbed of business activity, combining lifestyle choices, entrepreneurship, and significant profits and revenues. The SBA estimates that home businesses now account for over 50% of all firms in the United States, and generate over 10% of the nation's Gross Domestic Product. But even as more home businesses dot the economic landscape, most continue to face the burdens of local zoning and use restrictions in residential neighborhoods, turning many home-based businesses into underground outlaws.

Just as its name implies, the "atmospheric" lead invokes an image or feeling. This type of lead is especially effective for human-interest stories where the purpose is to generate an emotional response from readers.

Phang-Nga Bay, the idyllic, 400-kilometer body of water off the Andaman Sea in southern Thailand, is one of the great natural wonders of Southeast Asia. It offers warm, emerald green waters, plenty of equatorial sun, and an occasional fisherman casting a net from a long-tail boat. Declared a national park in 1981, the area became famous after the James Bond adventure, *The Man with the Golden Gun*, was partly filmed there, and has since become a favorite destination for outdoor enthusiasts.

Create a Framework You've captured an editor's attention with a powerful lead. Don't let up. Your second paragraph must keep an editor reading, expanding the promise of the first paragraph and placing your idea into a larger contextual framework, as in the following example:

Communication with the Click of a Mouse—
How to Start Your Own E-mail Newsletter

Terry Alton, principal of Computer Wizard in Lincoln, Nebraska, is a popular guy. Each month 5,000 people from all over the country await *PC Secrets,* his monthly e-mail newsletter of computer tips directed at small business owners. Unlike other consultants who constantly seek new business from strangers, Alton gets himself all the business he can handle without spending a penny on printing, mailing, or advertising.

E-mail newsletters (e-zines) are an effective tool to help small businesses keep in touch with their clients, customers, and prospects. The goal of e-zines is to provide readers with useful information on a regular basis that creates a win-win situation—readers get news they can use, e-zine publishers establish goodwill and credibility—an ongoing gesture that builds a bridge for future sales.

In the third paragraph, explain how you will tailor your idea to the needs of the publication. Here's where you discuss the slant and focus of your topic.

Use the fourth paragraph to talk about your expertise as it relates to the article. Discuss your credentials. Mention sources of information you will use. Be prepared to discuss opposing opinions. List any writings you've published. (If you haven't published before, skip that part.) An exceptional query letter can compensate for lack of experience.

Finally, sign off gracefully. A one-word statement will suffice: "Interested?"

Sample Query Letter

Query: Barter—Cashing In on an Old Idea

Robert Pritikin, owner of the Mansions Hotel in San Francisco, was having a bad day. His finely plumed macaw had taken sick in the hotel lobby. He needed lots of props for the "miraculous snowstorm," part of the evening's magic show. His magicians needed to be paid. And, to top it off, there was a plumbing leak in the restaurant.

As usual, Pritikin relied on bartering, an idea as old as civilization, to handle these business needs. Through a simple phone call to his barter exchange, Pritikin obtained a veterinarian, props for his magic show, compensation for his employees, and emergency plumbing service—all without spending a dollar in cash.

By definition, bartering is any cashless trading of goods or services. But it's far more sophisticated today than when our ancestors traded chickens for horseshoes; today's savvy business people are, with the help of barter exchanges, swapping hotel rooms for printing, paging services for computer repairs, and advertising space for timeshare condos in the Caribbean.

Part accountants, part matchmakers, today's barter brokers bring their members new business. As a business activity, barter is huge. According to Tom McDowell of the National Association of Trade Exchanges, there are between 400 and 600 barter exchanges in the United States, with over a quarter million members generating the equivalent of billions of dollars in trade revenue each year.

I would like to write a feature article explaining the benefits of barter exchange membership to your readers. I will define bartering: how it started, what it entails, and how it can be used to boost profits. I will explain the basics of barter exchange membership, provide quotes from national experts, and provide reports of experience from business people across the United States who have benefited from bartering.

I am a writer and marketing consultant based in San Francisco. I have been involved with four different barter organizations over the past four years. I am intimately acquainted with the barter industry, and understand the considerations small businesses face when joining an exchange. I have enclosed some previous clips and a SASE for your response.

Interested?

Steven Van Yoder

Submitting Your Query Letter   Since your query letter is supposed to be the beginning of a relationship, don't act like a door-to-door salesman by sending anonymous "Dear Editor" letters. Direct your letter to the right editor by calling to inquire which editor handles topics like yours, and make sure you have the correct spelling of his or her name, and the preferred delivery method.

It's also important not to send query letters to competing magazines simultaneously. Create a priority list and propose your piece to the first on the list. If the first magazine rejects it, send it to the next magazine on your list, and so on. An editor who discovers that you've been two-timing him or her will drop you forever.

Be professional in your presentation. Avoid flowery stationery or garish logos. Don't detract from your presentation by calling attention to insignificant details. Editors buy well-presented ideas, not attempts to compensate for basic weakness by ornate packaging.

It never hurts to include samples of any previously published work. The more they relate to your query letter, the better. If you don't yet have clips, just make sure your query letter is as strong as you can make it, and rely on the quality of your presentation to help you make the sale.

You've Sent Your Query Letter. Now What?

One of three things is likely to happen after you submit your query letter.

1. You will receive a go-ahead from the editor "on speculation." This means the editor likes your idea and wants you to write the article, but won't commit to publishing it until approving the completed manuscript. Your chances of getting published are excellent if your article is well-written.

2. Your query is rejected. Don't take this personally. Send your query letter to the next editor on your list.

3. You hear nothing. If you have not heard from a publication after a few weeks, send a follow-up message. After a few more weeks, you can call.

Writing the Article

Congratulations! You've sold your idea. Now it's time to gather your thoughts, incorporate the editor's feedback into your plans, and meet your deadline. The editor will give you some idea of how long the article should be, and may also provide guidelines on how to best slant and focus your article so that it appeals to his or her readership. Here are guidelines for writing a good article.

Outlines and Research

Just as you wouldn't begin building a house without a blueprint, don't begin writing an article without an outline. Without an outline writing can be tough going, an upstream swim. If your outline is complete, you can cruise downstream as you write.

A well-organized outline prevents writer's block. Inspiration goes only so far—you must take the time to get organized, either before you write, when it is much easier, or during the writing, which inevitably makes even a small writing project take twice as long and leaves you frustrated.

Some writers love research, others hate it. Whatever your inclination, writing well depends on researching well. When you have the facts in hand and understand the context of your subject, you will be able to reach out to your readers with a sense of authority.

Formulas Make Writing Easier

Outlines and research make the process of writing easier; formulas can be used to provide an instant structure for articles. Formulas are set patterns for expressing your ideas. Most articles follow one formula or another. Here are some of the easiest and most common formulas that can be applied to articles:

The List Just as it sounds, a list article presents a number of items tied together by a binding idea. "Ten Common Sales Objections" and "Eight Ways to Avoid Workplace Injuries" are examples of list articles that promise an easy grasp of a cluster of facts based on an overall theme.

The Roundup Article The roundup article gathers information around a question or a common theme, and presents it in an organized manner. This format calls for the opinions of various authorities, making the article easy to write and sell. A roundup article is like a conference on paper, bringing together a group of people to talk about a particular topic.

The Case Study Case studies provide extended examples of how someone has met a challenge, sold a product, or communicated an idea. Your own company might be the subject of a case study if you can show you helped a client solve a common business problem.

The How-To This is one of the most common formulas, and a favorite among writers, editors, and readers. Its plan is simple; show readers how to achieve something on a step-by-step basis. Examples of the how-to formula include "Ways to Include Humor in Speeches," "How to Recession-Proof Your Business," and "Strategies to Resolve Workplace Disputes."

Rights and Contracts

If you plan to reuse your work after it's published, you need to understand the basic principles of copyright before you agree to write for a publication. Here are the most common copyright arrangements between freelance writers and the publications they deal with.

First Rights When a magazine buys first rights, it purchases the right to publish the article before it appears anywhere else, and it has exclusive use of the article for the lifetime of the issue in which it appears. When that issue is no longer current, you are free to republish it in any way you choose.

One-Time Rights Under this arrangement, the publication buys the non-exclusive right to publish the piece once. The writer can sell the same article to other publications at any time.

All Rights This means you give a publication complete ownership of your article for a period defined under copyright law. Under this arrangement the publication owns the article, not you, and you'll need to get their permission for any further use of it, including publishing the article on your own website. Avoid this arrangement if you plan to reuse your work.

Work for Hire Under this arrangement, you sell your copyright and any claim on your article. They own the copyright, and don't have to give you credit. This arrangement doesn't work as a *slightly famous* marketing strategy.

Electronic Rights More and more an issue with regard to written works that previously only appeared in print, these rights refer to the use of your words on websites or CD-ROMs. Many publications will want you to grant them permission to archive your article on their website. If you agree to this arrangement, make sure you retain the right to reuse your work in any form.

Always ask the editor whether they will be sending you a contract. It's best not to write anything before you have a signed contract that includes your copyright agreement.

How to Get the Most from Your Articles

In addition to increasing your company's visibility, articles can generate immediate response from readers. Here are some techniques to maximize the results.

The Extended Byline

A byline is the author's name as it appears attached to a published article. An extended byline includes not just an author's name, but contact information and/or a short description of the company he or she represents. Extended bylines are common in trade and specialty publications, and if you are contributing an article for little or no money, it is a reasonable expectation.

An extended byline should be a concise but accurate profile of your company, expressing your identity and the benefits of doing business with you. Here's a byline I have used on many occasions.

How Jeff Dobkin Promotes Articles through Self-Syndication

"Every few months, I mail out a packet of 15 – 20 articles to a list of 100 carefully selected magazine editors whose publications reach my audience of small business owners and direct-marketing professionals," says Jeff Dobkin, the author of *How to Market Your Product for Under $500*. "In an average month, about 10 of the editors publish one or more of my articles, which cover topics like '12 Places to Buy a Mailing List,' and '18 Marketing Assumptions That Aren't True.'" His most popular article, 'The One Evening Marketing Plan,' has appeared in over 50 magazines."

Dobkin makes the articles available for free on a non-exclusive basis to editors, the only catch being that they must include his phone, fax, and other ordering details at the end of the story. This method has paid off very well. In four years of steadily mailing out articles, he has sold more than $400,000 in books (some direct and some through bookstores). In addition, the name recognition he has earned has allowed him to increase his speaking fees to $5,000 per engagement and brought a steady stream of direct-mail copywriting and consulting clients.

"Most of the magazines running my articles are niche market trade magazines (for example, *Office Systems, Mortgage Press*), regional magazines (*Business Strategies of Eastern Ohio*), or second-tier national publications," says Dobkin. "The two common characteristics are a willingness to run non-exclusive material, and very tight editorial budgets."

Here are more details on his approach:

Develop a list of magazines. Dobkin's first step was to build a mailing list of 300–400 publications that addressed his audience and seemed to be open to running non-exclusive how-to articles.

GET THE WORD OUT! Communications can help you become a recognized expert in your industry. We develop, write, and place feature stories in publications read by your prospects and clients, and can help you get quoted in publications that reach your target market. Ask about our custom-tailored Media Interview, Article Coaching, and Strategy Programs to help you harness the power of PR for your business at a reasonable cost. Learn more at www.getthewordout.net.

Target the Top Editor In the case of small magazines, Dobkin mails his article packet to the top editor listed in the publication's masthead (typically the Editor-in-Chief).

Titles are Key By far the most important part of the article is the title. When drafting each article, Dobkin says he typically begins by writing many possible titles in an effort to find the one that's most compelling.

No Fluff Dobkin's articles average 600–2,000 words, but most are around 1,200 words long and include practical how-to information. He suggests making them easy to read by using subheads and keeping paragraphs short.

Easily Editable Since magazines use articles of varying lengths and need to slant articles for their readerships, many of Dobkin's pieces are lists of tips that can be easily shortened and adapted to individual publications. For instance, "The 23 Best Lines in Marketing" can quickly become "The 18 Best Lines for Marketing Florists" if an editor doesn't have space for the entire list or needs to slant the article accordingly.

Supply Multiple Formats Dobkin's typical package includes a set of 15–20 articles on 60 lb. white offset-quality stock. He also includes a black-and-white photo of himself, plus a cover letter that mentions that he'll gladly e-mail the articles or provide the text on disk. The latter options save editors the time and hassle of retyping the article.

Customize Articles If They Pay While Dobkin's primary focus is on finding editors who will run his existing articles for free in exchange for a resource box mention, occasionally editors contact him who are willing to pay him to tweak an article just for them—or even write a new one from scratch. His fees vary from $250 to $1,500, depending upon how much customization is required.

The Offer

How do you ensure that readers, who are ultimately prospects, have reason to contact you? Draw readers toward your company by offering something free— a booklet, product sample, consultation, special report, or other such enticement—related to your business. You can do this in your extended byline.

Make sure prospects feel that requesting your information will be painless, risk-free, and unaccompanied by sales pressure. If possible, let prospects request information by writing or e-mail.

Marketing with Reprint

Savvy marketers get maximum mileage from their efforts by using reprints of their articles as creative marketing tools. Not only do reprints cost a mere fraction of the price of an original brochure, but they carry far more credibility. While a brochure will always be perceived as a sales piece, reprints read like news, making prospects more receptive to your marketing message.

Here are several ways to use reprints to your advantage.

• Include reprints with proposals. You have a better chance of impressing prospects with your abilities if you are a newsmaker.

• Use reprints to keep in touch. You can mail reprints of your published article to prospects, customers, and clients. You can do this at a fraction of the cost of writing, designing, and mailing a newsletter.

• Frame or laminate articles to display in your lobby or reception area. Everybody likes to do business with a winner. Show your customers and clients how you stand out.

• Turn reprints into special reports and booklets. You can reprint your article in other forms to give away as sales incentives.

• Post published articles on your website. You can show off what you have done while keeping your website fresh with new content.

• Republish articles in other magazines, websites, and newsletters. Make the most of each article you write by looking for likely publications and websites that would be interested in reprinting them as is or with a few changes.

• Use reprints as trade show handouts. You can send reprints to key vendors, customers, and clients with a cover letter announcing your presence and location at the show. An effective article can lure prospects to your booth.

How to Become a Columnist

Articles are usually a one-shot deal. Columns, on the other hand, are regular engagements that allow a writer to build relationships with readers. Columns appear on a weekly or monthly basis in newspapers, magazines, and websites. They can brand the authors not just as experts, but also as friends, confidantes, and mentors.

Columns are appealing promotional vehicles because of their regularity. Becoming a columnist is not easy; there are fewer opportunities for columns than articles, which makes landing a regular column a competitive contest. But if you succeed, becoming a columnist can turn you into a recognized authority within your target market.

"My column gave me an opportunity to touch people in a meaningful way and enhance my reputation," says former *San Francisco Examiner* career columnist Pat Sullivan. "People would forward my column to their friends and associates and many times I'd hear people say, 'This column really started a discussion in our workplace.' My column also helped me get invitations to speak and even land some new clients."

You don't have to achieve "Dear Abby" status to be a successful column writer. As with any *slightly famous* marketing strategy, your column only needs to reach the right people in your target market to position you as a resource.

Years ago, motivational speaker Bill Hodges was frustrated by what he felt was a constant barrage of negative news in the media. He approached his local newspaper editor, saying that the paper should devote more print space to uplifting news. The editor told Hodges to fix the situation by writing something himself.

A few weeks later, Hodges came back to the editor with thirteen columns on the power of positive thinking. The editor was so impressed he made Hodges a weekly columnist. In the years since, Hodges has expanded the reach of his "Positive Talk" columns, which now appear in 16 weekly papers in 37 countries around the world. With titles such as "Even the Bravest Need a Shove," "The Fear Is False," and "The Art of Human Relations," these columns have brought a tidal wave of speaking engagements and book sales.

Hodges maintains that writing a column is a grueling but ultimately rewarding experience. "I don't generally care what they pay me for the columns, because they're usually worth well over ten times the amount I receive," says

TIPS FROM THE GURU

An Interview with Jay Conrad Levinson

Jay Conrad Levinson is the author of the acclaimed *Guerrilla Marketing* book series. When *Guerrilla Marketing* was first published in 1983, Levinson revolutionized marketing strategies for the small-business owner.

How did you come to appreciate the value of getting your name into print as a way of building your business and reputation?

It happened by accident. I was teaching a course at a local college in the mid-1980s, and my students wanted to know if I could recommend inexpensive marketing books. Because there weren't that many devoted to small businesses at the time, I wrote *Guerrilla Marketing,* which not only took on a life of its own, but also became the name of my course.

The book led to speaking engagements and media interviews. Soon, I started writing columns, and though the pay was nominal, it got my name out there along with contact information. Then I was able to take columns I had written and incorporate them into books.

Now, my agent markets my columns to publications that reach small businesses. I don't receive financial compensation, but the name recognition of having my name in print leads to other things. Publishing helped me land a job teaching a course at U.C. Berkeley. And other unexpected opportunities always result from publishing.

When I give a talk, say to a national convention, they always ask if I would write something for their newsletter, and I almost always agree. So my message is always out there, often in publications I'd never even heard of.

What's your advice to businesspeople about using article and column publishing to promote themselves and their small businesses?

Hodges. "The thing that I stress is that consistency counts. Getting my name out there and getting in papers has delivered many benefits. Furthermore, the discipline of writing the weekly columns allowed me to write a book and to put a set of tapes together."

Marketing and selling a column requires work—often more work than writing the column itself. Here are some possible markets.

The easiest way to get into print is through websites. Search for sites that match your expertise and industry. Websites provide one of the most accessible and inexpensive ways to get your message out there. There are about 50,000 newsletters online. These are excellent sources for the beginner. Online newsletters are more willing to say "yes" where magazines might say "no." By publishing on the Internet, you can generate published articles quickly, and move on to bigger things.

What's one of the most interesting things that happened to you as a result of publishing articles and columns?

I have a mind-boggling success story. A San Francisco Chronicle reporter wanted to interview me years ago about my book *Earning Money without a Job*. He was especially interested in my assertion that I've been working a three-day week since 1971. He wrote the article, which included my phone number, and in a few days I received 1,000 orders for the book that translated into $10,000 in sales.

After the interview, the reporter was so impressed by my self-determination that he vowed to quit his job and make a similar move. In the end, the reporter quit his job and went on to found Banana Republic.

What's your advice to people who lack the confidence to get started?

You can do it. There are millions of websites out there hungry for material from people who know their stuff. And there's very little downside to it. If you take a little time to learn the ropes and tailor your writing to the needs of others, it's almost rejection-free. And, you can make copies of everything you've published and use them as marketing materials or brochures. Once you get started, and your name begins to appear in new places, it will open up a whole new frontier.

Daily Newspapers Although competition is fierce, 1,600 daily newspapers make this market worth exploring. Newspapers that don't have print space for your column may be interested in publishing it on their website. Some newspapers also have online-only supplements to their print versions, including many columns that are online-exclusive.

Community Newspapers These weekly publications have experienced

EXECUTIVE BRANDING

Patrick McLaurin Leverages One Published Article into a Comprehensive Executive Branding Campaign

As Director of Diversity and Multinational People Strategy at Booz Allen Hamilton, one of the world's largest management consulting firms, Dr. Patrick McLaurin dedicated himself to promoting corporate diversity. In the process, he was able to showcase Booz Allen Hamilton's diversity efforts, particularly a Board Diversity Initiative that he led.

McLaurin began by approaching *MWorld,* the flagship publication of the American Management Association (AMA). The editor was impressed with McLaurin's unique insights on global diversity. She asked that he participate in a roundtable discussion for an article entitled "Leading Diversity in Times of Change," which included other Booz Allen executives, and set the stage for other AMA articles and a white paper distributed globally to their members.

The *MWorld* article prompted McLaurin to refine his ideas, take stock of his expertise, and differentiate himself in the field of corporate diversity. He created a thought leadership platform around the concept of "global talent management" that distinguished him and his firm as innovators in this growing sector.

From there, McLaurin identified other media where he could reach a broader

steady growth, and can make good markets for your column. You might need to "localize" your column, but if the subject is universal, it could be as simple as finding different examples for each market.

Alternative Press Weeklies These newspapers are often free, usually urban and eclectic, and sometimes left of center politically. Many are unofficial entertainment guides for their cities.

Magazines Although the sheer number of magazines now being published may seem promising for the aspiring columnist, breaking into magazines is not easy. The best place to begin is to forge a relationship by writing freelance articles that may, over time, prove you are a good bet for a regular column.

Internet Publications Don't reject the potential benefits of reaching your audience. Editors were receptive, and within a few months he placed articles in *American Executive, Employment Relations Today*, and *Leadership Excellence*.

At the same time, he applied to be a speaker at several global conferences, and was selected to give the keynote address at the Consulting World confer ence sponsored by the Institute of Management Consultants. His talk, "Consulting With Multi-National Multi-Cultural Companies," was designed to provoke a lively discussion on global diversity issues.

McLaurin then launched a blog, which he called "Leadership and Diversity," that allowed him to comment on diversity issues. His postings carried titles such as "The Global Graying Workforce: Implications for Leaders," and "Institutionalized Bias or Systematic Faults in the Retention of Talent? Walgreens Under Fire."

All of these accomplishments led to an invitation to submit a book proposal to a major publishing company for *Talent without Borders*, a book concept inspired while writing the *MWorld* article.

"Publishing helped me focus my thinking and finally take action. It was a tremendous motivator and springboard for other opportunities," says McLaurin. "Within one year, I went from relative obscurity in my field to laying a strong foundation for my expertise and industry thought leadership around corporate diversity. Moreover, by cultivating my own reputation as an industry thought leader, it reflects equally well on my employer and their commitment to advancing diversity."

audience via the Internet. What may appear to be an insignificant website or electronic publication could be an opportunity to raise your stature and provide an inroad to your target market.

Read Other Columnists

Find out where your column concept might fit in the marketplace by carefully reading what others are writing on your subject. Being able to articulate how your column fills a unique need in the marketplace will give you an edge.

While you may be the only person writing about tax planning for your hometown paper, there are probably many columnists addressing the same subject in various publications throughout the country. So if you want to go national, you'll have to differentiate yourself from them.

Before you get too far into your column project, run your idea by a few editors. Tell them what you have in mind—your column idea, your selling strategy, and an overview of your column's position in the marketplace. You'll find most editors helpful and willing to give feedback and guidance.

Selling Your Column

If you're serious about pursuing a column, you will need to put together a sales package that includes:

- a cover letter describing your proposed column
- six to ten sample columns
- the copyright terms you are offering
- reprints of published articles
- a biography and business background
- a self-addressed, stamped envelope for editor response

If a publication is interested, they will most likely name a price for the column (yes, you can get paid for this) that will probably range between $30 and $150.

8 Broadcast Media

Doctor Douglas Markham, a Los Angeles-based chiropractor and nutritionist, approached dozens of radio and television producers with the message "Eating Fat Does Not Make You Fat." As a nutritionist who'd recently developed a new dietary system, Markham asserted that the "low-fat, high-carbohydrate diet that has gotten so much attention does not work." Moreover, he said, the studies that promoted these diets were biased, possibly even corrupt, because they had been financed by the food industry.

His message hit a nerve with the media because he touched on what broadcasters are often looking for, controversy. Markham received 25 phone calls from television and radio stations eager to interview him. His media strategy even landed him on *Larry King Live,* where he appeared with one of his celebrity clients who testified that Markham's dietary system worked.

Radio and television producers are always looking for interesting and informative guests, and compelling content that informs and entertains audiences by bringing a fresh and insightful angle to the day's news. You don't have to be a celebrity to be a guest on radio and television shows. All it takes is tailoring your expertise to the needs of particular audiences, and presenting your message in an enjoyable and interesting way.

An Overview of the Airwaves

Broadcast media provides a great way to reach large local, regional, or national audiences. Unfortunately, too many potential beneficiaries of the media are intimidated by radio and television, and think them unapproachable.

Radio and television stations rely on interesting guests, including those from the business world, to fill airtime and add authority to their news stories. And they are always looking for businesses and products that offer some novelty or special angle that will grab their audience's attention.

The broadcast media reach the ears and eyes of your target market, delivering these powerful benefits:

Greater Reach Consumers today spend much more time watching television and listening to radio programs than they do reading traditional print media like newspapers and magazines——some studies indicate that the ratio is on the order of 5-to-1 or more.

Personal Connections Unlike print media, where you appear only indirectly, behind a wall of words, radio and television programs enable you to reach out directly and make a more personal connection.

Celebrity Status The more you appear on radio and television programs, the more you'll be seen as a celebrity, which will boost your brand and reputation.

Enhanced Credibility People who appear on radio and television are seen as leaders in their industries.

Increased Sales If you target the right radio and television programs, your media appearances can make you money. Appearing as a guest on a local program that reaches your target market can attract many clients and customers. National television shows like *Good Morning America, Oprah*, or *Larry King Live* reach millions of people.

Understanding What Radio and Television Want

Broadcast opportunities are abundant for experts in everyday subjects such as travel, taxes, health and fitness, parenting, and home safety, to name just a few. Unique products can be good material, and colorful individuals and personalities that offer excitement and entertainment value are always in demand.

Compelling News

You must craft your message in a way that gives it obvious news value. "What most business owners need to do is put themselves in the position of the editor or producer," says publicity expert Paul Krupin. "You have to look at what they do. The key to being successful is to give them news that's better than anything else they have. It's that simple."

Radio and television producers consider items usable when they have broad consumer appeal. Producers particularly want information about current events, new industry developments, and business and product innovations. For example, if you are a local dry-cleaning operator who has embraced the use of non-toxic cleaning solvents, you could generate media exposure through your environment-friendly practices, especially if they challenge industry norms.

Captivating Material

Radio and television producers need material that keeps audiences tuned to their programs. They want guests who evoke an emotional reaction from their audiences. If you can provide material that's so riveting, entertaining, or even outrageous that no one would think of changing the station while it's on, you will be in demand.

Many producers use the term "sexy" when rating the media value of a subject. They ask themselves, "Is this sexy? Does it hold strong appeal?" This does

REAL-WORLD SUCCESS STORY

The Surreal Gourmet Gets Real Attention

Bob Blumer makes a big impression when he rolls into town. Blumer (a.k.a. The Surreal Gourmet) travels in a custom-made Airstream Trailer, a one-of-a-kind kitchen on wheels dubbed the Toastermobile due to the giant sheet metal pieces of toast protruding from the roof.

As one of today's most imaginative food personalities, Blumer is a good example of how any business can make itself interesting, exciting, even outrageous, and enjoy media attention.

Blumer designed the Toastermobile to promote his third cookbook, *Off the Eaten Path*. "When I'd seen Airstream trailers in the past they always reminded me of the shape of an old classic toaster," Blumer explained. "So when I was getting the trailer ready for the tour, I thought, 'why not?' and had two 12-foot-wide pieces of 'toast' installed on top."

Blumer became a food personality when he published *The Surreal Gourmet: Real Food for Pretend Chefs*. It was an instant hit that established his brand and earned him a loyal following. "The success of my first book made me live up to my

not mean the content is sexual, it means material that is attractive to their audience. If your business doesn't appear exciting, look for ways to add interest, even an outrageous twist, to make news-hungry producers take notice. Depending on your situation, industry, and inclinations, you might dress in an outrageous costume, hold a wacky contest, or stage an elaborate publicity stunt at a public location. Even humdrum businesses can cut through the clutter and get noticed by the media when they develop creative strategies.

Seasonal Appeal

Broadcast media may give you some coverage if your topic is timely or tied to a holiday or seasonal event. Certain broadcast media segments that appear every year are tied to seasons and holidays. For example, radio and television programs regularly provide tax tips in April, and discuss educational products own moniker of the surreal gourmet," says Blumer. "I saw the potential to get a lot of publicity on television shows that are always looking for interesting people."

It's a strategy that's paid off. His 30-city, three-month book tour for *Off the Eaten Path*, fueled by Blumer's knack for showmanship, not only got a lot of media attention on CNN, QVC, *Entertainment Weekly*, *People Magazine*, and over 100 daily newspapers, it also helped him land his own show on the Food Network.

Now, whether he's traveling the country in his Toastermobile for the Food Network, designing a surreal meal for the Salvador Dali Museum, or creating a supermodel diet for RuPaul, Blumer continues to build his personal brand identity in ways that make the media take notice.

"In the world of cooking, I've carved out this one little niche that is very unique and attractive to the-public and the media," says Blumer. "Because I so passionately and completely live my brand, and go out of my way to make it fun and interesting, the media love it! I make their job easy by developing my own surreal bag of tricks and culinary theatrics."

Blumer's trump card is salmon fillets poached in the dishwasher and topped with a brightly flavored cilantro sauce. According to Bob, "Not only do the media love it, but you can cook salmon, wash the dishes, and have your plates warmed all at the same time."

during the back-to-school season. Look for ways to tie your business to these "evergreen" calendar events.

Be on the Spot with Your Expertise

Radio and television stations don't have the time, money, or staffing to fill every second of airtime themselves. Almost anyone with inside understanding of some widely interesting subject area can present himself as an expert to radio and television audiences.

Michelle Burke, author of *The Valuable Office Professional*, created a niche that helped executive assistants more effectively work with their bosses. Each year, she pitched herself as an expert on media stories related to Secretary's Week, and got several interviews on radio and television programs that in turn generated book sales and established Burke as a leading figure in her industry.

Media Kits

A media kit, including the pitch letter and press release discussed in Chapter 5, is a standard tool in any publicity campaign. In addition to these basic elements, when approaching broadcast media you should include:

A List of Interview Questions A list of interview questions is an important part of any broadcast media kit, particularly for radio programs where the question and answer interview format is standard. Many radio producers don't have time to research products, guests, and issues for upcoming segments, and rely on the questions you provide as the basis for the show. You should list the questions in order of importance to assure that your main points are covered in case time runs out.

A Biography Create a personal bio to introduce yourself to the various people at the media outlet that you'll be working with. Keep your bio short, no more than 200 words. Support your statements with credentials, educational background, or professional experience that boosts your credibility. Write your bio as a broadcast producer would want it read on air, tight and concise.

Visuals When approaching television, you should include your photo and/or a photo of your product.

Video Footage (B-roll) Often, television stations would like to cover your story but don't have the resources to videotape your business on location. In such cases, they rely on video footage—B-roll, as it's called—provided by the subject of the proposed story. Your provision of B-roll increases your chances of getting on the air by making it possible for television producers to create stories without sending a film crew.

You create B-roll video footage with the help of a video production company that specializes in your business, product, or event. Once it's created, the video company edits the footage into several television-friendly segments, ready to be sent to appropriate producers. The footage can then be broadcast by the station or network, with a voice-over provided by you or a news anchor.

The cost of creating B-roll ranges from several hundred dollars to several thousand dollars. Its creation is best left to professionals; it must be shot in a format suitable for broadcast (producers rarely use VHS format). Generally 5–7 minutes of B-roll is sufficient, and this much usually takes a half day to create.

Your product offering and individual situation will determine if it's right to make this type of investment. If your story includes something such as a new product or manufacturing process, for example, you may be able to tell your story better visually.

Video News Releases (VNRs) A video news release is a two- or three-minute-long, professionally produced video in the format needed by news programs. It may be distributed through local and national news outlets, or even more widely via satellite broadcast organizations. With a professional voice-over, it provides a dynamic, visual press release that can be used "as is" by a broadcast outlet. If you are creating B-roll, you will have the raw footage to produce a VNR as a by-product when the B-roll is edited, and this can be archived for use at a later date.

Television Press Kits Sample footage on VHS tape is fine for inclusion in a television press kit. If you've been on television previously, or had some successful speaking engagements, include tapes of these events in your media kit. This sample footage shows producers that you are "ready for prime time."

Radio Press Kits An inexpensive five-to-ten-minute audiocassette interview should be included in your radio media kit. Radio producers need to know that you're an articulate, engaging guest. If you haven't been a guest on a radio broadcast previously, create your own mock interview by using your well-crafted interview questions.

Professional videotape suppliers generally carry audiotapes that can be purchased in 15- and 30-minute lengths. Finish them off with professional-looking computer-generated labels. You can add the plastic cases or simply tuck them into your press kit as is.

Identifying Broadcast Opportunities

How do you determine which broadcast media are right for your business? You are probably already familiar with the radio and television programs that reach your target market. Look closely at the types of topics that get airtime on them. Pitch programs that pertain to your geographical area. Look for programs likely to feature guests and segments related to your business. Here are a few considerations to keep in mind:

Local Media: Your Best Bet Again, you are probably already familiar with most of the programs you want to be on. You watch the local newscasts and have a favorite morning show. You listen to radio talk shows or the latest gardening tips while driving. You've probably seen or heard other businesses tell their story and wondered, "How did they get on this program?" This section answers that question.

Determine the Station's Format First, find out which radio or television programs have guest segments. Some stations limit programming to what is termed "hard news." This means that there are no guests, only interviews usually done at the site of breaking news.

Newscasts or programs that feature guests conduct interviews either in the studio or in the field. This means that either you would travel to the studio and be interviewed on a set, or a reporter would come to your place of business and interview you on-site. Once you've learned which radio or television programs book guests, you can target those that are a fit for your story.

Do You Have a Local or a National Pitch? Most *slightly famous* entrepreneurs have a story that is locally or regionally focused, so if you're typical, your business and your customers are limited to a geographical area considerably smaller than the whole United States. However, you may be an exception; you may have a product or service that is available nationally, meaning your broadcast opportunities are much greater.

Regional Considerations Consider regional factors when targeting radio and television stations. Is the area urban or rural? Is the population conservative or liberal? If your product or service is impacted by these factors, keep this in mind when pitching producers. Some stations producing nationally syndicated programs have websites providing information on past guests and subject matter.

Radio versus Television

There's no formula for determining which broadcast media should be part of your campaign. Obviously television is more suited to a visual presentation, but radio often dedicates more time to a presentation or interview, so you have a greater opportunity to tell your story. Here is a more detailed discussion of the major attributes of radio and television.

Radio

Radio is generally considered a more forgiving medium than television. Radio interviews usually offer larger time slots to tell your story. You can be interviewed in your office, your home, and even your car if your story is related to breaking news.

Radio producers generally have longer lead times than television producers, so you may have more time to prepare for your appearance. Understanding the overall time constraints in radio programming can help you better target those programs appropriate to your business.

Drive Times Radio has two "prime time" slots, the morning drive time (roughly 5–9 AM) and the evening drive time (roughly 4–7 PM). The audiences in these slots are mainly commuters. The formats are news, traffic, and short guest interviews that are often rebroadcast.

Other Time Slots Non-prime time slots are the longer stretches between the drive times. Midday programming audiences are often largely of retirement age. Travel, food, and leisure subjects are often the best subjects for these slots. However, there are many business and consumer issue programs in these time slots as well.

How Alex Carroll Scored Huge Book Sales Giving Radio Interviews

Alex Carroll's battle against traffic tickets began more than ten years ago when he took his first job as a courier driver and accumulated ten moving violations over four years. Because the company allowed drivers only one ticket, Carroll had two choices: beat his tickets or lose his job.

Carroll challenged his moving violations in traffic court. To his surprise, he managed to beat 8 of his 10 tickets. From this experience the idea for writing a book, *Beat the Cops*, was born.

Lacking money to spend on promoting the work, he began looking for very cheap—or better, free—ways to promote his book. Radio was the answer. Discovering that the thousands of radio stations across the country need approximately 10,000 guests a day to fill their programming schedules, he decided to create a morning drive radio tour to target audiences trapped behind the steering wheels of their cars during commute hours.

Alex started conducting interviews on smaller radio stations before moving up to the really large radio stations, those with over 100,000 listeners. He created a press kit, pitched himself as a guest, and quickly established himself as a radio personality, reaching national radio audiences several times a month.

"The best part is I didn't even have to get out of bed," says Carroll. "Radio stations would call and wake me, then I'd do the interview and go back to sleep. I'd wake up later and see that 200 to 500 orders worth thousands of dollars had

Evening programming may lean towards authors, public issues, or the arts. If you are a therapist, attorney, or artist, these time slots may be your best targets. Weekend programs typically deal with health and fitness, parenting, gardening, and other home-related topics.

Local Radio Programming Local radio is usually simple to approach. You can easily become familiar with the content because it's available on a daily basis, and most local radio stations want to keep their finger on the pulse of a community, so they make themselves accessible to local people with messages to deliver.

National and Syndicated Radio Programming If your story has national appeal, you can pitch to national and syndicated programs. These been placed by listeners while I slept."

Since writing *Beat the Cops*, Carroll has been featured on *ABC News* with Sam Donaldson, *E!*, *The Learning Channel* and Howard Stern-—-and has been a guest on more than 1,200 radio shows worldwide, selling over 100,000 copies of his book.

Carroll has become a vocal opponent of speed traps, insurance surcharges, and unfair tickets. He was a leading spokesperson for the National Motorists Association during their successful campaign to repeal the 55 mile per hour speed limit.

The secret to effective radio publicity, says Carroll, is targeting the types of shows that make sense for your business and message. Carroll also stresses that radio publicity requires both persistence and phone calls. "You can't just send your press release everywhere and expect good results," says Carroll. "One month, I booked 77 interviews by making 1,500 phone calls. You have to keep calling until you reach the right producer."

Most important, successful radio guests see themselves as partners in the programming process. "When you decide to do radio, you're in show business," says Carroll. "You've got to be able to come up with great ideas for shows and make yourself intriguing.

"Can you help people save time? Can you make them rich? Can you tell an amazing story? Can you make listeners laugh? If you can engage listeners and keep them from changing the channel, producers will welcome you

programs usually have a specific focus, such as health, parenting, travel, or personal finance. It's easy to identify which ones may be best for your pitch. National programming generally has long lead times, and the programs may be taped weeks or months in advance of the actual airdate.

Radio as the First Step to Broadcast Radio is a great medium for first-timers. For many it may be the most appropriate broadcast vehicle, but even for those aiming for a television appearance, it can serve as a good stepping stone. It gives you the opportunity to polish your story, and get a feeling for being interviewed. You can hear what your voice sounds like when telling your story, and learn the difference between being interviewed and carrying on a normal conversation.

The Lure of Television

Television is best for stories and products that beg for visual demonstration. It is also ideal when you have a physically attractive spokesperson to convey your message. Television interviews can be conducted in television studios, your place of business, a customer's location, or possibly a tradeshow or other commercial event.

Unlike radio, television affords little margin for error. Television cameras not only capture but also magnify your every gesture and nuance. However, if done well, television appearances offer some of the most powerful broadcast opportunities available to the *slightly famous* entrepreneur.

Local Programming You are most likely familiar with the local television or cable programming in your area. Once you have watched the programs to determine which shows have guests, identify your targets and move on to pitching the producers of those programs.

Carol Watson-Brand began rock climbing at age 40. She earned certification as a walking instructor and created a fitness program called Carol's Challenge. This program trained small groups for climbing expeditions from Mt. Whitney in California to the peaks of Nepal.

Because Carol's Challenge was so unusual, she got herself booked on a local morning television show for four consecutive Fridays, demonstrating exercises meant specifically for backpacking-related strength building. Carol was later interviewed for a cable television program produced for climbers.

National Television Before you approach producers at national networks like ABC, CBS, and NBC, or cable news networks like CNN, CNBC, and CNN Headline News, gather information about their shows. Investigate their websites. Most producers or programming departments can provide audience demographics. Within the framework of these national networks, there are several possible opportunities for *slightly famous* entrepreneurs.

Newscasts News programs are half-hour to one-hour programs that cover breaking news, sports, and other subjects. Guest formats vary from show to show, so make sure you understand the formats of the particular shows you want to appear on. Generally, business segments are aired on morning news, midday news covers leisure or human interest-related subjects, and evening news covers a broad, general range of subjects.

Morning Programs Morning programs offer numerous opportunities for businesses and entrepreneurs. This type of programming is usually aired in one-, two-, or three-hour segments, and generally appears on independent stations that run parallel to the nationally broadcast morning shows. Interviews are conducted either in-studio or in the field.

Magazine Format Programs This type of programming is usually aired in the afternoon or early evening, between the evening news and nightly prime-time programming. Segments may be longer, and have more entertainment or human-interest focus. Generally, there are no business segments, but if your story has entertainment value, this could be a great vehicle for it.

Pitching Your Story

Big radio and television stations don't go looking for guests. Guests come to them. You need to introduce yourself to producers, usually with an initial phone call that you follow with e-mail, snail mail, or media kit. Many producers prefer the initial pitch via e-mail.

When you pitch producers, the first step towards being a guest is coming up with something that makes the "facts" about your business or product interesting. Here are three ways to grab a producer's attention.

1. Be controversial. Producers love to get their phone lines going, and nothing does the trick like a highly provocative statement.

2. Be entertaining. If you can make people laugh and tell them fascinating stories, you'll always be in demand as a guest.

3. Be informative. Give people useful, timely information so they'll say, "Wow! That's amazing! I didn't know that!"

If you are targeting news shows, target the assignment manager, assignment editor, or the assignment desk. This newsroom gatekeeper will route stories of interest to the appropriate producers or reporters. Don't try to talk to anchors or anyone else who appears on the air.

The AM Desk is responsible for the morning and noon news shows. There is usually an early-morning meeting of all of the producers, at which they determine which camera crews will go to film particular segments. If you have a newsworthy event coming up that day, get the pitch to the AM Desk early, even the night before. The night person will make sure they see it.

The PM Desk is responsible for the evening and late night news shows. The producers usually meet in the afternoon, between the noon and evening news, to determine which segments to film. While most evening news programs provide extensive coverage of national news and local breaking news, newscasts often end with a light human-interest story that is filmed in advance.

It's critical to target the right person at any program you approach. Most television and radio programs have at least one producer who's responsible for booking guests. A program that airs daily books many guests, and will probably have several producers who book guests, each responsible for one or more specific segments. Whenever possible, tape shows and note in the credits the name of the person responsible for producing segments relevant to your story. For all other programs, you can determine the appropriate producer for specific segments or programs through any of the media directories mentioned in this book, or by contacting the station.

Radio and television newsrooms operate at high speed. When you're ready to call a producer, have your pitch down to a few sentences. Don't dive into a pitch; instead, ask the producer if they are on deadline. If they're too busy to talk, ask for a convenient time to call them back, and whether it's all right to fax or e-mail your pitch.

If the producer asks to hear your idea, give your pitch directly in a few words. Examples:

"The hottest trend in _____ is _____. This is a subject very popular among your viewers/listeners."

"The new tax laws are stumping even seasoned CPAs. I can inform your viewers/listeners on these complicated new guidelines."

"There's a demanding exercise fad called _____ which is causing lots of injuries. I can show/tell viewers/listeners how to properly execute this new routine."

There's no substitute for being familiar with a program. Radio and television producers appreciate it when you take time to understand their format. If you've come across radio or television segments or guests that have dealt with topics similar to your own, mention it when you pitch your own story.

Interview Tips

Preparation is key to any broadcast interview. The mantra is practice, practice, practice. Practice your interview questions in a mirror and with your family and friends; tape yourself on video or on audiocassettes, practice in the shower.

Beg, borrow, or steal a video camera to tape yourself if you are doing television. Pay for it if you have to. You've got to have concise, sound bite responses to the questions you'll be asked by your interviewer.

A poorly prepared interview is easy to spot. The subject looks nervous and ill at ease, either answering too hastily or giving protracted responses without a clear focus. A seasoned guest delivers crisp, concise responses, and appears relaxed and at ease with the host or anchor. If you're well prepared for interviews, you'll be less nervous, better inform audiences, enjoy a more natural exchange with the host, and present your business in the best possible light.

Rehearse

Find a partner to play the part of the host as you go through practice interviews. For radio, tape your practice interview on an audio recorder, and have your partner use a stopwatch to time responses. For television, obtain a video camera with a tripod, and besides timing your responses, watch yourself later for distracting gestures or nervous tics. Your partner should ask your interview questions off-camera, usually sitting next to the recorder so you are looking at each other. This gets you accustomed to not looking directly into the camera.

TIPS FROM THE GURU

Donald Moine on Using Previous Radio and Television Appearances

Dr. Donald Moine, co-author of *Ultimate Selling Power*, is a pioneer in sales psychology who has appeared on more than 100 talk radio shows and several television shows in the U.S., Canada, and Australia. His secret? He uses prior media appearances, including articles that appeared about him in newspapers, to generate interest in other media outlets.

"*The Los Angeles Times* interviewed me on November 29, 1992, and published an article about some of my work," says Moine. "I then took the article, reproduced it on two pages, added some potential interview questions, and sent it out to about 150 talk radio shows."

Moine's campaign generated better results than the original newspaper story, helping him get booked on more than 30 shows. Some of them gave him a full hour of radio time and took call-in questions. Many shows let him mention his phone number and the name of his book. "A few interviewers even commanded their listeners, 'Folks, go out and buy Dr. Moine's book today!'"

Moine's strategy works because media outlets have a follow-the-leader mentality. "If they see that another highly respected news outlet has done a story on a given topic or person, and if it looks interesting and of value, they are likely to follow along and jump on board," says Moine.

When reviewing practice interview tapes, listen for awkward delivery; notice hand gestures, become aware of how fast or slowly you speak, and above all, count the number of times you say "Uhm." (Your "coach" should be on the watch for "uhm's" too.) Buying time with "uhm's" is a bad habit that even a seasoned radio professional may fall prey to from time to time. It will distract from and muddy your message. It is said admiringly in media circles that Bryant Gumbel has never uttered an "uhm" in over 20 years on the air.

Anticipate Questions

Most producers provide a list of questions that will be asked by hosts. These questions often mirror your interview questions, but you should be prepared for possible deviations from your prepared questions.

Try to anticipate interview questions that might occur on the fly. Although you may be well prepared, your host may not be, or may not adequately understand your subject. In this situation, being prepared to deal with common misconceptions about your subject will help assure the interview goes smoothly.

If you are asked questions that stray from your subject, take a deep breath, think for a second about your response, and try to restate the question to fit your prepared responses. If the question is stated in such a way that it's not possible to do so, keep these points in mind:

- Don't be defensive
- Stick to key points that you can quickly articulate
- Maintain friendliness
- Use colorful anecdotes
- Avoid jargon
- Ask the host to clarify if you don't understand a question

Develop Sound Bite Responses

It's important to master the art of short responses, because long, rambling responses may be edited out or edited in a way that changes your meaning. A good response to an interviewer's question should take no more than 30 seconds. You may not think this is long enough to answer a question, but if you take longer than this, your listeners will stop hearing what you are saying.

At least some of your responses should take the form of a sound bite, a very short comment or phrase, anything from a few seconds to 10 or 15 seconds long that is designed to be memorable. This is the exact statement or phrase you want viewers or listeners to hear and remember.

Some Extra Radio Guidelines

Here are a few extra guidelines to remember when doing radio interviews.

For interviews done in the studio, be sure to:

- Arrive at least 15 minutes early
- Get the direct telephone number of the producer or sound engineer in case of emergencies

- Bring your media kit or interview questions, even if you've already sent them to the producer

For radio call-in interviews, you should:

- Call from a quiet area
- Let anyone around know that you cannot be disturbed
- Have a glass of water handy
- Disable call-waiting on your telephone
- Turn off the radio to avoid feedback
- Keep pets out of the area

Look Your Best on Television

You want to look your best on any televised appearance. Take that one step further and make sure you feel good. Don't try to squeeze into something that doesn't fit because you think it makes you look slimmer. Don't wear a fabric that may irritate or be too hot under studio lights.

Here are a few basic appearance guidelines for television:

- Don't wear prints, stripes, or patterns. These tend to "vibrate" on camera.
- Don't wear a white shirt or blouse; they glare. Creams and blues look good on camera.
- Women should avoid wearing lots of jewelry; anything that makes a sound is distracting, and will be picked up by the microphone.
- Avoid the perspiring anchor disaster, as seen in *Broadcast News*. Men should make sure that their foreheads and noses don't shine by using powder. Practice at home with loose, matte-finish powder. Place tissues around your collar to avoid getting any on your clothes.
- Women who don't wear makeup should use matte powder and lip-gloss at the very least.
- Practice your makeup; hire a professional if the situation warrants.
- Don't appear in a new hairstyle or hair color unless you've had a chance to wear it at least a week before the interview. If you don't feel you look great, your lack of confidence will be conveyed during your interview.

- Pull your clothing tight behind and under you as you sit in the interview chair. Do this after the microphone has been run under your clothing (a production assistant will do this for you). Men, ensure your shirt is wrinkle-free in front; your jacket is tightly smoothed (yet comfortable). Women, ensure your clothing is tightly smoothed, but loose enough to shift in your chair effortlessly.

- Don't look at the camera, unless instructed to do so. Keep your gaze at a consistent place, usually towards the host. You will be directed on this just before airtime.

- Don't hit your microphone. Practice hand gestures that avoid the left side area around your heart, which is where the microphone is placed.

During the Interview

Keep your energy up. A lively, energetic guest will get lots of bookings. When you come across as lively and stimulating, not only will the radio show love you, but so will the audience.

As noted in previous chapters, it is important to conduct your interview as an opportunity to share information. What will you give your audience? Hosts and producers hate it when they ask a guest a question and the guest responds, "Oh, that's in my book," or "You'll find out if you come to my seminar." Never hold anything back. After all, the simple fact of being on a show confirms your credentials.

If you are appearing on radio, the host will introduce you and, with luck, mention your company name; if not, it's your job to mention it in your responses. Practice an opening response to your introduction that easily flows into mentioning your company name: "That's a good question; we at ABC Company feel that. . . ."

If you're on television, a graphic of your name will appear at the start, end, and possibly in the middle of your segment. At the end of a program, either radio or television, try to interject your name again. It may not always be possible when ending, as commercial breaks may abruptly end an interview, but be ready.

EXECUTIVE BRANDING

Susan Fahnestock Gives a Face to the Green Car Company

The Green Car Company opened its doors in March 2005, with a mission to help consumers choose environmentally-friendly vehicles to meet their driving needs. The Kirkland, Washington-based car dealer sells fuel-efficient microcars and vehicles powered by electricity and biofuel. The company has experienced robust growth, due in part to positioning its executives as media-friendly experts in green transportation issues.

Green Car Company co-founder Susan Fahnestock embodies the company's approach. "We don't hard sell anyone and we don't just preach to the choir," says Fahnestock. "We seek first to educate the public about innovative ways to think about personal transportation, choosing appropriate vehicles based on individual transportation needs, and how to make appropriate lifestyle choices that reduce greenhouse gas emissions.'"

To aid in this process, the company developed its Green Car Scores system that compares the environmental impact of different vehicles and conducts research on consumer and fleet transportation. The company's Education Center is a 6000-square-foot showroom with copious information on all aspects of environmental responsibility, including books, videos, and is a venue for presenting educational public presentations and community events.

Your 800 number may not flash during a telecast or be given on the air, most stations provide their guests with the equivalent of a reader inquiry card. When interested viewers call the station about someone they saw or heard on the show, the station will usually provide a contact name and phone number. Many stations post this information on their websites for a brief period of time.

Green Car Company jump-started its PR coverage shortly after opening, when it orchestrated an event at downtown Seattle's Pike Place Market. "We took ten smart cars, and we did a parade around downtown Seattle," says Fahnestock. "We drove through the market a couple of times and ended at the baseball stadium just before a game. We had two television stations, public radio, and several print media come out of that one event."

Fahnestock credits her personal involvement and visibility within her community as central in the company's PR process and instrumental in establishing the company in the community. "People do business with people, not with abstract companies," says Fahnestock. "I function as The Green Car Company's public face and spokesperson, and that's helped us forge an emotional bond with our marketplace."

By positioning itself as an environmental resource, the company has also become the go-to source for local media seeking information about green transportation. Fahnestock has appeared on a dozen television segments, seven radio spots, and in numerous magazine and newspaper articles. Much of the media attention Green Car Company enjoys is the result of the commitment to promoting ways consumers can reduce their environmental footprint.

"The media coverage we've gotten over the past two years has really legitimized our business. Consumers see us as a partner in finding the most appropriate green vehicle," says Fahnestock. "The media attention we've generated has been much more valuable than advertising. I recently did a public radio interview, and it hit our demographic straight-on. After the broadcast, we were bombarded with e-mail inquiries. We got so much business out of that one appearance, and it still keeps coming."

Get a Tape

This is relatively easy if you do an in-studio interview. Just bring a cassette or VHS tape with you, and have it brought to the sound engineer in the booth. Some stations may not do this, but most will be happy to. If you've been interviewed remotely, you may have to purchase the footage from the station or a duplication service. Fees for this may range from $75 to $150. Keep in mind, this footage will not be broadcast quality, but can be used as a learning tool and is also valuable when pitching other programs.

PART III

Reaching Out in All Directions

CHAPTER 9 The *Slightly Famous* Website

With most *slightly famous* marketing strategies, you are an actor on someone else's stage: a contributor to a magazine, a speaker at a conference, or a guest on a radio or television program. But when you have a website, you are the writer, producer, director, and star of your own show, with the opportunity of becoming a mini-celebrity reaching a large number of people.

A website is a powerful branding tool that tells your story, showcases your expertise, and puts a human face on your business. A website expands your reach to thousands of prospects. It can also create new profit centers, and literally make money for you while you sleep.

You need a website if only because people today expect you to have one. Not having a website these days is like doing business without a phone or fax machine. This chapter will help you create a website that advances your *slightly famous* marketing strategy, attracts new business, and dramatically expands your market by building a loyal online following.

Master of Your Domain: Make Your Business Web-Centric

Your website can become the flagship of your *slightly famous* marketing strategy, achieving its full potential when you fully integrate it into your business. A website is not a static, online brochure you create and forget about; properly set up and maintained, it becomes a virtual branch office and around-the-clock salesperson.

As a resource for your industry, your website can feature lots of useful information, including articles, links, downloadable files, customer resources, and anything else of use to your target market. Its also one of the most effective channels for establishing strategic alliances, facilitating co-promotions, promoting online classes and seminars, and reaching a global audience.

Design: Keep It Simple

Remember your website is a marketing tool, not a design showpiece. Web users are notoriously impatient. They want information, and they want it quickly.

A simple website design is easy to navigate, and avoids fancy graphics and theatrical elements that look impressive but serve no marketing purpose. Excessive embellishments can actually work to your disadvantage by slowing down your website and driving away impatient viewers.

As you consider your website design, write down adjectives that describe the ambiance you want to create. Make sure your website is aligned with your overall branding strategy. Use colors that evoke the feelings and moods you want to convey. Consider your business style and the way you want to be perceived. Your website design needs to match expectations about your type of business. If your site sells high-end financial services, you must convey a professional image.

If you choose to work with a professional Web designer, look for someone who possesses a solid understanding of marketing (both on and off the Internet), design, and technical know-how. Avoid Web designers who are primarily artists with little understanding of marketing. Also, avoid technical wizards who want to impress the world by loading your site with spectacular bells and whistles at the expense of usability.

How a Professional Speaker Clicked His Way to Success

A few years ago, speaker, author, and Internet marketing expert Tom Antion decided to learn Internet marketing techniques that would help him book more speaking engagements. By systematically pursuing this goal, he's developed a powerful Internet presence that attracts plenty of speaking opportunities, and earned him a reputation within the speaking industry as an Internet marketing guru.

"I'm not all that computer-literate, nor do I want or need to be," says Antion. "I just know where to click to make money, and that's all I, or any other business-person, needs to care about."

Antion uses the Internet to sell a line of products, seminars, teleclasses, and e-books on Internet marketing. Not only that, his speaking fee has gone from $5,500 to $10,500 per day, and he regularly speaks at conferences on Internet marketing (one audience bought $52,000 worth of his products after just one of his speeches). In addition, he publishes the speaking industry's largest e-mail newsletter, having signed up more than 100,000 subscribers in just two years.

Antion also leverages his online marketing to establish greater visibility and credibility within his target market. His site ranks high on most major search engines. He encourages hundreds of related sites to link to his website, which serves as an endorsement and traffic-generating tool. All of this tends to convince people that Antion knows what he's talking about, a fact that draws audiences to his events in droves.

"I wouldn't cold-call anybody if you put a gun to my head," says Antion. "That's why I cultivated a lot of visibility and credibility online, and sell my knowledge from

Choosing a Domain Name

Choosing the right domain name is critical; it needs to be memorable, it must differentiate you from competitors, and it must support your brand. The perfect domain name describes what you do, and is simple enough that people can type it in easily on their computers, and pass it along to friends. The maximum length for domain names is 67 characters, but for marketing purposes, the shorter the name the better.

Here are some of the most common options for choosing an effective domain name:

my website. I learned that people do not hire a professional speaker or a marketer per se, they hire an expert. I merely use the Internet as another tool to demonstrate my expertise in a way that attracts prospects and opportunities."

Antion has succeeded because he makes his website the center of his marketing activities, while using e-mail to affordably reach his target market. His many articles, which he publishes on a variety of website, help him grow his online mailing list.

"The best part is that I don't have to beg for business!" says Antion. "My Web presence is so well-established, and my credibility so much beyond question, that my reputation draws prospects to me. I now land speaking engagements directly from my website, and sell tons of products and get participants for my mentor program. Because prospects see my name hundreds of times in search engines, or read my articles on other websites, they call me ready to do business."

The most spectacular testament to Antion's strategy came when his website helped him land a job as spokesperson for Switchboard.com, one of the most heavily visited websites in the world. "A journalist for the *Miami Sun Sentinel* subscribed to my e-mail newsletter," recalls Antion. "After reading several issues, the journalist was apparently convinced of my expertise, and interviewed me for an article about Internet marketing."

Soon after, a representative from CBS read the article. "CBS just happened to be looking for an Internet marketing spokesperson for an upcoming business seminar series," recalls Antion. "Because of that article, prompted by my e-mail newsletter, CBS offered me the deal and I beat out thousands of Internet experts. It was the easiest six-figure deal I ever landed!"

Your own name If you are a solo professional, such as a writer, attorney, or fitness trainer, this is the most direct approach. Using your own name is also effective when you establish yourself as an expert. Speaker, author, and marketing consultant Larry Chase uses his own name to brand his website, larrychase.com. If you are seeking to develop personal brand recognition, then naming your URL after yourself makes sense.

Your company name If your branding strategy revolves around promoting your firm, use your company name as your URL. Be sure to use easy spelling and pronunciation. If it's long, shorten it to something that still suggests your full company name. For example, the Small Press Action Network opted to use an acronym for its URL, www.span.org.

Your main concept or idea It can makes sense to name your URL after your core business concept or solution. Author and simplicity expert Janet Luhrs' domain, simpleliving.com, clearly expresses the central theme of her books, her speaking engagements, and her publication, *The Simple Living Journal.*

When acquiring a domain name, it's good practice to also reserve names that are closely related to your chosen URL. If the name of your company is Spring Advertising Services, make sure you acquire spring.com, spring.net, and spring.org, then go a step further by getting springmarketing.com, .net, and .org. There's no reason you can't have more than one website or have multiple domain names pointing to the same site.

The website of a small, non-computer business usually resides on a dedicated Web host, a computer owned by a service company that specializes in storing (and possibly maintaining) websites. For this reason, when registering domain names, it's imperative to protect your ownership and control. If you have a third party, such as your Web host company, register your domain name(s), make sure you are listed as both "registrant" and "administrative contact." This assures that you maintain full control over your website should you need to switch Web-hosting companies.

Web Pages and Navigation

Make it intuitively easy for visitors to find their way around your website. Imagine yourself as a first-time visitor as you consider your website's navigation scheme. The first rule is not to burden the visitor to your site—especially the first-time visitor—with excessive options.

Developing a user-friendly website should not constrain good design, but it needs to be an integral part of the design process. According to Gerry McGovern, co-author of *The Web Content Style Guide*, your navigation scheme should:

- Help readers quickly find what they are looking for
- Let readers know where they are at all times

- Provide context
- Be consistent
- Provide feedback and support
- Never surprise or mislead a reader

Because navigation is an aid for visitors, start your design from their point of view. Involve people in the design process who represent your customers' or clients' point of view. Find out what they want from your site.

The Home Page: Your Virtual Kiosk Easy navigation begins at a home page that functions as a virtual lobby or kiosk. This is where you orient visitors to your business, and guide them to subsequent pages of your website. If your home page doesn't grab visitors' attention and make them want to enter and explore your website, you risk having important pages go unviewed, regardless of the toil that went into their construction.

Because your home page is the first thing visitors will see, it must speak directly to your target market, letting them know they've come to the right place. Keep the message on your home page down to a few paragraphs and boldly convey the core benefit of your business. Focus on the keywords, features, and images that will capture the attention and interest of your target audience.

Provide a summary of your ultimate business benefit. This will help visitors decide whether your website contains information relevant to their needs. Be as direct and clear as you can. A travel site might say, "Are you a single mother who needs help planning your next family vacation?"

Next, describe how your company provides the answer to that question. Using the above example, your next line might read, "A Mother's World is a travel service that works exclusively with single mothers. Our unique focus helps single mothers enjoy fun, educational vacations with their children."

Finally, state how your company is the best choice for visitors, promising what they will find throughout your website when they dig deeper. "We help clients plan exciting, hassle-free trips within the United States, and provide a range of travel options to meet your needs and budget. Our site is filled with useful information to help you plan your next vacation."

By delivering relevant content, you guide visitors through your website to your e-mail sign-up pages, and—ultimately—your services.

About Us Once visitors get a picture of who you are and how you can help them, you need to show how your business is uniquely qualified to help them. You can do this by:

- Positioning yourself against your competitors
- Highlighting your approach or process
- Emphasizing your experience
- Featuring or demonstrating your expertise

Staff Profiles Visitors need to know and trust the people behind your site before they put their faith (and their dollars) in your business. Staff profiles give visitors reassuring background information about the qualifications of the human beings behind the website.

List in order of importance the most relevant qualifications or experience of each of your principals and other key staff people. List everything about them that sets you apart from competitors. List the professional affiliations and anything else that makes a case for their experience and expertise.

Products and Services Provide a description of all the products and services you offer, with enough detail for visitors to see the benefits and value of each. Depending on the price and complexity of the items you offer, you may need to provide separate pages with highly detailed descriptions, specifications, and pictures.

For example, if you are a martial arts instructor offering a variety of programs, you might provide separate pages for programs aimed at children, teens, and adults. By focusing on individual client groups, and emphasizing the benefits that apply directly to each, you'll attract more customers.

Clients, Customers, and Case Studies To earn visitors' trust, it helps to name customers you've already served. You can do this with a simple list of past clients, but it is more effective if you provide details about how you've helped those clients and customers. If you present a lengthy list, you can create subheads for different categories of customers.

Case studies are great for conveying how you achieved favorable results for your clients and customers. Choose situations that are broadly representative of your target market. Describe the customer's situation both before and after they worked with you, and be very clear about the results you achieved for them. You want your potential clients and customers to see themselves receiving similar benefits.

Testimonials Develop a dedicated testimonial page and keep it constantly updated. Ask satisfied clients to describe how your organization solved a problem for them. Because they don't come directly from you, these stories have greater credibility.

In addition to, or instead of, a testimonial page, you can place customer testimonials throughout your site. You can put them in the margins of individual Web pages or intersperse them in stretches of sales copy.

Articles Because content is king on your *slightly famous* website, you should include articles you have written or that are about you. Such materials demonstrate your expertise. If you have more articles than will fit, include a list. This makes a case for your expertise and also attracts Internet keyword searches.

You should also consider including articles and columns from "guest experts" who can address issues that are important to your readers. By inviting others to help you create a compelling website, and publishing thoughtful pieces written by others who are respected, you make your site a valuable resource.

Resources and Links Whenever possible, include pages with valuable information—either in full or in the form of links to other sites—and update them regularly. This gives visitors a reason to return to your website even when they're not ready to buy. You might have links to all the professional associations in the area, or links to related business services. You might offer a list of relevant books, with key excerpts from the best of them—in short, any resources that your visitors might find useful.

Press Room Many websites fail to provide the kind of fast, basic information journalists are looking for. That means lost publicity opportunities, since harried journalists looking for information will quickly move on to another source or subject.

In contrast, a well-designed website with an easy-to-use press center will attract reporters who are writing about your industry or community. To design a website that meets the media's needs, keep these tips in mind:

- Provide a direct link from your home page to your press center.
- Give reporters what they are looking for: press releases, media clippings, and other information that facilitates their research.
- Make company facts and information easy to find and read.
- Prominently display contact information and include phone, fax, pager, and cell phone numbers, as well as e-mail addresses.
- List people in your company who are expert in particular subjects.
- Include links to relevant sites, including industry organizations, clients, and governmental agencies.
- Invite reporters to register to receive future company news and updates.
- The Haddon Group, an IT consulting firm, fulfills these requirements by offering a list of areas on which they can provide industry commentary, some samples of their work, and articles and white papers that demonstrate their expertise.

Contact Information As mentioned above, make it easy for visitors to contact you. Your contact information should contain an e-mail message form so that visitors can send you a message without leaving your site, your e-mail address, phone number, fax number, postal mailing address, and any other relevant information (like the best times to call you).

Include contact information on every page of your website, and make sure it's visible. Nothing is more frustrating than searching a website in vain for a telephone number or other basic contact information. As a test, ask others to find such information on your site, and see how long it takes them to find it.

You might also offer visitors a questionnaire they can complete before you contact them. This demonstrates your ability to diagnose their needs, and it shows them how your services fit their needs. Use questions about common problems and situations, and be sure you respond promptly.

Newsletter Sign Up Once someone has visited your site and liked it, don't lose contact with them. Many new visitors, even those who have enjoyed and benefited from your website, will forget about you unless you capture their e-mail addresses and stay in touch. So it's important to have a vehicle, such as an e-mail newsletter, to make that possible.

"Think of your website as your car or vehicle. It can take you where you want to go with your marketing," says Robert Middleton of Action Plan Marketing. "Then think of the e-mail newsletter as the gas for that vehicle. Without gas, the vehicle may look beautiful, but it simply won't go very far."

Create a page that offers your latest newsletter, along with a simple sign-up form on each page of your site asking for visitors' names and e-mail addresses. Motivate visitors to join your e-mail list by offering something free, such as a special report or article. Your goal is to continue marketing to them with their permission, and keep the door open for them to become customers or clients.

Writing for the Web

The main thing people seek from your site is to know if you can provide something they want. Don't waste their time (and yours) with anything else. Rather than provide entertainment and flash (unless that's the nature of your business), help people get the information they want when they need it.

Strip away the glamour of the design and technology, and you're left with words. Your website lives or dies by the quality of your writing—specifically, your ability to write in a manner friendly to online readers. People rarely read Web pages word for word. Internet readers are skimmers, and that means that information must be presented in short chunks that stand on their own.

Here are some strategies for writing effective Web copy:

• Highlight keywords, phrases, and sentences.

TIPS FROM THE GURU

Dr. Ralph Wilson on Making Your Site Trustworthy

Web users worldwide have been buzzing for years about the insights of Dr. Ralph Wilson, aka Dr. Ebiz. A widely acknowledged Internet guru, he's given hundreds of thousands of people Internet marketing advice since 1995 through newsletters, e-books, articles, seminars, and his book, *Planning Your Internet Marketing Strategy*.

Wilson realized early on that trust was paramount if consumers were to use the Web as a commercial resource. Creating website credibility, and overcoming what Wilson calls "the central problem of fear and distrust," is key. You need to overcome the fact that, as he says, "You can't shake hands with a Webmaster."

"Tell your story," Wilson suggests. "Rather than a corporate-sounding 'About Us' section, provide insight into the people behind the company, their passion for the business, their struggles to achieve success, and their plans for the future." Developing a chatty, person-to-person rapport gives you an advantage over larger, impersonal business entities.

Wilson also suggests including a photograph of the business itself, when applicable, and getting involved with trust organizations, such as the Better Business Bureau; if you can, display their logos. Include any awards you've won. Also, promise that all visitor information will be kept confidential and never sold to third parties.

Wilson emphasizes that writing articles and providing expert content plays a large part in establishing visitor trust, and has helped him grow his e-mail newsletter relationship with his more than 120,000 subscribers. "Publishing instantly makes you an expert, and expertise instills trust," says Wilson. "Not even a politician could easily shake 120,000 hands, yet I do it figuratively a couple times a month."

• Use immediately intelligible subheadings, not "clever" ones.

• Use bulleted lists for groups of short, related items. Develop one idea per paragraph.

• Use the inverted pyramid style, starting each page and section with the most vital information first, followed by supporting ideas.

• Reduce the word count to half (or less) that of conventional writing.

• Avoid overtly promotional claims, such as "hottest ever."

While practicing tight writing, don't overdo it to the point of stripping your personality and voice from your Web copy. The best Web-oriented writing is done in a conversational style that creates a personal bond with readers. Web users want to experience the person behind the website. Don't be afraid to write using your own voice. We all love stories. Use them to personalize your writing, and help readers latch onto and remember your narrative and, ultimately, your business.

Marketing Your Website

The Internet is billions of pages large, so it doesn't take too much analysis to appreciate that the chance of someone finding your site by accident is close to zero.

There are three ways people will get to your site. First, they come to it because you can tell them the URL, either directly or through your advertising. Second, they find it through a link on another site. Third, they find it through search engines.

The best place to begin promoting your website is within your existing contact network. Plaster your website address on everything that represents your business or touches your buying public—your business cards, invoices, letterhead, and Yellow Pages ads. It's also worthwhile to announce your website through a mailing to vendors, associates, and business contacts.

Don't merely tell people that you have a new website, offer them an incentive to visit: a free report, a sample product, a free teleclass, anything with perceived value. You can provide extra motivation to people by offering special benefits that carry an expiration date.

The Role of Search Engines in Buying Decisions

Some of the most prime "real estate" in the world these days is at the top of the search engine listings. Search engines help potential customers find you, evaluate you, and decide whether to do business with you. For example, a Harris study showed that 54 percent of online searchers used Google instead of a phone book, and that 58 percent of those searchers are looking for information on local businesses.

Another study by Internet research firms Marketing Sherpa and Enquiro entitled, "The Role of Search Engines in Business-to-Business Buying Decisions," demonstrated that search engines are now the dominant force driving most business buying decisions involving both products and services.

In this study, participants were asked where they would go to research an upcoming business-to-business purchase. A full 93.2 percent indicated they would go online; 63.9 percent indicated that a search engine would be the first place they would turn; 54.6 percent indicated they would begin researching from one-to-three months early; and over 50 percent would turn to a search engine, regardless of the price of the purchase.

There can be no downplaying the importance of online research in purchasing decisions, as well as the critical role that search engines play in the ultimate outcome. Factoring search engines into your marketing mix is a necessity.

Search Engine Strategies

Search engines are a major source of website visitors, but to optimize their effectiveness you need to understand how they work. Search engines do not search millions of websites anew each time someone orders a search. Rather, they search their existing indexes of websites, which have been ordered by keywords. When users type their search terms and hit "search," search engines scan their indexes, returning links to those websites whose listed keywords match the search terms the visitors used.

Search engines form their indexes in a couple of ways. Most "crawl" the Web with electronic "spiders," scanning millions of sites to collect keywords. This collecting and cataloging of information enables them to make some sense out of what would otherwise be the chaos of the Internet. Search engines get some keywords by scanning the contents of sites, and some from the keywords submitted by site owners for inclusion in search engine databases.

To make the most of search engines, you must optimize your website before you submit such information to them. You must also employ tactics that ensure Web spiders find and catalog your site accurately. Most major search engines allow you to register your site free. You can simply go to each major search site, click on the button marked "Add Your Site" or "Submit URL" or something similar, and fill in your site information.

It's important to regularly monitor your search engine listings to make sure they are working to your advantage. Getting and staying listed in search engines is part art, part science that requires ongoing testing and detective work. It's a continual battle to keep your site indexed on the major search engines. (The next chapter will discuss the vital role of content in this process.)

Choosing Keywords Keywords play a central role in ensuring that prospects find your site. Search engines use the number and relative importance of the keywords associated with a site to determine whether a site will be found by a given search. When people search for topics related to your website, you want to rank high in the search findings. For this to happen, you must optimize your chances by ensuring that the best search phrases and keywords appear in various areas of your website, including title pages, section headings, and site descriptions.

Determining keywords related to your business is pretty straightforward. But you will still need to test your assumptions about the words that are most likely to be used by prospects. Ask people to suggest words they'd be inclined to use when searching for businesses like yours. The results may surprise you.

You can visit competitor sites to study their keyword usage. (You can view a website's meta tags by bringing up the site page, and then looking in your Web browser under View/Source. This will show you the meta tags they are using.) You can also compare the relative ranking of various sites by looking them up with popular search engines.

Finally, there are several online services that provide keyword analysis based on the most popular search terms.

The most important place to include keywords is in the body text of your pages. It is the percentage of keywords within the total number of words of your individual pages that constitutes what search engines call their "density." Keyword density matters in different ways to different search engines; most prefer a per-page keyword density of between 5 and 7 percent.

Site Description Once you have a list of keywords, write a site description that makes use of them. For example, if you're an attorney specializing in bankruptcy cases in Chicago, your list of keywords might be:

- Bankruptcy
- Chicago
- Attorney
- Bankruptcy attorney
- Consumer bankruptcy

Make sure that your description both reads well and includes your strongest keywords. Starting from the above list of keywords, a good description might read, "Bankruptcy attorneys specializing in consumer bankruptcy in the Chicago area."

Page Titles You need to give a title to every page on your website, and you need to consider these titles carefully. The title is something that you program behind the scenes in HTML code, the language that describes how text should be formatted when a browser displays it on the screen. The tags are simple but play a very important role in your search engine strategy.

The title of your home page is given extra attention by search engines seeking to catalog your site. You need to make sure it includes the keywords you want to have associated with your site, and those keywords must be included in the page content. Page titles appear in search engine results, and they are what visitors see at the top of their Web browsers when your web page loads. Write page titles that are not just key-word-relevant, but compel people to click through when your site appears in search results. A sample page title might look like this: "Chicago Law Firm Specializing In Consumer Bankruptcies."

Meta Tags Meta tags are also descriptions that work behind the scenes in HTML code. Although visitors won't see them, they play an important role in determining how search engines treat your site. There are two meta tags to address.

The "description" is a short description of what your site is about. It goes a bit further than your site description and page titles. The keyword meta tag is a place to list additional keywords related to your site. This is where you will pick a few additional words to expand your description in a way that gives users more opportunities to find your site through the search engines.

The following examples show how meta tags might appear on a website:

META NAME="description" content="We are a Chicago-based law firm specializing in consumer bankruptcies.":

META NAME="keywords" content="bankruptcy, bankruptcy attorney, filing bankruptcy, Chicago, Chicago attorney, Chicago bankruptcy, consumer bankruptcy":

Search engine optimization is an evolving field that involves many variables. There are several good books and online resources if you are handling your own website. In addition, you can hire a professional search engine consultant or Web developer with expertise in basic search engine techniques. Avoid search engine marketing services promising "instant success" or shortcuts to improving your overall Web rankings. Search engines aggressively circumvent search engine spammers, those who try to manipulate Web rankings with tricks and shortcuts.

The Role of Inbound Links

The quantity and quality of third-party sites that link to a website play an important role in search results. Because you can't build a website and expect that people will find it on their own, cultivating inbound links helps promote your site by pointing the way via good-quality content.

Inbound links help search engines find your website, better indicate the overall theme of your site, and indicate its overall popularity within the overall Web community. Search engines are attracted to sites with high link popularity and consider those websites more relevant than others in their results for a search query.

Google, for example, uses a link scoring system called PageRank, which is fundamental in determining value, and ultimately the website's placement in search results. According to PageRank, the more links a website has, the more "worthy" it is, and the more likely it will rank higher in Google.

You can increase your link popularity by cultivating inbound links through content you distribute online. Distributing content related to your business and getting inbound links from other websites, particularly sites that score highly on PageRank, can be an extremely powerful site promotion tool.

Having many inbound links also adds to a positive virtual first impression by showing within search results that other websites value your business. Following are several online content strategies you can use to increase your online findability.

Pay-to-Submit and Pay-Per-Click Search Engines

Everything was once free on the Internet, but many online businesses, including many search engines, are now charging for access.

Yahoo!, one of the first and still one of the most important search engines, charges a fee to include your site in their database. Unlike "spider"-driven search engines, Yahoo! is a directory. Instead of trawling the Internet and organizing its findings, Yahoo! uses live people to evaluate websites and decide whether to include them in their directory.

Yahoo! now uses a pay-for-consideration strategy. If you want your site to be listed in Yahoo!, you must pay them a few hundred dollars just to be considered. There are no guarantees that they will actually list the site, and the fee is nonrefundable. Despite the fee, Yahoo! is still a great place to list your website. You have a good chance of being listed if you submit a well-designed, genuinely useful website, with smartly optimized keywords.

Another new concept is that of pay-per-click search engines, which allow websites to bid on keywords, and in effect buy their way to the top of the list of sites found when people search on those keywords. These search engines operate on a commission basis: you determine a dollar amount, list your site, and bid for keywords related to your site. You pay a deposit against future click-throughs. When users search on your keywords, your site comes up higher in the listings than those who've paid less or nothing.

The pay-per-click strategy is becoming more popular. It can work for you if you select good keywords, optimize your site to encourage sales, and bid on keywords for reasonable prices. What's reasonable? That depends on the number of visitors who turn into paying customers.

Monitoring Results

There are many software programs to help you keep track of the various aspects of your Web marketing efforts. Some help you determine the types of keywords people are using to find your site. Others show you where people are spending time within your website, and at individual pages.

By taking advantage of the many tools available to track your Web marketing efforts, you continually perfect your marketing strategies and website to build a powerful Web presence. Such tools can also save you a lot of time and money by showing you ineffective keywords, those that nobody is using in search engines. You can also learn where people go on your site, and revamp areas that are getting little attention. Your Web host may be able to provide these functions as part of its package.

Keep in mind that the world of Internet search engines is complex; the material in this chapter is just an introduction. Several excellent books on the more technical points of Internet marketing are widely available and you should take their advice seriously.

The Online Sales Cycle

In addition to its marketing value, your website is a sales tool. But because skepticism runs high in the world of online commerce, you'll need to earn visitor trust over time in order to realize sales. This means turning one-time visitors into subscribers who either return to your site on a regular basis or sign up for an e-mail newsletter.

Successful websites give their online visitors a reason to keep coming back by providing fresh, evolving, up-to-date content. They also provide a sign-up

REAL-WORLD SUCCESS STORY

Seth Godin Unleashes the Power of Viral Marketing

Word-of-mouth is one of the oldest ways businesses become successful. Viral marketing, a new twist on the old idea, is word-of-mouth conducted at Internet speed. Given its nature, viral marketing is a natural for promoting your *slightly famous* website.

"Sometimes it seems as if everyone you know is watching the same television show, reading the same book, or talking about the same movie, Website, or television commercial," writes viral marketing guru Seth Godin in an article in *Fast Company*. "It usually happens because an idea spreads on its own, not because a company behind a product spends a ton of money advertising it." Viral marketing imitates this phenomenon by encouraging Internet users to pass marketing messages to others by e-mail, thus raising brand awareness exponentially.

Godin put this idea to the test with his book Unleashing the Idea Virus. Published initially as an e-book and later in print, it became one of most successful e-books of all time when he made it available for free from his website (www.ideavirus.com) prior to publishing it as a hardcover a few months later. More than 100,000 people downloaded his e-book, and many more forwarded it electronically to friends. Not only did the success of his e-book validate Godin's theories, it secured enough advance orders for a hard copy version that justified a 28,000-copy print run, a distribution deal with a major publisher, and translation deals with publishers in Brazil, Japan, and Korea.

button or banner on every page. The easier it is to respond, the more subscribers you'll get.

Many visitors will need an inducement to move from an anonymous visitor to a card-carrying member of your *slightly famous* world. Offer them something valuable in exchange for their e-mail addresses. Give away free

Godin believes that any viable commercial concept can become an idea virus as recipients become "infected" and pass it on to others. "This wasn't all premeditated. I did almost nothing fancy to make this work," says Godin. "The bottom line is that it doesn't take cash to distribute a book any more. You can now build an asset on the Internet, and then transfer it through a publisher, distributor, or partner."

He offers the following advice for creating successful Internet viral marketing campaigns:

- Create an online experience that offers your users something completely new, something they can't get offline.

- Fill the vacuum in the marketplace with your version of the idea so completely that competitors will first have to eliminate your virus before they can unleash one of their own.

- Get permission from users to maintain an ongoing dialogue with them, so that you can build a relationship that gives them a beneficial experience and gives you a profit stream.

- Continue creating noteworthy online experiences to spread new viruses. Always begin by infecting your core audience.

"The future belongs to marketers who establish a foundation and process where interested people can market to each other," he writes. "Ignite consumer networks and then get out of the way by offering something new and valuable that will attract people to your website and get them talking."

e-books, reports, articles, or anything else of obvious benefit. Downloadable files—particularly those offering timely content, such as special reports—have high perceived value, and cost you nothing to deliver, while offering your online visitor a good reason to give you an e-mail address.

CHAPTER 10 Marketing in a Virtual World: Internet and Web 2.0 Strategies

B efore the Internet, most businesses reached prospects through advertising, brochures, direct mail, cold calling, and networking. The smallest businesses were often limited to a local market and hoped that customers found them through word-of-mouth or a Yellow Pages ad.

A decade ago, marketing meant "getting in front of customers." Now, customers usually "google" to find someone with your skills, and they turn to independent websites, blogs, mailing lists, and online communities to research products. They expect to find you online, that you will make a virtual case for yourself. If people can't find you and your business online, you don't exist for them, and if they find your competitors, you've lost their business, for sure!

This chapter will discuss online marketing strategies that all businesses, from global corporations to small firms serving a local market, can embrace to factor the Internet into their *slightly famous* marketing plans.

The Virtual First Impression

Prospects you've never met are forming opinions about your business, at the click of a mouse, twenty-four hours a day. You need to ensure that they get a positive virtual first impression.

In *Blink: The Power of Thinking Without Thinking*, author Malcolm Gladwell discusses the phenomenon of first impressions that occur in seconds and are often more reliable than deeper analysis. He calls this phenomenon "thin slicing," whereby our minds focus on the most relevant facts and impressions to form snap conclusions. Gladwell's premise can be applied to the world of online searching as well. The Internet first impression is, in part, a coping mechanism, a way for online browsers to quickly size up whether a business is worthy of further investigation.

Developing a positive virtual first impression is something within your control, but you must be proactive. Just as you would never wear a threadbare suit to a meeting with a prospective client, you need to factor in how your business appears to prospects in those vital first seconds. You must communicate that your business is relevant and trustworthy. And above all, you must be findable. When evaluating your Web presence, ask yourself the following questions.

- How does your business look in the first couple of seconds when somebody types your name in to Google or another major search engine?
- Does your business come up at all?
- Do top websites in your industry link to your site?
- Does any media exposure appear in your search results?

The Emergence of Web 2.0

Over the last few years, the Internet has evolved from a universe of static Web pages to an interactive online community. Driven by new technologies collectively labeled "Web 2.0," the Internet now enables people to collaborate, co-create, and share information online rather than simply peruse information.

These new technologies, also called "social media," include blogs, podcasts,

TIPS FROM THE GURU

Dave Taylor on Using Content to Increase Your Online Findability

Website content is central to enhancing online findability. By creating relevant, useful content that helps search engines find you, and that serves prospects when they arrive at your website, you not only attract potential business but encourage prospects to engage your business.

Relevance and Credibility Many websites focus on the sale, on the pitch, but neglect to consider that many visitors have no experience with the business or its owner. You must share your experience and credentials right up front to maximize your online credibility.

"If I search for 'family therapist-Dallas,' and I find a therapist's website with just background information about her qualifications, I have little to assure me that this woman can help me," says Dave Taylor, author of *The Complete Idiot's Guide to Growing Your Business with Google*. "But if I find helpful articles dealing with family relationship issues, a blog about child psychology, and see that the therapist was quoted in the Dallas newspaper, I'd think, 'Finally! Here's a person who knows their business!' and I would be more likely to enquire further."

Traffic Does Not Equal Customers Too often, people focus only on generating traffic, but give little consideration to whether website visitors are likely to convert into customers.

"It's a Catch-22: I have a website, but, it doesn't seem to drive much traffic to it, so should I focus on simply generating more traffic, or do I need to look at

social networking websites, social bookmarking websites, and online communities. *Wikipedia*, a user-generated online encyclopedia that allows visitors to add, edit, and change available content, describes Web 2.0 as a shift toward online market conversations, open communications among Web users, and decentralized authority.

Because Web 2.0 delivers unfiltered market feedback and opinions, it increasingly influences public perceptions about products and services. Web 2.0 frees consumers from the limitations of seeking advice from a small circle of friends, relatives, and work colleagues, offering a vast diversity of knowledge and a source of collective intelligence.

who is visiting? Often, it's not working because you're just not appealing to your customers," Taylor comments.

If your website is a useful resource, a hub for those seeking information related to your business, it will then quite naturally increase its findability by being relevant to your target customers.

Frequent Content Additions Strive to produce a few hundred words of new content at least twice a week to ensure that your Website is search engine-friendly. The best content attracts prospects, helps them clarify their decision-making process, and ultimately make the right purchase decision for their situation and needs.

"There are so many ways to produce content on your site," says Taylor. "Develop case studies that feature your customers. Include press releases about your company. Write questions-and-answers, FAQs, and troubleshooting information about your products and services by turning common business questions into useful content."

For people who may feel intimidated by this change in the business landscape, Taylor insists that findability marketing strategies are enjoyable ways to market yourself. "Trust me, it's so much better than cold calling, and it's rewarding when you receive e-mail from people saying how much they appreciate your website and the role you play in helping them," says Taylor.

A Forrester Research 2004 study showed that over 60 percent of consumers trust product recommendations found in online sources like discussion boards. Social media content regularly finds its way into traditional media. A recent Columbia University study found that 51 percent of journalists use blogs and social media regularly, with 28 percent relying on those sources for daily reporting.

"The public turns to social media to supplement traditional information sources and to seek the opinions of others," says Jen McClure, founder and executive director of the Society for New Communications Research. "When businesses embrace this shift, Web 2.0 tools provide a way to reach and deeply engage clients and customers and other core audiences on a global scale."

Online Content Strategies

A core strategy for boosting your online findability involves sharing your knowledge, giving your expertise generously and frequently in a variety of online formats. Sharing your knowledge by creating and distributing content online contributes incrementally to growing your business brand.

The following strategies focus on developing and distributing useful content on the Internet to build your reputation as a thought leader, attract visitors to your website, and improve your online findability.

Syndicate Articles Online

Many websites have an ongoing need for content, and they simply can't produce all of it themselves. Whatever your niche or area of expertise, there's an audience out there who wants to learn more, and online publishers who are looking for free content.

Online article syndication is a strategy based on writing and publishing articles on websites that reach your target market. You offer your articles for free, and in return include a short description of your business and a link to your website at the end of the article.

People interested in topics as diverse as Java programming, retirement planning, or landscape architecture seek content on websites devoted to these subjects. The trick is to provide useful content that ultimately drives readers back to your website to see what you have to offer. When prospects read your articles on a trusted website and click to your site, it's the online equivalent of being introduced by a friend or associate. Moreover, articles can remain online for years and bring you thousands of visitors.

Anatomy of Online Articles

Much of the advice contained in Chapter 7, *Getting an Article into Print*, applies here. Following are some special considerations for online articles:

Write for Ease of Online Reading Because most people reading on their computers simply skim the content, make your writing especially easy to read.

Write headlines that catch attention Keep paragraphs short, typically no longer than two or three sentences. Use subheadings to separate long stretches of copy and bullet points for noting lists and action steps. Most websites expect articles of less than 1000 words; 500-750 words is ideal.

Write for the search engines. Include keywords and phrases that are popular with searchers within your target market. Research potential keywords and phrases relevant to your business and include them in your articles.

Create a Compelling Resource Box The resource box, which appears at the end of your article, should contain biographical information about you, an overview of your business, and an incentive that encourages readers to click back to your website. Here is a box that I have used:

> Steven Van Yoder is the author of *Get Slightly Famous*. His company helps executives, consultants, and professional business owners become recognized thought leaders in their fields and attract more business with less effort. Visit http://www.getslightlyfamous.com for free resources and to download his free marketing guide.
>
> Copyright 2007 – Steven Van Yoder. All Rights Reserved. You may reprint this article with the original, unedited text intact, including this resource box and URL link.

Keep in mind that if you use overly promotional language in your resource box, you risk compromising the goodwill you established by the valuable information in your article. You can, however, encourage people to visit your website by offering something of value as I have done.

Include Keywords in Links and Anchor Text These give readers information about the website they're linking to, and helps search engines better understand what your website is about in a way that can boost your rankings. For example, a link for a Detroit copyeditor's website might include the anchor text "Detroit copyeditor," using your word processor's "insert hyperlink" tool.

When including your website address, use the full http://www.yoursite.com format to ensure that search engines properly index the link to your site. Also, when formatting your link, never put a period at the end, which in some instances can cause the link to fail.

Submitting Your Articles

There are two ways to syndicate your articles--through article directories, or manually, by researching websites on your own and submitting your articles.

Article directories are databases where writers can post free articles that editors can publish in their e-mail newsletters or websites. When you post articles on these directories, you make your articles available to anyone who chooses to download and use them. Perhaps making the process easier, several software packages and automatic submission services have recently emerged that promise to syndicate articles to hundreds or thousands of article submission sites and directories. This approach necessarily delivers quantity over quality, and you have no control over who publishes your articles. So this method needs to be approached with care.

Since potential clients and customers will often judge you by the company you keep, the best strategy for syndicating articles online is to target websites with both credibility and relevance to your target market. Manual article syndication provides this control, and, while it takes time, it is worth the effort. You can seek out the most relevant sites and get links from "authority sites," those that are deemed by search engines to be of strong importance on a certain subject.

Above all, you need to maintain a regular publishing schedule. The greatest real value of publishing online articles comes to those who make this an ongoing strategy.

Use a Blog to Boost Your Business

Blogs, short for Web logs, differ from standard websites because they tend to be less formal, more frequently updated, and convey the unique voices of their authors. Powered by special blogging software, blogs read like diaries, with postings arranged in reverse chronological order.

Blogs are a user-friendly, cost-effective way to build a brand, provide useful information, and establish personal connections. Without a doubt, blogs are growing, both in number and influence. In its April 2006 "State of the Blogosphere" study, leading blog search engine Technorati reported:

- 19.4 million active blogs (defined as having a new post three months after creation)
- 3.9 million blogs are updated at least weekly
- 1.2 million new posts are created per day
- 70,000 new blogs are created each day
- The universe of blogs is 60 times larger than it was just three years ago.

A Cost-Effective Web Presence

Ideal for small businesses with limited marketing budgets, a blog can be produced for little or no cost, with virtually no technical skill. For some people, a blog can substitute for an expensive website. Another plus, due to the casual, informal nature of blog writing, is that even business owners who are not professional writers can develop blog content that effectively promotes their businesses.

"Blogging allows people to know my opinions before they engage me as a consultant, saving time and potential frustrations," says Harold Jarche, an independent business consultant based in Atlantic, Canada. "Through blogging, I have raised my profile on the Web, increased my site traffic by a factor of 1000 in less than one year, and I met a number of business partners. This is cheap marketing."

Unlike traditional websites, blogs are easy to update, customize, and maintain, eliminating both the delays involved and the costs of hiring a programmer to maintain a website.

"I paid someone way too much money to develop our website, and then I had to argue and fight with them every time we wanted to change something," says Ben Williams, co-owner of the Horsefeathers Restaurant in North Conway, New Hampshire. "Now with the blog, I just grab my computer and

REAL-WORLD SUCCESS STORY

Blogging Earns Ted Demopoulos a Thought Leader Reputation

Ted Demopoulos is a speaker, author, and consultant specializing in business technology. He started blogging in December 2004 and within a short time, saw that blogging was having a real impact on his business.

"Blogging doubled my site visitors in the first month, and has become instrumental in helping me sell speeches, consulting, and training classes," says Demopoulos. "Blogging has delivered other additional benefits that go beyond selling my services."

Demopoulos credits his blog with helping him beat competitors when landing high-profile speaking engagements. "Less than a month after I started blogging, I was asked to apply as a potential keynote speaker for a conference," recalls Demopoulos. "I'd been highly recommended by an associate, but so had two other speakers. I was told that the organization would contact me when they made the final selection."

"Thirty minutes later, the meeting planner called back and said 'I don't know what a blog is, but I've been reading yours since we got off the phone. You're perfect for the job. If you want to speak, we'd love to have you.' I knew I was on to something then!"

Blogging has positioned Demopoulos as a thought leader in his field, and enables him to interact with other influential bloggers. "When you blog, your target market can see your thoughts and expertise, as well as interact with you. You earn your thought leadership in a very public forum, where everyone can see and respect it, even if they don't always agree with you." In addition to attracting new prospects, Demopoulos' blog has helped him stay in front of existing clients. "My blog helps to keep me in touch with longtime clients, many of whom have realized the breadth of my expertise and experience though my blogging," says Demopoulos. "I've taken on additional roles, such as one client who previously used me only for technical training, but now retains me for a wide range of consulting."

"When I attend conferences, I frequently run into people who comment on my blog, and it's like meeting old friends. I've been asked to take part in panels because of my blog. Blogging has made me a recognized leader in my industry, and has increased my business network tenfold. Best of all, my phone rings more often!"

write up the stuff we're talking about every day in the restaurant—the Red Sox, the weather, the ski conditions."

How Businesses Benefit from Blogs

People prefer to do business with people they know and trust. A blog adds a personal touch that can facilitate a sense of community around your business. Blogs allow readers to comment and give feedback, fostering interactive online discussions.

"All of my advice is simple and straightforward," says Susan Stewart, president of Charter Financial Group, whose blog, stopstealingmydough. com, educates women investors about financial matters. "We don't blatantly plug the company, but see the blog as a place to stimulate online discussions with our target market about financial practices that investors should be wary about."

Expand Your Reach

Many bloggers say that blogging holds the potential to create online networking opportunities to interact and network with people you might not otherwise meet personally. If you want to network with insurance brokers, or those who influence them, you can create strategic blog posts that serve as virtual conversation starters.

"Recently, a technology firm contacted me about a lead generation campaign after finding my name mentioned by another blogger," says Jill Konrath, author of *Selling to Big Companies*. "Microsoft contacted me about being a featured blogger, and a new podcasting group contacted me about being a featured podcaster. These opportunities happened because my blog creates opportunities to become part of new networks, and these lead to new relationships."

"Blogs are alive and fun and can help you make connections with total strangers who can advance your business," says Konrath, who specializes in sales training. "Five years ago I was a consultant from White Bear Lake,

Minnesota. Not a soul knew who I was, except my clients. Today, because of the Internet, I am ubiquitous. My ezine has nearly 20,000 subscribers and my blog has many readers, too. All my clients now find me online. And it's easy! I started learning all this when I was fifty years old. I hate technology. I can't even do my VCR. I only have four names programmed into my phone, and my husband did it for me."

Build a Virtual Platform

John Jantsch, a marketing coach and author of *Duct Tape Marketing*, developed the Duct Tape Marketing blog in 2003; it was recently chosen as Forbes magazine's favorite small business blog. Jantsch credits blogging with quickly positioning him as a leader in his field of small business marketing and helping him land a book deal with a major publisher.

Jantsch suggests that a blog can amplify your other marketing activities. "A blog is not a be-all, end-all marketing tool. But, as part of your overall marketing strategy, a blog can help you build Web traffic, enhance your online presence, grow your reputation in your industry, and attract new opportunities," says Jantsch.

Keep in Touch with Your Target Market

Many business owners use blogs to complement existing client communications strategies, such as e-mail newsletters. Because blogs are easy to update, they provide a way to stay in front of your target market and existing clients and customers.

Sallie Goetsch launched the FileSlinger™ Backup Blog as an alternative to sending clients weekly e-mails reminding them to back up their computers. "I realized that I had enough content after years of sending informational emails to my client base," says Goetsch. "I took my existing content, added to my blog, and now have my clients subscribe to receive new content and reminders."

Now, Goetsch not only uses her blog to write about her core business of computer backup technology, but also to attract prospects for tech support, trademark research, and business writing. "It's definitely increased the profile of my website generally and provides a showcase for my writing services," says Goetsch.

Search Engines Love Blogs

Search engines pay special attention to websites that offer fresh, constantly updated content. Blogs can raise your page rank in search engines, sometimes dramatically, in a short time.

The secret to getting your blog ranked high in search engines is frequent updates. When a blog is regularly updated, that actually trains search engines to visit more frequently, and this boosts your search rankings. A blog that offers useful, fresh content based on relevant search words and phrases can pull ahead of more static websites, even those of larger companies.

How to Create and Launch a Blog

Although launching a blog is relatively easy, don't think about blogging just because it's the latest trend. Determine to make the most of the medium you need to stay focused on your primary goals.

Think Strategically about Your Blog

Consider how your blog will deliver value to your target audience and how you can integrate it into your other marketing activities. Your blog's key strategic objectives may include:

- Building brand awareness within your target market
- Establishing thought leadership in your industry
- Providing customer service and support
- Communicating the "human" side of your business
- Acting as an employee communications vehicle
- Creating an ongoing dialogue with prospects, customers, and clients

It's also important to research the "blogosphere" (the collective term encompassing all blogs as a community or social network). Don't try to create your blog in a vacuum. Identify blogs that influence your target market to discover what others are saying. A useful tool is the popular blog search engine, Technorati, where you can search for blogs that relate to your business, or any other topic. Observe the distinctive voice, style, and content of different blogs, and look at reader comments to see how the blogs are received.

Choose a Blog-Hosting Platform

The easiest way to start a blog is through a hosted blog service, which offers an affordable way to get your blog up and running. Best of all, no technical knowledge is required on your part. A free, user-friendly blog platform owned by Google called Blogger enables you to create a blog using design templates. Typepad is a popular low-cost option that offers more features and starts at $4.95 per month.

Most blog services allow you to customize your blog by using design templates. You can design the theme for your blog, including colors and number of columns. You can include your picture, lists of books you're reading, and details to personalize your blog. If you work within the hosting company's core functions, you can actually set up your blog without a Web programmer.

Brand Your Blog

A blog contributes to your business brand, so it's important to maintain consistency with your overall brand identity. Choose a name for your blog that reflects your business brand identity, and that is consistent in tone and style with your overall objectives.

Design your blog in a style consistent with your website. Orient readers to your blog by creating an "About" page that lists biographical data about the blog's author. Allowing readers to become familiar with the person behind the blog is a vital part of the blog experience.

Writing Your Blog

Successful blogs focus on a particular theme or niche. This principle, which goes to the core of any *slightly famous* marketing strategy, demands that your blog offers your target market relevant, meaningful information of value, that is not easily found anywhere else.

Consider the tone and overall thematic style of your blog, and make sure it will help you meet your objectives for engaging your target market while enlarging your audience. Cultivate a strong voice that expresses your brand and your personality. Along the way, keep these guidelines in mind:

- Establish an open, credible tone
- Keep the blog updated regularly—ideally, a few times a week
- Keep blog posts in the first person
- Include resources and links to other websites and blogs
- Keep your blog focused on your business objectives
- Maintain an honest, engaging, conversational quality

Express Your Passion

Concentrate on short, frequent entries and let yourself go as a writer, allowing your authentic voice to emerge. Plan a content strategy to keep you on track. Keep a file where you note ideas and inspiration for blog posts as they arise in your daily life.

The more you get into the rhythm of blogging, you'll see blog-worthy material in daily e-mail correspondence, articles in trade magazines and newspapers, talks you attend, and on other blogs, discussion forums, and websites.

Know Your Keywords

Including keywords in your blog posts can help customers find you when they are searching on Google or other sites. However, don't overdo it, as readers will quickly become annoyed at awkward postings obviously overloaded with particular phrases.

Maintain Consistent Blog Postings

Try to designate a regular time and schedule for writing and posting blog entries. At a minimum, post a new entry at least once a week, preferably two

TIPS FROM THE GURU

Debbie Weil Makes the Case for Corporate Blogging

Debbie Weil, author of *The Corporate Blogging Book*, believes that company executives should embrace blogging as a way to "come down from the mountaintop" and have authentic conversations with their most important stakeholders, including customers, employees, the media, and the broader business community.

"Blogs provide a tremendous opportunity for executives to engage in a conversation with their marketplace," says Weil. "Executive bloggers contribute their insights and expertise, as well as define and shape the overall discussion within their industries. Blogs complement existing marketing strategies and allow companies to interact with anyone who has a stake in their company."

As word-of-mouth moves online, executive blogs create a sense of community that can cultivate passionate customers. "Blogs are a way to build social networks around brands and products, and a way for executive bloggers to interact with their market on a personal level unattainable from traditional marketing strategies," says Weil.

General Motors, for example, provides commentary from GM leaders on topics relevant to the company and the industry on its FastLane Blog. FastLane offers car enthusiasts a chance to connect with GM leadership and provides "pure and unvarnished" feedback from car buyers. "These people have a great deal of influence, not just on what we read, but on the cars their friends and family purchase," says Bob Lutz, the vice chairman of GM, who writes his own posts and then e-mails them to the tech staff, who drop them into the blog.

Weil sees executive blogs as public relations channels that can enhance traditional PR tools, including press releases, contributed articles, and media interviews. The media increasingly turn to blogs as they research stories, and executive blogs allow companies to get their message out on their own terms, which can enhance or prompt media coverage.

"CEO and executive bloggers who are perceived as being open, intelligent, accessible leaders in their industry niches demonstrate their company's commitment to its target market," says Weil. "In today's marketplace, bottom-line benefits go to companies that shape the public conversation within their marketplaces and listen to what people are saying."

or three times a week, or more. Strive for succinct posts that pump pertinent new information into the "blogosphere," and then move on. Keep it short and sweet so visitors can pop in, read up, and click on. Your blog will have a cumulative effect.

Promoting Your Blog

There are several strategies you should pursue to promote your blog. Here are some of the most effective ways you can grow your readership.

Make Your Blog a Central Part of Your Marketing Strategy Don't just create your blog and hope people find it. Tell your target market and your existing contact network about your blog by promoting it as a source of useful information.

Integrate Your Blog into All Aspects of Your Marketing Include your blog address on your business cards, e-mail signature, and other marketing materials, and reference your blog in any PR activities you pursue, including press releases, interviews, articles, and talks.

Enable Your Blog's Feed Features Although there are several feed technologies, the most prominent is Real Simple Syndication (RSS). By enabling your blog's RSS feature, readers can keep up with changes to your blog without having to check back to see if it's been updated.

Here's how the blog feed syndication process works:

- Readers subscribe to your blog through a feed reader
- You create new content and post it to your blog
- Whenever your blog is updated, subscribers' feed readers will receive downloads of your most recent content

You should familiarize yourself with the blog feed syndication process by downloading a "feed reader" and subscribing to blogs of interest. There are several free feed readers, including Feedburner and Newsgator (programs that run on your computer) or Bloglines, a popular Web-based feed reader.

Consider adding signup forms to allow readers to receive your blog posts by email. Free services like Bloglet and Feedblitz can be added to your blog for those readers who opt for e-mail notification over RSS feeds.

Use Blog Search Engines and Directories There are several blog search sites and directories—that thousands of people search every day—where you can list your blog and attract potential readers. Some popular blog directories include blogsearchengine.com, technorati.com, and yahoo.com. There is also the free search engine blog notification service Pingomatic.

Connect with Other Bloggers Successful blogs are two-way conversations between a blogger and readers, which is why some of the best blog promotion opportunities exist in the blogosphere among fellow bloggers.

Sometimes blogging can allow you to enter into a direct conversation with the most famous people in your industry. If they have a blog, you can reach and build relationships with people who are already centers of influence.

Create a Targeted List of Bloggers Read blogs related to your niche, then make your presence known by commenting on posts that get your attention. You can agree, rebut, or expand on particular blog posts, always referencing and providing a link to your own blog.

You can also provide links and commentary on other blogs within your own blog posts. This is effective, because bloggers often monitor what other bloggers are saying about them via blog search engines. Make sure to include links to the original blog post.

Stick with It Building a steady readership for your blog takes time. Blog experts suggest that new bloggers should expect three-to-six-months, updating routinely, before search engines and other bloggers find you. Successful blogging is about committing to the long haul, regardless of the amount of feedback from readers.

Podcasting

The word "podcast" combines the terms broadcasting and iPod, the latter referring to Apple's popular music player. Although a relatively new technology,

Podcasting is emerging as a cost-effective marketing tool to help businesses reach prospects, employees, and customers via the Internet with radio show-style programs, corporate training programs, teleconferences, audio newsletters, new product information, and how-to seminars.

According to a recent eMarketer report, podcast audiences in the United States will reach 10 million in 2006, increase to 25 million by 2008 and 50 million by 2010. A recent Knowledge Storm/Universal McCann report exploring podcast use noted 32 percent of respondents said their usage of podcasts has increased in the past six months. The survey also noted that 58 percent of respondents would welcome traditional marketing information, such as white papers and reports, delivered as podcast content.

Podcasting can help businesses turn their online presence into a dynamic, multimedia enhanced marketing channel. Podcasts can make a small businesses appear large and give larger companies an executive platform. The medium has been embraced by such household names as Virgin Atlantic, Purina, General Motors, IBM, and Whirlpool as well as vast numbers of individual entrepreneurs.

John Baldoni, an executive coach, speaker, author, and communications consultant, created a podcast series called Coach Casting, designed to help IT managers plan, manage, motivate, and lead more effectively. Each podcast is comprised of a two-minute segment that focuses on topics such as dealing with people you can't stand, developing your message, delivering bad news, prioritizing, and asking for a raise.

"I use podcasting for my leadership and coaching practice, and it has helped me share my point of view and reach my target audience of front-line and middle managers," says Baldoni, whose podcast is now sponsored by CIO magazine's website, his podcast now averages 5,000–8,000 listeners per week. "Podcasting has enhanced my public profile, attracted speaking engagements, and increased my book sales," he says.

Similarly successful, Technomic Asia, a market entry and growth strategy consulting firm, launched a "China Business" podcast in 2005. Providing information on business opportunities and precautions, in a little over a year

Two Financial Advisors Create a Platform through Podcasting

Jason Papier and Peter Johnson are principals of PW Johnson Wealth Management in Los Altos, California. In 2005, while exploring marketing strategies for their financial services firm, they got interested in podcasting. After some initial research, they made a $29 investment in a microphone and were soon hosting the Pro Money Talk podcast.

Pro Money Talk covers a wide range of personal finance issues, such as asset class investing, zero coupon bonds, taxes, and retirement planning. The show includes educational discussions, interviews with financial experts, and success stories of ordinary people. Within its first year, Pro Money Talk attracted a following in more than 100 countries, and it has been consistently ranked in the top ten podcasts in Apple's iTunes Music Store.

"Our marketing strategy centers on communicating with people frequently," says Papier. "We chose audio because it's an intimate marketing medium. Our podcast allows us to talk for 45 minutes on topics that demonstrate our expertise. We show in a personal way how we are different from other financial planners."

Papier and Johnson were pleasantly surprised at how podcasting has helped them leverage their time and reach more people. "Our podcast provides educational resources for potential clients, consumers and our own peers. We made a conscious decision not to promote, not to say anything about our business, but

the podcast gained 1,000 subscribers with segments being downloaded more than 2,000 times per month.

This podcast series generated considerable media coverage. Within the first week, it was featured on National Public Radio's *All Things Considered*. The podcast has been cited by CNBC, *Business Week*, and many major newspapers and is now a critical component of Technomic Asia's marketing efforts.

Creating Your Own Podcast

Podcast production can be surprisingly low-tech and inexpensive, or it can be done in a studio with professional recording equipment. You can edit the everyone knows, obviously, we're financial planners. Podcasting helps us position us as leaders in our niche by delivering value to our broad marketplace," says Johnson. "It's an educational tool for existing clients, and it attracts an audience of other financial professionals."

Pro Money Talk guests have included former presidential candidate Steve Forbes, and Nobel Prize winner Bill Sharp. "Bill is one of the giants in our field and one of the fathers of modern portfolio theory," says Johnson. "He appeared as a guest, and afterward invited me to his house. Our podcast connects us to high-end professionals in our industry who are honored to be on our show, and often return the favor by referring us business. Additionally, being publicly linked to these high-credibility people helps our reputation and search engine rankings."

After a year of steady podcasting, Pro Money Talk has grown in reach and sophistication. Papier and Johnson have invested in professional recording equipment to boost the quality of their broadcast and include more high-profile guests.

"Podcasting provides a tremendous opportunity for businesses with limited resources to create their own platforms," says Johnson. "We find that the more we tell our story and communicate our expertise, it opens up more opportunities. A podcast is one way to build up a passionate community. It also enables people to go deeper into the topics of interest."

audio, and add other production elements, like music, using software such as Audacity, a free, downloadable software program for recording and editing digital audio. Once a program is recorded, it is converted into an MP3 file (the de facto standard, which is compatible with most digital audio players) and uploaded onto the Internet.

Most podcasts are modeled on audio programming formats that are similar to radio talk shows. Consider your target market by asking clients and customers for suggestions. Will you interview others, host a teleclass, or record yourself delivering informational content? How frequently will you deliver your podcasts?

EXECUTIVE BRANDING

Mena Trott: The Unofficial Spokesperson for Blogging

Mena Trott is the president and co-founder of Six Apart, the largest independent provider of blogging tools and blog hosting services. Before that, however, she had a long history of being an online public persona.

Mena started blogging on Dollarshort.org, a fledgling weblog created with the help of her husband Ben, a software programmer. It began as an online diary where she frequently wrote entries on a variety of subjects, her childhood, musical tastes, pets, and hobbies. Her blog somehow grew in popularity and soon complete strangers checked in daily to see what was on Mena's mind.

One day, she created a humorous post about how she wanted to buy a banjo, but that her husband Ben wouldn't let her. Although intended as a joke, several readers wrote and angrily suggesting she get a separate bank account, or even leave him. This provided the husband/wife team with a profound insight: the Internet was now a personal, two-way medium. If people enjoyed reading Mena's personal blog, there might be a market for blog software. What started as a hobby eventually led to the launch of Six Apart and Mena's central role in advancing the company brand.

Since 2001, Six Apart has attracted millions of customers, largely through positive associations with the Six Apart brand and its founders, Mena and Ben Trott. Mena, in particular, is widely regarded as the public face of Six Apart.

"Part of the brand appeal is Mena and Ben's story as a young couple that launched a successful company," says Anil Dash, vice president of Six Apart. "Our customers strongly identify with the personality and humanity of our founders, to the extent that 'Ben and Mena' is often used as shorthand for discussing the entire company. But what really comes through is their commitment to making tools that enable people to connect and communicate online."

Given the relatively small size of the company, Six Apart gets an extraordinary amount of national press coverage, and Mena has earned a reputation as the unofficial spokesperson for the wider phenomenon of blogging and online social media. She has been featured in the *New York Times*, *The Wall Street Journal*, *CNN Headline News* and as a *Fortune* cover story. She regularly speaks at industry conferences and was named one of Fast Company's Fast 50 for 2004 and *PC magazine's* "People of the Year" for 2004.

Mena still maintains several blogs, including Mena's Corner, where she documents company milestones and initiatives, and Vox, an community blogging service created by Six Apart. When Six Apart launches a major initiative, Mena is a frequent guest and contributor on industry blogs and podcasts, such as Marketwatch and Wired News.

In addition, nearly all Six Apart senior executives engage in online thought leadership though blogging, interviews, and online discussions. In this way they provide a consistent message about the opportunity blogging presents for everyone on the Web, and ongoing education about the basics of blogging and their belief in the medium.

"Online social media provide executives with low-cost, accessible channels to establish an intimate relationship with everyone in their target market," says Dash. "Blogs and other online tools allow executives to expand their traditional communications such as press briefings and industry announcements and share them with a larger audience."

Moreover, says Dash, blogging and social media technologies allow for a direct connection to clients and customers by facilitating feedback and online conversations. When executives make direct connections to customers online, companies develop a level of trust and brand affinity that's hard to beat with more traditional marketing channels.

"Your customers are already talking about your brand, and you should take part in the conversation," adds Mena Trott. "It's important for entrepreneurs and executives to get out there and participate in online discussions and communities. There are now tremendous new opportunities to connect in meaningful ways with the broader online world of your marketplace."

Audio teleconferencing offers a simple, cost-effective way to produce a podcast. Several teleconference services offer built-in features that allow you to record a telephone call discussion and then convert the recording to a podcast-compatible audio file.

Audio Acrobat, a nominally priced based audio service, provides a full suite of functions, including telephone conference recording, audio file hosting, and syndication capabilities to make your podcast easily available online. This is a user-friendly service for anyone starting out.

Promoting Your Podcast

Popular business podcasts tend to provide focused information not easily found anywhere else. The Burchfield Group, for instance, produces the Pharmacy Benefits podcast for benefits managers at large companies. Each segment discusses the details of drug insurance and reimbursement costs to employers and their employees.

When considering your podcast title and subtitle, tend to the literal. You want a title that clearly describes what your podcast delivers. Include your keywords in your feed title and description to boost your podcast's search engine findability.

Syndicate Your Podcast

Like blogs, podcasts can be syndicated through RSS and other feeds to listeners. The easiest way to publish your podcast is through a hosting service that notifies various directories about the availability of your new podcast.

To subscribe and manage podcast feeds, listeners use an aggregator software program, sometimes called a podcatcher or podcast receiver. There are several free feed readers available; the most popular is the Apple iTunes program, which allows users to access a podcast library and subscribe to podcasts.

Consider getting a syndication link through Feedburner, a free service that provides custom RSS feeds and management tools to bloggers and podcasters.

Submit Your Podcast to Libraries and Directories

This is perhaps the most important thing you can do to attract new listeners. Although iTunes is the most popular podcast library, there are hundreds of others, including Yahoo!, podcast.net, iPodderX, Odeo, and Podcast Alley. When submitting your podcast, identify directory categories where your podcast is likely to attract listeners.

Use Other Slightly Famous Techniques

You can employ a whole range of marketing strategies to get the word out about your podcast. Issue a press release when you interview famous and interesting people, form strategic partnerships with other businesses or groups that will co-promote your podcast, mention your podcast on other blogs, and include it in the resource box of your syndicated online articles.

Engage your listeners by encouraging feedback. This two-way communication will not only help you improve your show, but will foster a sense of community. Announce and provide ways to call and/or send e-mail feedback, and read positive listener comments during your podcast.

11 Stand and Deliver: Speaking Strategies

Harriet Schechter, founder of The Miracle Worker Organizing Service in San Diego, is the author of three books, including *Let Go of Clutter*, that have been published in five languages. She has been interviewed on *Good Morning America* and numerous radio and television programs, and has been quoted in hundreds of publications including the *New York Times, USA Today,* and the *Atlantic Monthly.* Harriet's media exposure has played a large part in her success, but she points to her public speaking and seminars as primary causes of that success, helping her get nearly 75 percent of her business.

"I founded The Miracle Worker Organizing Service in 1986, and by 1988 was presenting speeches and seminars," says Schechter. "I had not planned on becoming a speaker; it was something that evolved. After I spoke to local organizations like the Lions Club, Rotary, and Kiwanis, my business really took off. Soon I was offered paid speaking engagements, and was prompted to become an author because audience members kept asking me if I had a book."

Public speaking is the perfect *slightly famous* marketing method, because it showcases your knowledge in polished form to people who are interested in hearing it. A person who takes the podium is seen as somebody with something worth saying—something audience members would like to know themselves. Speaking can be the fastest, easiest, and cheapest way to establish yourself as an expert, and it gives you tremendous credibility that increases over time. When done well, a speech can help you close sales before you leave the room. Having heard you speak, people feel they know you personally, and are more confident about hiring you.

Get on the Program

Speakers are in great demand—especially those willing to speak for free. Dottie and Lilly Walters, authors of *Speak and Grow Rich*, estimate that there are over nine thousand speaking opportunities a day in the United States. Clubs, organizations, and associations are eager to establish relationships with speakers who present useful, interesting material to members at meetings, seminars, conferences, and workshops, and you don't have to be a seasoned speaker to get started.

Even so, just because it's easy to get booked somewhere as a speaker doesn't mean it's worth doing. Before you commit yourself, try to find out about the audience. Most organizations can answer these questions:

- Are audience members really members of your target market?
- How many people are likely to show up for the talk?
- What kinds of speakers have recently presented to the group?
- If expenses are involved, will the organization reimburse you?
- Can you hand out materials and/or gather audience contact information?
- Can you sell your books or other materials at the talk?

It takes time to prepare your speech, travel to a speaking venue, and give a talk. Before you pursue a speaking opportunity, or accept an invitation to speak, make sure it has a high probability of benefiting your business.

Here are a few of the most common venues for promotional speaking.

Service Clubs Clubs like the Kiwanis, Lions, and Rotary provide ample opportunities for speaking. Start with organizations where you're already a member.

Chambers of Commerce Local Chambers of Commerce typically have several program meetings each month that require outside speakers on topics of interest to local businesses, from marketing and sales to technology.

Industry Associations Every industry has at least one association, such as the Council of Realtors or Financial Women International. These groups have monthly meetings and quarterly conferences and conventions, most of which utilize outside speakers.

Professional Associations There are several groups not specific to a particular industry, such as Leads Clubs International and American Business Women's Association, that are always looking for speakers.

Continuing Education Programs Teaching a class is a great way to gain credibility in your community. Continuing education programs, adult education programs like the Learning Annex, community colleges, and university extension programs provide opportunities.

Hold Your Own Event You can host an event in your office, in a rented hotel room, or in a conference room at the office of a friend. Such an event allows you to showcase your business in the best way possible.

Online Chats and Teleconferences You don't have to be personally present to give a talk that reaches your target market. Online chats and teleconferences, using your own or others' Web sites or telephone lines, can help you reach a lot of people eager to hear your message.

Approaching Speaking Venues

Once you've compiled a list of potential speaking venues, do whatever you can to become familiar with your targeted organizations. It's always helpful to attend a few meetings to determine whether the organization prefers individual speakers or panels. Read the organization's newsletter to familiarize yourself with member concerns and interests. Then choose a few topics you can tailor to that audience.

Contact the program chairman for each group on your list. Ask to be considered for speaking opportunities and describe how the group will benefit from your talk. Keep in mind that many programs are scheduled from six to twelve months in advance.

Send the program chairman an introductory package, including a cover letter naming other groups that have sponsored your presentations, and citing comments from attendees (when applicable), a personal and company biography, and any other materials that validate your expertise. Briefly describe one to three potential speaking topics, so as to give meeting planners a choice. Each topic should highlight your expertise, while allowing for opportunities to tell stories about your work.

The National Speakers Association notes that most speakers rely on word of mouth to land repeated speaking engagements. Even though it takes some legwork to land your first speaking engagements, the more you speak and the better you become at it, the more you will be in demand.

Preparation

According to the *Book of Lists*, speaking in public produces more fear and anxiety than any other activity—death comes in only seventh. The good news is that the more you speak, the easier it becomes. Public speaking can be both rewarding and enjoyable.

Although you don't have to be a master orator to be effective, you do need to take time to prepare your speech; you want to avoid damaging your reputation by appearing disorganized, inarticulate, or uninformed. Spend time practicing to build your confidence and abilities. Remember that all great speakers worked to develop their speaking abilities. Martin Luther King gave countless sermons at small churches before his famous "I Have a Dream."

REAL-WORLD SUCCESS STORY

Roseann Sullivan on the Power of Public Speaking

Ever since she unexpectedly won a speech contest during a summer school session, Roseann Sullivan has been hooked on communicating effectively. Today, she coaches corporate CEOs and conducts workshops for organizations on how to communicate more effectively. Her clients include Hewlett-Packard, Pepsi-Cola, Apple Computer, and Clorox Company.

"Too often, beginners don't realize the benefits speaking will bring to their businesses, and how much they have to contribute," says Sullivan. "Years ago, when I booked speakers for the Learning Annex, my job was to find independent business owners who could speak about hot topics. I'd approach people and say, 'You have a booming business. Wouldn't it be nice to share it with people?' The response I'd always get was, 'What would I possibly tell people?'"

Eventually, she'd talk them into it, and they would give their speech. And time and again she would see them generate prospects and sales as a result. "That was when I recognized the power of speaking," says Sullivan. "Even if there are only five people in a room, you never know what will come of it because each of those five people knows five people and so on."

The most important thing to remember is that you don't have to be a great speaker to get started. "If you can just get up there and do a decent job you will immediately position yourself as an expert," says Sullivan. "The value of speaking is that it gives people a taste of what you offer in a non-threatening environment. I hired my caterer because I saw her doing a cooking class, and my house cleaner when she gave a presentation at a Chamber of Commerce."

"Speaking before a group about your business is the cheapest, best way to market your product or service, and expand your customer base," says Patricia Fripp, a Certified Speaking Professional (CSP) who started with a career in the beauty industry more than 25 years ago. Since then she has gained a reputation as an award-winning speaker, author, sales trainer, and in-demand speech coach. "I started talking about my business at organizations such as Rotary, Kiwanis, and Optimists. I didn't have any public speaking experience, so I studied the pros."

Her practice paid off. Since 1980 she has spoken to over 100 groups every year. This includes Fortune 100 companies and major associations world-wide. The National Speakers Association, with more than 4,000 members, elected her their first female President in 1984. She has since received every mark of prestige given by the NSA, including membership in their Hall of Fame, and their highest honor, the Cavett Award, considered the "Oscar" of the speaking world.

Fine-tuning your public speaking skills will also improve your performance in other areas, such as conducting meetings and making sales presentations. Every time you speak with confidence, style, and ease, you enhance the reputation of your company, attract more business, and generate credibility for yourself.

Toastmasters (www.toastmasters.org), an international nonprofit group that helps people speak more effectively, is a great resource for aspiring speakers. For a nominal fee, members learn how to speak to groups in a supportive environment. A typical Toastmasters club is made up of 20 to 30 people who meet once a week for about an hour. Each meeting gives everyone an opportunity to practice.

You can further hone your speaking skills by participating in networking groups that require you to talk about your business. These groups usually give members plenty of opportunities to introduce themselves at meetings, give short business presentations, and profit from audience feedback. Practice the basics: planning what you want to say, using positive body language, pacing your speech, and interacting with your listeners.

Your Public Speaking Engagement

Larry Bird, the basketball great from the Boston Celtics, was known to dribble the ball for hours on a basketball court in order to identify the dead spots on the floor and avoid them during the game. On the day of a speech, good speakers, like good athletes, arrive early to become familiar with the room, microphone system, slide projector, and audiovisual equipment. Nothing detracts from the beginning of a presentation as much as testing the equipment by asking the audience, "Can you hear me?" or "Would someone adjust the focus on the slide projector?"

Before the speech, greet guests at the door as they come in to become familiar with the audience and make yourself less nervous. Once you interact with people, you can visualize conversing with them as friends rather than as strangers.

Write Your Own Introduction

Don't leave your introduction in the hands of the meeting planner. Prepare your own introduction, send a copy to the meeting planner, and bring another on the day of the speech. Keep your introduction short, no more than one minute in length, and craft it in a way that creates an interest in your subject matter and establishes your expertise. Your goal is to inform and arouse interest, not to give an exhaustive (and exhausting) infomercial.

Nine Rules for Strong Presentations

1. Effective speeches come in three segments—beginning, middle, and end. Create your speech around this simple formula. Introduce the scope or nature of your topic in the beginning, go into more detail, background, or illustrative stories or examples in the middle, and point out conclusions, or issue a call to action, at the end.

2. Don't read from notes. Excessive note reading while speaking keeps you from creating a bond with the audience. Use handwritten notes only as an outline to keep yourself on track. Have written bullet points to capture main ideas. They're easy to see and will jog your memory. The briefer your sentences, the easier the speech will be to deliver. Practicing your speech beforehand will make you more confident and less reliant on written notes.

3. Use a microphone when necessary. A microphone not only adds volume, it also invests you with an aura of authority. Make sure you have a microphone available for your talk if the size of the room and audience warrant it.

4. Start with a story. Launch your talk with a short personal story about an incident related to your business. Make sure the story "humanizes" you, so as to develop a reservoir of good will that will extend to the rest of the speech.

For example, "Today, I want to talk about the five most common mistakes people make when starting a consulting firm, and how I made every one of them."

5. Use client examples. Use client examples to illustrate the main points of your talk. Describe a problem a client had, and what you did to help. This gives your audience a greater understanding of what your firm does, and shows in a positive light how you serve clients and customers. Using client examples in your speech is also a sales tool that encourages audience members to imagine themselves as your clients.

6. Ask your audience questions. Good questions engage the audience and help provide direction and momentum for your talk. By asking the right questions, you can determine the concerns and interests of your audience, and tailor your presentation to those concerns. By asking for answers from the audience, you also encourage people to become involved.

7. Body language sends a message. If you look confident, the audience will perceive you that way. When you want to emphasize a point, use simple, understated gestures.

8. Make regular eye contact with audience members. This will help you draw listeners into your speech. Nodding to emphasize points also helps make a connection with the audience.

9. Your voice is an instrument of persuasion. Use it that way. Don't rush your delivery. This can be difficult if you are nervous, but take time to gather your thoughts. Try to set a relaxed, conversational pace. When you make a particularly relevant point, emphasize it by pausing before and after the point.

Concluding the Talk

Be prepared to answer questions. In fact, encourage them by seeding the audience with questions. Have a few prepared questions on note cards, and give them to a few carefully selected members of the audience before you speak. Have these individuals ask the questions on the cards if there's a dead spot during the question-and-answer session.

The time immediately following a speech is critically important for promoting business. Don't be in a hurry to pick up your slides and leave after it is over. Make yourself available to the audience. If you have books, booklets, or other information products to sell, now is the time. When audiences have just heard you speak, they are usually primed to take your advice and move to the next step.

Creating Promotional Opportunities

Since your main purpose in speaking is to build your business, you need to go into each speaking engagement prepared to maximize your return.

Ask the group if they will seek media publicity for your talk. If not, ask if you can supply a press release of your own to appropriate media. Because most organizations have a newsletter, ask them to publish an article by or about you, mentioning your speech, either before or after your talk—or both! As an alternative, you can ask them to include your brochure or other materials related to your company in their next mailing. Point out that this will help to boost attendance at the meeting you'll be speaking at. Develop handouts that have value for your audience, and make sure they include your name, address, telephone number, and Web-site address.

Speaking engagements are a way to gather prospect names, addresses, and e-mail addresses. Offer an incentive, such as a free book or consultation, to get people to drop their business cards in a box. Tell them that you would like to send them your free newsletter—or something else that might have value for them—and that they can unsubscribe at any time.

Audience members may not need you today, but if you make a good impression and continue to send them something on a regular basis, you will build a list of prospects that will grow and bear fruit for years to come.

Seminars

An experienced public speaker who bills himself as "The Mole Man," Jeff Holper promotes his business, Holper's Pest & Animal Solutions, through a workshop for homeowners. To standing-room-only crowds at home shows, trade shows, and wildlife conferences, his program, Holper's Terminator

TIPS FROM THE GURU

Caterina Rando on Handouts That Get You Clients

Caterina Rando, international speaker, life-and-business success coach, and author of *Learn to Power Think*, suggests creating "tip cards" to give out at the end of each talk. As its name implies, a tip card contains useful information, but it is formatted to be posted in homes and offices. Once on the wall it's a constant reminder of your talk. The following tips are excerpted from her special report, "Attracting Clients with Ease."

• Always have something to give audience participants when you speak. Audience members will forget you when they walk out the door if they don't have a part of you to take home with them.

• In addition to the information you conveyed in your talk, consider giving participants an article you have written on the topic. This makes you look like an expert.

• Always have your brochures and business cards displayed for the taking. Include a flyer on your upcoming seminars or a schedule showing where you will be speaking next.

• Put your business name, address, Website address (URL), and phone number on the bottom of each sheet of paper you give your audience.

• Use an evaluation form to ask audience members for feedback on how your presentation can be improved. While you have to be pretty thick-skinned to do this, it can be helpful.

• Use an action sheet. This is a sheet that asks audience members what action they are going to take now that they have heard your talk.

Ask audience members for their contact information. You will at least get their e-mail address if you offer to send them your monthly newsletter or articles.

• Ask qualifying questions to help you determine if you should follow-up with an individual. For example, "Do you or does your company use (fill in the blank with your product or service)?" or "Would you be interested in a complimentary consultation to discuss (fill in the blank with your product or service)?"

Hold a drawing to make sure everyone turns in their forms; give away one of your products or services, or a book of interest to audience members.

University, offers ten easy steps to dealing with moles and other rodents that invade lawns and gardens. These workshops are a way for Holper to sell his many books, reports, videos, and mole traps.

Bringing a group of prospects together in one place is an efficient way to generate leads and sales. You can charge an admission fee, but you won't get as many attendees. So you have to decide in advance on whom you want to attend and what their attendance is worth to you. And remember that people who have paid want, expect, and deserve more.

Whether for free or for the cost of a ticket, people attend seminars because they want to learn something. They understand that you're there because you have a product or service, but they don't want to feel pressured to buy. You may sell home security systems, for example, but the seminar should focus not on your products, but on benefits such as safety or peace of mind. Useful information is the key. People feel cheated and trapped if you give little more than a sales pitch for your company. In contrast, if you inspire trust by giving away some of your knowledge—and thus demonstrating your expertise and fair-mindedness—attendees will turn to you when they are ready for more help.

The easiest way to launch a seminar is through a local organization, community college, or continuing education program. These institutions have positive reputations that will boost the credibility of your seminar, plus they have the infrastructure for making the event happen, catalogs, mailing lists, and meeting rooms. These institutions will also be able to give you feedback on what kind of response you are likely to get.

Trade associations or other industry groups are often willing to promote seminars to their members, if the seminar topic is relevant to their membership. If you can get such an association to sponsor the event you have gone a long way to establishing credibility.

Join with Others for Panel Discussions

Partnering with related businesses to create discussion panels and group seminars lets you share the cost and labor involved in organizing an event, while at the same time creating value from the consumer's point of view. Moreover, if you're not an experienced speaker, taking part in a panel or team presentation reduces the pressure on you.

The ideal panel comprises people from related businesses and professions, but without much overlap. An accountant, for example, could team up with a retirement planner and an accounting software expert for a seminar about small business financial strategies. If each partner can attract attendees from among their clients, then they all can benefit from referrals.

If you're in charge of the panel discussion, make sure everyone is clear about what the discussion is supposed to cover. You don't want to be too general, nor do you want to cover the same points. It's also important to enforce time limits. A panel can quickly fall apart when one person talks well beyond the appointed time limit. Ideally, a 50-minute panel discussion with four panelists would give each panelist 10 minutes to speak, and then have 10 minutes left for questions and discussion from the audience. Have somebody in back of the room hold up a "one-minute" sign, a "30-second" and a "stop" sign that everyone on the panel can see.

Be clear about how you will handle questions from the audience. One common method is to take questions at the very end. Try to make sure that at least one question goes to each person on the panel.

Teleclasses

Teleclasses are, in essence, virtual classrooms created with an automated conference call system called a "bridge line." Students register for a teleclass, receive the virtual-classroom telephone number, and call it at the appointed hour to get connected to the host and other attendees in a format that is part lecture, part interactive classroom.

Teleclasses are a great way for businesses to provide information to prospects, clients, and customers all over the world, with minimal cost and effort. Unlike seminars and other meetings, they eliminate the need to travel. Both hosts and participants can attend from their offices, their favorite easy chair at home, or even by mobile phone while on vacation. Teleclasses make it easy to connect to prospects all over the world.

Business coach and teleclass leader Michael Losier took his first teleclass

REAL-WORLD SUCCESS STORY

Steve Dubin Learns the Power of Seminar Partnering

Steve Dubin of PR Works embraced partnering when he helped a Boston-based moving and storage company plan a joint seminar to reach business prospects.

He advised the moving company to partner with related businesses to create a more valuable seminar with more crowd appeal, rather than go it alone. The result was a panel of "relocation experts" for a Home Buyers and Sellers Seminar that included a mortgage broker, a real estate attorney, a realtor, and the moving company.

The seminar was a success. Not only did the moving company and its partners generate leads, they now hold their seminars on a regular basis, and attract free media coverage to help promote them.

"I've found that teaming up with a group of related businesses generates more interest among potential attendees," says Dubin. "Bringing together a broad-based panel of experts, instead of one company sponsoring a seminar, gives people a sense that the event is truly an informational opportunity and not a sales pitch."

Here's a press release that Dubin used to promote this seminar:

For Immediate Release
Contact: Steve V. Dubin, PR Works
sdubin@prworkzone.com, (781) 878-9533

three years ago and was impressed with the potential for this type of meeting. Because it was so convenient and so much fun, he decided to try running one himself, and set up a teleclass about exhibiting at trade shows. "I had 60 students in my first class, which was very profitable, and many later hired me as a consultant," says Losier.

Since then teleclasses have helped Losier expand his market, and gotten him a stream of international clients. "After just six months of teaching teleclasses I was able to leave my desk job. I ended up writing two books on my teleclass courses, thanks in part to the feedback my students gave me. I also became a teleclass trainer to leaders across the globe."

FREE SEMINAR ON BUYING AND SELLING
YOUR HOME IN TODAY'S MARKET

MILTON, MA. Humboldt Storage and Moving continues its series of FREE seminars on "Buying and Selling Your Home in Today's Market" on Monday, October 18, from 7 – 8:30 pm at the Braintree Sheraton Tara, Exit 6 off Route 128 (across from the South Shore Plaza).

Expert panelists will outline the necessary steps to selling your home at an optimal price, as well as "buying smart" in today's market. Acquiring bank-owned properties will be emphasized.

This ongoing series is sponsored by Humboldt Storage and Moving, one of Boston's oldest and largest relocation firms, and an award-winning United Van Lines agent in Lower Milton Falls.

The seminar moderator is Howard Goldman, President of Humboldt Storage and Moving. Panelists are Claire Garrity of Coldwell Banker Residential Real Estate, who will give the inside scoop on buying and selling homes; Attorney Kenneth K. Quigley, whose topic is "How to Look at Equity in your Home"; and Mary Ellen MacInnis of the Salem Five, who will advise sellers on "How to Obtain the Best Mortgage for the Next Residence."

At the conclusion of the seminar, there will be a question-and-answer period, followed by complimentary refreshments.

Attend this seminar and get information on the housing market from the people who really know. Please R.S.V.P. by calling Claire LeSage of Humboldt Storage and Moving at (617) 696-9500.

According to Anne-Marie Rennick of Learningbyphone.com, teleclasses offer an alternative to live presentations and seminars that doesn't put added stress on people's already jam-packed schedules. "Teleclasses enable you to bring together 10, 20, or 100 people to listen to you talk about your business for an hour, allowing you to engage them and display your mastery," says Rennick.

Rennick's teleclasses generally meet once a week for three to four weeks, with each meeting lasting 55 minutes. "This gives students a chance to absorb a topic in bite-sized pieces, like a short college course, with time in between classes to apply what they've learned."

REAL-WORLD SUCCESS STORY

Josiane Feigon, TeleSmart Communications

During the economic slowdown starting around 2000, many companies slashed their training budgets. This affected Josiane Feigon, president of TeleSmart Communications, whose traditional sales-skills training seminars, directed at sales and customer support professionals, became an easy target for budget cutting.

"The economic slowdown really hit my client base," says Feigon. "As they tightened their belts, it became much more difficult for managers to justify bringing me on-site. They were very reluctant to invest their salespeople's time, pulling them off the phones or out of the field, to travel to training."

Feigon realized that her clients needed training more than ever. So she started offering teleclasses as an alternative to on-site seminars. She reformatted her previous multiple-day, 3-hour seminars into a series of 60-minute teleclasses, using the same delivery principles that made her successful with her on-site training.

"I've always been a big advocate of the telephone as a primary business tool," says Feigon. "And I've always been committed to teaching people to sell by phone. It makes perfect sense to replicate the same environment where salespeople work. Now, I create a memorable experience without being face to face. I time each activity, question, and learning objective to make an impact immediately—within seconds."

Feigon owns a 10-seat license on her telephone bridge line, and places a limit of 8 participants on the sessions. Before the session, she gets a list of attendees, sends out e-mail reminders before placing each call, and offers fifteen 60-minute topics, following the same formula to deliver each.

"My main goal is to engage the team immediately, and keep it going until the last minute," says Feigon. "All the skills I teach are designed to be tested the moment the participants get off the phone. I want to get the salespeople 'addicted' to this type of training. I've designed 3-, 6-, and 12-month teleclass plans that would ideally be incorporated into every training schedule."

Feigon continues to expand her use of teleclasses, constantly looking for improvements. "I don't think we've even begun to scratch the surface of this type of technology," says Feigon. "I constantly attend different teleclasses to discover new possibilities. Teleclasses are the answer to so many issues today. It's had a big impact on my business and quality of life. I'm traveling much less, practicing my trade with clients around the country from my office."practicing my trade with clients around the country from my office."

Many businesses are also offering free teleclasses as an affordable way to connect to groups of targeted prospects and attract new business. "A lot of businesses offer a free initial teleclass to attract people and build a list of prospects," says Rennick.

As in any class, the quality and effectiveness of the experience depends on getting people to participate and interact. And by their very nature, teleclasses are more interactive. They make it easier to participate, because in a roomful of strangers, many attendees are too shy to speak up.

That's why teleclasses often experience increased participation among attendees. They are highly interactive, more like tele-discussions, which make it easier to share and be heard, to ask questions and get answers (they also, of course, make it easy for the very shy to just sit and listen as if they were hiding in the back row of a classroom). "In teleclasses, there's no worry about body language, or turning red when you speak," says Rennick. "Participants are more free to engage in the teleclass."

One of Rennick's popular teleclasses covers how to design, conduct, and market a great teleclass. "It's the longest running and most popular of my classes," says Rennick, who usually has from eight to twelve people taking part in her class. She supplements phone time with a manual. "I use that manual as the backbone of the class—then we're all on the same page, so to speak."

12 Info-Products: Create Multiple Income

I f you run a small business providing services only, your ability to earn is limited by the number of hours you have available—once you're fully booked, that's it. Information products are especially appealing, therefore, to service businesses whose only saleable asset, otherwise, is billable hours.

It may take some effort to turn your skills, knowledge, and advice into products, but once you've done it, you've created assets that can then be sold and resold over and over again. If you create and market information products that are in high demand, you can literally make money while you sleep.

Anybody Can Be an Info-Entrepreneur

You don't have to be a high-end consultant or established author to produce information products; anybody with special knowledge can use that knowledge to create saleable products. And these products, in turn, will advance your *slightly famous* marketing strategy.

REAL-WORLD SUCCESS STORY

Bill Brooks Reaps Multiple Rewards through Products

Bill Brooks, CEO of The Brooks Group, a sales training and consulting firm, is the author of nine books and over 150 information products that appear in a wide variety of formats: audio tapes and CDs, videos, CD-ROMs, DVDs, books, manuals, and Internet training systems.

"One of the great things about developing information products is they position you as an expert in whatever niche or segment you want to establish yourself," says Brooks. "The more knowledgeable you are, the more perceived value you have with prospects. Information products position you as an industry leader by distilling your wisdom into concrete form."

According to Brooks, successfully embracing information products begins by taking an inventory of everything a company can provide their target market. "We market training programs for salespeople," says Brooks, "and in working with them we realized they needed advice for overcoming objections, staying motivated, and better managing their time. We address these topics in e-books, manuals, CDs, and special reports."

These information products have generated handsome profits for Brooks' company over the last 25 years. In addition, he also uses these information products as "premiums" to attract new prospects.

An exterminator, for example, can produce a "termite-proofing" report for homeowners, and offer it to prospects on a Yellow Pages ad or his website. A kickboxing instructor can develop a video training program that can be sold through local gyms to generate income and attract prospects for live training. A corporate communications consultant can develop an employee training program and workbook that can be sold to companies that don't have their own training programs.

Establish Credibility

Why do so many of the most respected business pros make sure that their names appear on books, articles, and other information products? Because having their names on a dust jacket, the byline of a white paper, or an audiotape training course has a way of convincing people that they know what they're talking about.

The added prestige of being an information-product developer lends you the kind of credibility that allows you to increase your hourly rates and project fees. Information products also let prospects sample your approach, your expertise, and your skills before they hire you. Businesses that produce and market information products regularly report that prospects not only buy those products, but also are more likely to inquire about additional products and services.

Expand Your Market

If you're a practitioner selling customized services to individual clients, you're excluding people who can't afford to hire you one-on-one. You are also limited to working with those in your immediate geographic area.

Turning your expertise into a product lets you serve all those potential customers who can't afford your personal-consulting rates, or who live outside the area you can easily travel to. You can expand your market because your information products provide a range of options at different price points. A small service business, for instance, could offer a one-on-one consulting package priced in the thousands of dollars, an online training course for a few hundred dollars, and a book priced below twenty dollars.

The result is a business that has "something for everyone," and converts many smaller prospects, who would otherwise pass you by, into paying customers. And although you make less per sale on these clients than you would for in-person service, you can make many more such sales.

What Products Are Best for You?

Here are some of the most common information products, along with production tips and suggestions for including them in your *slightly famous* marketing strategy.

REAL-WORLD SUCCESS STORY

David Garfinkel Gains Independence and Respect

David Garfinkel, president of Overnight Marketing, is a long-time copywriter who became an information product entrepreneur. Garfinkel developed information products related to his copywriting expertise because he knew that many business marketers wanted to learn to be better copywriters.

His home-study copywriting course included an audiocassette album and workbook. He also created a Web-based tutorial, and wrote an e-book devoted to advertising headlines. Garfinkel then partnered with others to get the word out, and created an online marketing campaign. "I put together structured sessions that teach people how to be their own copywriter; I give them what they need to know to do what I do.

Garfinkel credits his information products with helping him establish a widespread Internet reputation. "My information products have positioned me as a go-to guy about selling information online," says Garfinkel. "People also want to joint venture with me for projects.

"Having products puts you into a whole other category. You are seen as an instant guru. Not only do you get more respect, people don't argue about your prices or question your abilities. I now pick and choose my clients, and almost all of my prospects come through the reach and reputation I've established with my information products."

Booklets

Producing a booklet is one of the simplest ways to turn your knowledge into a saleable object that is easy to create, and inexpensive to produce and distribute. In particular, the ever-popular "tips" booklet is easy to write, and suited to almost any business topic. A common 8.5" by 3.5" booklet, which fits easily into a standard business envelope, can be produced for less than a dollar a copy, and sold for anywhere from three to ten times that amount.

The process of creating such a booklet is simple. You choose a subject and title (such as 151 Travel Tips or 20 Ways to Keep Your Car New), and jot down every fact and idea that comes to mind about that topic. After you have accumulated enough material to fill an eight- or 16-page booklet, group your tips under appropriate headings, and create a table of contents. There you are.

REAL-WORLD SUCCESS STORY

Paulette Ensign's Booklet Journey

In 1991, long-time professional organizer Paulette Ensign, now the president of Tips Products International, spotted an offer for a free booklet called *117 Ideas for Better Business Presentations*. Upon seeing it, her first reaction was, "I could knock out something like this about organizing tips."

Ensign began collecting ideas for a booklet about business and household organizing tips. The result was not one but two 16-page tip booklets, *110 Ideas for Organizing Your Business Life* and *111 Ideas for Organizing Your Household*. Ensign printed 250 copies of each.

She sent review copies of her booklets to magazines and newspapers, inviting them to use excerpts as long as they included an invitation to readers to send her $3 plus a self-addressed stamped envelope for the booklet. Several publications accepted her offer, and the orders started dribbling in.

Ensign continued to cast "seeds" all over the place, targeting publications through library directories. In February 1992, a 12-page biweekly newsletter with 1.6 million readers ran nine lines of copy about one of her booklets, which resulted in 5,000 orders.

"I distinctly remember the day I went to my post office box and found a yellow slip in my box that said, 'see clerk.' There was a tub of envelopes that had arrived that day, about 250 envelopes as I recall, all with $3 in them."

Some "very wonderful" things began to happen as Ensign sold her booklets. A seminar company hired her to record an audio program based on her booklet. A manufacturer's representative ordered hundreds of booklets to send to his customers, and she began licensing reprint rights, including one deal with a mail order catalog company that resulted in an agreement to print 250,000 copies.

If you're a proficient editor and designer, you can prepare the whole piece for the printer, but for most businesspeople some production help at this point is probably in order.

Video, Audio, and CD-ROM

Audio and video products are well suited to presenting certain kinds of information, and can deliver benefits by allowing prospects to see and hear

REAL-WORLD SUCCESS STORY

New World Library Publishes Print and Audio

New World Library offers a model that many small and mid-size publishers would be happy to emulate. With a strong line of self-help, inspirational, and New Age titles, the company's audio line brings in 15 to 20 percent of their total sales revenue. Over the years they have had two titles that sold over a quarter of a million copies in audio: Shakti Gawain's *Creative Visualization*, with steady sales over almost 20 years, and Deepak Chopra's *The Seven Spiritual Laws of Success*, which sold that many in less than three years.

With rare exceptions, the audio line is adapted from books that the company has originated. All the presenting is done by authors, and while New World Library jobs out the recording, the editing is done in-house. A major key to their success with audio has been their ability to promote a book and its audio version as a package. Finding it difficult to promote a stand-alone audio cost-effectively, the company includes both print and audio versions in every advertisement, listing, and press release. Author appearances naturally help in the sales of both products.

For both print and audio distribution, New World Library works with Publishers Group West, and even though retailer orders go through wholesalers, the company supports retail sales through active marketing efforts. They mail almost 4,000 catalogs to bookstores, New Thought churches, and specialty shops, and have identified a core list of about 700 stores that account for most of their business. In addition to the retail sales, New World Library actively pursues other markets for their audio line. They license audio rights to audio clubs such as Columbia House, Audio Book Club, and Doubleday Direct, and they sell to direct mail catalog houses such as Audio Editions and Audio Adventures.

New World Library's success in the audio field reflects consistently high-quality content in a subject area that has been popular since the inception of spoken-word audio, and steady efforts at marketing. Above all, they have built up a niche identity that serves them well in either format. Publishers considering their own line of audio must attend to these factors.

Excerpted from *The Complete Guide to Book Marketing* by David Cole (Allworth Press)

you. Selling for prices ranging from $29 to $99, audiotapes can be highly profitable. Videos are usually priced between $30 and $150, but cost more to produce. A commonly sold form of audio is the taped talk recorded live at a workshop. While not always of the highest sound quality, these tapes are great ways to convey information in an easy-to-absorb format, and it's a format that people have learned to rely on.

Izzy Kalman, a school psychologist and psychotherapist, developed an audiotape called "How to Stop Being Teased and Bullied without Really Trying," which he sells from his website for $19.95. The tape is a way for Kalman to offer low-priced help to children and their families, bring in some income, and cultivate potential clients.

Special Reports and Downloadable Files

Tip sheets and special reports provide highly specific, immediately usable information. They are also profitable and easy to produce. An environmental consultant, for example, could compile a tip sheet listing businesses that sell office furniture made from recycled materials. That consultant could also develop a special report titled "Reducing Indoor Air Pollution by Going Green," which could be sold from a Website or used as a marketing and sales tool.

Creating tip sheets and special reports is relatively easy. Tip sheets can be easily produced in a word-processing program, and reproduced on a laser printer. Special reports, which can run anywhere from five to sixty pages, go into greater depth about a subject, and can be sold or given away as marketing incentives.

As the number of potential clients and customers with Internet access increases, tip sheets and reports are increasingly being distributed as electronic files. Distributing information by e-mail and posting on Websites is convenient for everyone. Information providers eliminate the need to print and mail documents, and recipients enjoy instant access to information that might take several days to arrive by mail.

E-Books

Homer McDonald, a long-time marriage counselor in San Antonio, Texas, spent years dreaming of seeing his name on a book jacket. He specialized

REAL-WORLD SUCCESS STORY

PinkMonkey Sells Downloads to College Students

A relatively new Web-based business, PinkMonkey.com (www.pinkmonkey .com), is now selling downloadable Literature Notes (study guides similar to the well-known *Cliffs Notes*), *Test Preparation Guides*, and *Course Guides* ("concise reviews of introductory-level course work such as Biology, Chemistry, Physics, Algebra, Geometry, Trigonometry, Calculus, Economics, Statistics, US History, World History, Government and more"). Files are stored and downloaded in PDF (Portable Document Format), a popular format for all kinds of Internet documents; it is read with Adobe's Acrobat Reader, a program available free via the Web. Both Windows-based PCs and Macs can access these files. The materials are competitively priced, easy to access, easy to download, and easy to pay for via credit card.

Free from the burden of maintaining a printed-book inventory, and serving a technologically sophisticated student audience, this company offers a model for creating electronic materials that may well compete successfully with their printed counterparts. PinkMonkey also benefits from the fact that the materials they are selling are relatively short, thus avoiding both the present resistance to reading book-length materials on-screen, and the need to print out a full-length book.

Excerpted from *The Complete Guide to Book Marketing* by David Cole (Allworth Press)

in working with couples on the brink of divorce, and he knew that a lot of people would like to know more about his successful strategies for avoiding marital breakups.

But when McDonald's marketing consultant, Dean Jackson, suggested that he might be better served by writing an e-book about his subject area that could be sold from his website, he was intrigued. In a period of 40 days, they distilled McDonald's years of experience into an e-book called *Stop Your Divorce*, which they sold as a downloadable file from www.stopyourdivorce.com.

Through search-engine key-word strategies, and partnerships with other divorce-related websites, since 1988 McDonald has sold over ten thousand copies of his e-book at $79 each. Not only was the book profitable, it has

REAL-WORLD SUCCESS STORY

Jim Edwards Teaches Home Sellers to Go It Alone

Jim Edwards had spent eight years as a mortgage broker when his wife suggested that he write a book about what he had learned. He considered approaching a major publisher, but ended up writing an e-book based on his real estate expertise. He called it *Selling Your Home Alone*.

Edwards set up a Web site devoted to the book that included a sales letter clearly explaining the benefits. Then, he used a number of devices to drive traffic to his Web site, including search-engine key-word strategies, joint ventures, and pay-per-click ads.

"In 1997, when I put my first book on the Internet, I had absolutely no clue what was going to happen," says Edwards. "Five years later, this same e-book sells consistently month after month, and now makes enough money to cover my house payment, two car payments, and the electric bill!"

Edwards emphasizes these elements in the creation and marketing of a successful e-book:

- Target your audience clearly.
- Find out exactly what they want and need that's not offered elsewhere.
- Help readers get quick results.
- Put your e-book on CD-ROM to distribute offline.
- Learn everything you can about marketing online, and be ready to adapt.

helped him convert a hefty percentage of book buyers to paying clients. "Some subjects beg to be sold online," says Jackson, the co-author. "Because our market niche is so specialized, and because we discovered that people on the brink of divorce seek help online, we did quite well developing this as an e-book."

Although e-books can be extremely profitable, they don't carry the credibility of a conventionally published book. Also, because they are outside the mainstream book distribution system, there are only a few places, other than your own Web site, where e-books can be marketed. Nevertheless, e-books, especially as problem-solvers, have shown they can work. Successful e-books have been published that address financial issues, relationships, emergencies, and emotional distress.

If you are self-publishing, e-books also offer some major advantages——no printing bills, no trucking, no packaging, no postage, and, at least for now, no sales tax. Readers get instant delivery. To create e-books, you merely need to convert your finished manuscript into a Web-acceptable format, such as PDF, HTML, or RTF files. These files can be read by most computer users right on their screens, and printed out on their own printers if they wish. As noted earlier, a popular program, Adobe Acrobat, is compatible with both Macs and PCs, and allows authors to encrypt e-books to avoid piracy.

Books

Having your name on a book can be an immense boost to your business. Of all information products, a book has the greatest potential to open doors.

"A book provides you with more credibility than anything else you can do: more credibility than an audiotape, a videotape, a seminar, a screenplay, or a song," says self-publishing expert Dan Poynter. "People place a higher value on a book than on a tape—even though the same amount of work may have gone into their production. The fact is, authors are highly valued in our society."

After spending 16 years working as a flight attendant for a major airline, Elliot Hester recounted his experiences in a book with plenty of attitude and self-deprecating humor, *Plane Insanity: A Flight Attendant's Tales of Sex, Rage, and Queasiness at 30,000 Feet.*

"My plan was to start as a travel writer, because I had free flights," says Hester. "I wrote stories about the places I'd traveled to, and sold them to several newspapers. Later, I used my work to land a travel column for Salon.com."

After his book was published, Elliott appeared as a guest on more than 150 radio talk shows, including *Fresh Air, The Savvy Traveler, The Today Show*, and *Inside Edition*. His success also helped him land a second book deal that paid him to travel around the world for a year, and chronicle his journey.

Finding a Publisher While certainly the info-product with the most status, a book is also the most difficult to develop. The traditional route is to go through a publisher who handles production, marketing, promotion, and distribution. Although publishing your book through a high-profile publishing house carries a lot of credibility, it's not a guaranteed road to riches. It takes a long time for your book to hit the shelves, and for most books royalty payments are usually small and slow to arrive.

Just to be considered, you must write a detailed book proposal, a table of contents, sample chapters, and a market overview. You will also need to develop a marketing plan for your book that addresses the competition; makes a case for you, the author; and outlines what you will do to promote the book once it's on the shelves. You then pitch the proposal to potential publishers on your own or through a commissioned agent.

If a publisher decides to take you on, as a first time author who is unknown, you will probably receive an advance against future sales in a range of $2,000 to $10,000. After the book is completed, you can expect to see it in print in 12 to 18 months. Payment to authors comes from royalties, typically 10-15 percent of the publisher's net revenue from the book, payable twice a year.

Big New York publishers are good at getting books into bookstores; they have sales reps who visit the stores, and a well-established pipeline. But even if you've placed your book with one of them, you will need to put forth a lot of personal effort promoting your book. Large publishers devote most of their promotional resources to their superstar authors whose books are likely to sell hundreds of thousands of copies. If their books are not to disappear in a frighteningly short time, lesser-name authors must usually fend for themselves.

For most authors with a specialized topic, the best bet is to look for a publisher with a history of publishing on that topic. A specialty publisher who is focused on your niche will already have established relationships with the people you most want to reach, and your book will be a more valued asset to that publisher. To find these specialized publishers, check your own bookshelf, and go to a library or bookstore to consult *Books in Print*, a multi-volume reference listing all the books that are currently available for sale.

REAL-WORLD SUCCESS STORY

Nancy Mueller Learns the Work, and Payoff, of Publishing a Book

Cross-cultural communications specialist Nancy Mueller had been conducting workshops about international business for many years when she decided that a book about finding work overseas would bolster her credibility.

Mueller bought a book about writing book proposals, followed its advice, and contacted an agent. While the agent was enthusiastic about the project, he couldn't convince any of the top ten publishers to publish it. Not one to give up easily, Mueller started searching on her own. She eventually found a small publisher and landed a book contract for *Work Worldwide*.

"Even though finding a publisher and writing my book was a lot of work, it's established my credibility and positioned me as a global career expert," says Mueller. "The media regularly call me, and I appear in newspaper articles and radio interviews. My book is like a business card that makes selling myself easier. Being an author means I get taken much more seriously.

"I found that there weren't good resources about international career strategies, and it was a subject I obviously knew very well," recalls Mueller. "I felt my how-to approach was different enough from other books on the subject that a book would go over well."

The Self-Publishing Alternative According to Dan Poynter, author of *The Self-Publishing Manual,* self-publishing has many advantages over traditional publishing, the most compelling being greater financial returns for the author. "When you self-publish, you keep all the profits," says Poynter. "Additionally, you get into print quickly, own the copyright, and take all applicable tax breaks.

"Self-publishing is good business. But aspiring authors need to realize that while writing a book is a creative act, selling it is a business," says Poynter. "Some people can do both, while others are more creative than businesslike. You have to ask if you want to be a publisher. Do you have an office, the time to conduct the business, and a place to store the books?"

While authors often feel there is greater prestige in being published by an established firm, this is an argument that self-publishing advocates dis-

REAL-WORLD SUCCESS STORY

Robert W. Bly on Why Every Guru or Would-Be Guru Should Write a Book

Robert W. Bly, a direct mail copywriting expert and author of 50 books, became a widely recognized marketing expert largely by writing and publishing books on his area of expertise. "I tell virtually every self-employed professional, as well as many small business owners, to define their niche specialty, write a book about it, and get it published," says Bly.

"Nothing has been as helpful in establishing my own career and generating a steady flow of business than the many books I have written on my specialties of direct marketing, business communication, and more recently, Internet marketing."

Bly points out that writing a book is part of larger strategy that brings a host of benefits. Here's what he says:

• In writing a book on a subject, you are forced to do additional research to fill gaps in your knowledge. Your knowledge therefore increases, making you a better authority to your clients.

• Writing a book also requires you to organize your material in logical sequence.

• Doing so increases clarity of presentation in all your communications, including individual consultations with clients.

• A book can serve as the basis for a profitable seminar or workshop. The chapters of the book become modules of the seminar.

• Potential clients who read your book will call you to inquire about the services you offer, and will be predisposed to hire you.

• Associations will ask you to speak at their conferences for handsome fees if you are the author of a book that interests their members.

• Listing yourself as the author of a book is an impressive credential on your Web site, brochure, and other marketing materials. It increases your status.

miss. "No one cares who published your book," says Poynter. "Nobody goes around saying: 'I love HarperCollins books. I buy everything they publish.' Potential buyers want to know if a book will solve their problem and whether the author is a credible person. They never ask who is the publisher."

You can give copies of your book to potential clients to familiarize them with your methodology and convince them that you are an expert in your field.

• You may be called upon to serve as an expert witness on your topic in court cases, at a handsome day rate.

• Editors will ask you to contribute articles to their publications.

• The media will want to interview you as an expert in your field. This can lead to appearances as a guest on radio and television shows.

"I specialize in writing direct mail packages," says Bly. "A few clients began asking me to write Internet direct mail and e-mail marketing campaigns. I liked this niche segment of Internet marketing for several reasons. And it has less competition than Web site development, which was already overcrowded."

Seeing an opportunity, Bly wrote a proposal for a book on Internet direct mail. He sent it to one of his publishers, NTC Business Books, and they gave him a contract to write the book. "During the next six months, I wrote e-mail marketing campaigns for clients. I read everything I could get my hands on about e-mail marketing. I also interviewed numerous e-mail marketing experts and users about what was working for them to research the book. And of course I wrote the book," says Bly.

The result? He became the foremost authority on Internet direct marketing.

"I now knew how to do it, and was doing it, at nice fees, for both new and existing clients," says Bly. "The interviews I had done, which I would not have gotten had I not been writing the book, showed me techniques that increased the effectiveness of my e-mail campaigns. And when the book was published, it cemented my reputation as a leading copywriter in the e-mail marketing field. Many factors contributed, but the book was certainly the catalyst and driving force that gained me early entry into this new niche market."

Excerpted from *Become a Recognized Authority in Your Field*, Robert W. Bly (Alpha Books)

On the downside, self-publishing can be expensive. You pay up front for all the production and distribution costs, and if your book doesn't sell, you'll be stuck with the leftover inventory. However, if your book is successful, you'll not only have the satisfaction and advantages of being a published author, you'll make more money.

Marketing and Selling Information Products

If there's a real need for certain information, and you do a good job of addressing that need with an info-product, that product will sell. Develop a plan tailored to your own goals and disposition. Be realistic and start small. Consider your available time, long-term goals, and production budget before embarking on any information product.

Test the Waters

Don't fall in love with your idea for a book, booklet, or tape series at the expense of the most important part of any successful info-product—a qualified, targeted market that is likely to purchase the product. According to Gordon Burgett, author of *Publishing to Niche Markets*, targeting means knowing specifically who will buy your product, why, how much they will spend (and won't), how they will hear about it, and what your promotion must say to get prospects to make a purchase.

Ask a lot of questions. Contact associations, editors of industry newsletters and magazines, and others who are intimately acquainted with your market. Talk to people who represent your typical buyers to determine their degree of interest in your proposed products, and make sure you have ways to reach them that are effective and affordable.

Price your products to be profitable, but not in excess of the value that customers will perceive in them. Know your costs. Study the marketplace. Ask around. Find out what similar products are going for and determine how your prospective product compares.

Promotion Ideas

Announce your products to your existing client base. List them on your Web site. Create flyers, and include them in all your mailings. Take samples with you to networking events, trade shows, and speaking engagements. As you conduct your daily business, look for every opportunity to announce your products to the world. For instance, you can:

REAL-WORLD SUCCESS STORY

Earthworks Press Customizes Books for Utility Companies

Earthworks Press, the publisher of the bestselling *50 Simple Things You Can Do to Save the Earth*, provides an immensely successful example of how to package a book for premium sales.

Having already sold a huge number of their lead title for premium use by companies that wanted to be identified as environmentally sensitive—mostly in response to inquiries from the companies themselves—Earthworks decided to develop spin-off titles for industries in particular need of educational and promotional materials.

At the top of Earthworks' target list were energy companies. Earthworks knew that these companies had been mandated by their governing utility commissions to allot money for conservation projects, and were in need of appropriate materials. With this need in mind, Earthworks approached their regional energy supplier, Pacific Gas & Electric, with two prospective titles, *30 Simple Energy Things You Can Do to Save the Earth* and *25 Simple Things Kids Can Do to Save Energy*. Earthworks offered PG&E the opportunity to customize the books for their audience, developed a working relationship, and eventually wrote an order for 500,000 books.

Building on this success, Earthworks' special marketing staff then made cold calls to over 100 energy suppliers and simply asked for the person in charge of environmental affairs. They used the book developed in conjunction with PG&E as an introduction, and ultimately made sales to about 25 companies, with orders ranging from 5,000 copies to 500,000 copies.

Each company received custom-produced books of either 64 or 80 pages, and paid a price per copy that depended on the quantity they ordered, and how much the book was customized for their use. Since the energy suppliers used the books as part of their educational efforts—giving them away free to customers, at Earth Day fairs, in school programs, and at appliance centers—none of the books carried a cover price, nor were they ever sold through retail outlets.

Excerpted from *The Complete Guide to Book Marketing* by David Cole (Allworth Press)

- Sell products "back of the room" at speaking engagements.
- Sell products through workshops.
- List your products in catalogs and directories.

- Sell through dealers and wholesalers.
- Solicit volume sales to trade associations, book clubs, and busines groups.
- Cross-promote products with those from other businesses.
- Cultivate free media exposure for your products, saving you money in promotional expenses. But remember, you need a news angle.

"The simple fact that your book or other information product is newly published doesn't make it news," says David Cole, author of *The Complete Guide to Book Marketing*. "To turn your information product into a newsworthy item, you need to develop a hook on which you can hang your story—something that people want to talk about, hear about, and read about."

Position your products within the larger context of the overall topic or problem they address. If you can tailor your products to the needs and interests of particular media audiences, you can get your info-products into the public eye without spending a fortune on advertising. Write articles based on the subject of your information products. This is a way to get a free mention of your products along the way in trade and business publications, association newsletters, and Web sites.

Get your products reviewed by the media. If you have a book, e-book, or anything that may be of interest to the public, send it, with a brief cover letter, to editors in charge of reviews at appropriate newspapers and magazines. Favorable reviews serve as third-party endorsements for your info-products.

Expand Your Offerings

Once you distill your wisdom into a book, booklet, or audiocassette, look for ways to broaden your product line. Go deeper into a subject with products that command a higher price, or round out an expensive product offering with a handful of reports or tip sheets. Your goal is to maximize your income by offering your knowledge at many price points, so as to have something for every need and budget.

With a website, you can develop an affiliate marketing strategy to get other businesses to help you sell your products by agreeing to sell theirs on

EXECUTIVE BRANDING

Books Are Amy James' Best Calling Card

Amy James, a third-generation educator and former social studies teacher, is an expert on the federal No Child Left Behind Act. She founded her Oklahoma City consulting firm, SixThings, in 2000 to help textbook publishers comply with state and federal curriculum guidelines.

In 2003, she published the first of the *Knowledge Essentials* book series to help parents understand the No Child Left Behind Act (NCLB). James was inspired to write the book series when she discovered there were no books on NCLB compliance. She wrote a book proposal, hired an agent who submitted her proposal for *Knowledge Essentials* to several publishers, and was awarded a seven-book contract by Jossey-Bass Publishers, a division of Wiley.

Now, with the series completed, she credits her books and her author status with growing her consulting practice from $100,000 to $2 million in annual revenues.

"I received my book contract because of my deep expertise in educational standards," says James. "When I published the books, it validated my expertise and elevated my status as a thought leader in my field. Becoming a CEO and published author has established SixThings' reputation as the expert on national education standards. Our credibility has skyrocketed, and our clients feel that our company deeply understands our subject area," says James.

---

your website. Affiliate programs are commission-based sales programs that can produce additional income streams. When you sign up as an affiliate or reseller, you can earn money for doing—well, just about nothing other than maintaining your Web site, which you were doing anyway.

James' growing status as an industry expert attracts media exposure, and she's been quoted in prominent publications including *Parent, Parenting, Child, Nick Jr., Scholastic, Good Housekeeping, Business Week,* and *Entrepreneur.* Her books led to appearances on Oklahoma City's CBS television affiliate, where she appears every month to discuss education-related topics.

"A book delivers instant credibility that can rocket a company to the top of its industry," says James, who says that executives should not be discouraged by the prospect of writing a book. "Executives are busy, but with planning, patience, and working with professional writers, even the busiest executive can write and publish a book."

While she wrote every word of her first book, James now works with professional ghostwriters. "There are certain chapters in every book I write on my own. But, there's plenty of material I outsource, sometimes to other highly qualified experts. If an executive approaches writing a book methodically and consistently, it is very manageable."

13 Strategic Partnerships

Everywhere from corporate boardrooms to Main Street America, savvy businesses are partnering with related businesses, even competitors, to forge mutually beneficial alliances.

According to *The Economist*, alliances now account for 18 percent of the revenues of America's biggest companies. Strategic partnerships can include co-op advertising, cross-promotions, sponsorships, and cause-related marketing. And while each represents a different twist on the concept, all involve combining the efforts of two or more organizations to enhance the results for all those who participate.

Whether partnering with a manufacturer, members of your local merchants association, or a company that offers products or services complementary to your own, the potential to form profitable relationships is around you all the time, and can become a core element of your *slightly famous* marketing strategy.

Partnering can help you create inroads into new markets by combining your skills, resources, and capabilities with those of other businesses. When Susan Grant, an executive recruiter in San Francisco, decided she wanted to tap into the biotechnology industry for clients, she looked around for professionals in related service fields who were already established within the sector, and would be open to joint marketing efforts. She hooked up with Carol Cherkis, a mergers and acquisitions consultant, and the two decided to collaborate on articles for relevant industry trade publications. They developed topics that needed their combined expertise, and pitched them as a team to those publications. The result was an article co-authored for *Pharmaceutical Executive* magazine, titled "Mergers & Acquisitions: Plugging the Brain Drain."

Consider your own business challenges. Maybe there are business expenses you can share with others: for instance, warehouse equipment or administrative costs. Or perhaps, like Susan Grant, you can partner with another professional to reach prospects for both your businesses. Sometimes you can ride on the coattails of another, already established business to build market awareness and credibility.

Where do you find potential partners? Talk to your suppliers to identify worthwhile businesses that already serve your target market. Ask trade associations, chambers of commerce, and the Better Business Bureau; talk to board members and staffers who are knowledgeable about your industry. Once you identify businesses that serve your market, look for ways to pool talent, capital, and experience to reach mutually beneficial ends.

Partnering with Competitors

For some, partnering with competitors is akin to sleeping with the enemy, but others have made it work for them. You can enjoy competitive alliances that are both emotionally rewarding and financially profitable. Competitive partnerships can sometimes open up opportunities for creating synergy and enjoying a larger potential marketplace. Such was the case with the Sonoma County Woodworkers Association mentioned in Chapter 1.

TIPS FROM THE GURU

Ed Rigsbee on Creating Successful Partnerships

Strategic alliances are commonplace among large corporations, helping them successfully compete in the global marketplace. Smaller companies can derive the same advantages of strategic partnerships by building win/win relationships with other businesses.

"The key is finding partners with the same core values before you start building a relationship," says Rigsbee. "You need to help your partner develop emotional ownership in the partnership. Without emotional ownership, any commitment will rest on a shaky foundation."

Rigsbee compares the act of establishing long-term relationships with partners to forging a strong and enduring marriage. To ensure that your partner relationships are built on a solid foundation, Rigsbee offers the following pointers.

The getting-married jitters. You must successfully deal with the fears and issues in synergistic alliance partnering. Sensitivity and understanding of your potential partner's situation are crucial at this juncture. Talk about both the upside and the downside with your intended partner. Talk about how you might deal with the relationship if things do not work out. Plan an exit strategy. Getting fears and issues out on the table rather than hiding them in the dark will serve all involved well.

Where are you going to live? Discuss your individual and combined marketing areas. Selecting the alliance's geographic marketing area and the service/product mix is no easy task. You'll need to pay close attention to both the small and large issues. Might you share warehousing or delivery facilities, or possibly even employees, to overcome personnel conflicts?

Who does the chores? Allocation of alliance partner responsibilities will make or break the relationship. Too often this is the area where unrealistic expectations of one another manifest themselves. Be clear about who will be doing what, and put it in writing. It is too easy to forget your commitments six months, a year, or a decade later.

Time to tie the knot. The partnering agreement should be in writing. It should contain detailed explanations of the authority, expectations, and responsibilities of each partner. This document will be your road map for a successful alliance relationship. When in doubt, you can refer to this "Partnering Charter."

Oh no, divorce! You tried, but it didn't work out. This sometimes happens. No reason to feel like a failure, or declare that you'll never again be in a relationship. In dealing with separation issues, be the bigger person, and again meet your partner more than halfway. Otherwise the rage and anger will fester, and you will become embittered. If there is "community property," dispose of it fairly.

The "Group of 8" Contributes to All Its Members

When eight professional speakers needed a way to get speaking leads, they put their heads together. The result was the "Group of 8," an informal leads exchange group consisting of eight professionals who meet regularly by phone to share leads and business development strategies.

"We take turns interviewing one another on an individual basis," says Mandi Stanley of Mandi Stanley Speaker Services in Memphis, Tennessee. "The idea is to spend about 30 quality minutes on the phone and find out the who, what, when, where, why, and how of each other's businesses, so that we intimately understand each other's areas of expertise."

Even though all members are professional speakers, and are nominally competitors, they still find plenty of opportunities to share leads with one another. "Even though we're all speakers, we do not speak about the same topics, and have different areas of expertise," says San Francisco-based Romanus Wolter of Kick Start Your Dream. "There is some overlap, but we are all different enough that it's not like anyone is stepping on anyone's toes."

The group meets every three weeks by telephone conference call to commiserate, brainstorm, and share tips and leads about potential speaking engagements. Between calls, members send one another information and leads about speaking opportunities as they arise. Even though members are spread around the country, they schedule time for personal connections with one another at national speakers' conferences and other events.

"Because the speaking industry is filled with so many potential opportunities, more than any one of us could keep track of individually, we alert one another to opportunities we'd miss otherwise," says Christine Holton Cashen. "One of our members is from Canada, and has introduced us to a number of Canadian associations where speaking opportunities exist. This is an area that many of us would probably not have explored on our own."

Setting up strategic partnerships with similar businesses can also help you target larger accounts. This is what a cabinet manufacturer did when his company was given a chance at what was for him a huge contract from Disney World. The problem was that he lacked the resources to complete the job within the required ninety-five days. The solution was a strategic alliance with three of his competitors that enabled him to land and complete the $2.5 million contract—something he could never have done on his own.

Co-Branding Alliances

Co-branding is about marketing two or more complementary products together, thus allowing each partner to "piggyback" on the reputation of the other in an expanded marketplace. In a successful co-branding relationship, companies share costs and command more attention than either could individually.

Cross-Promotions: Working Together to Get the Word Out

Cross-promotional marketing strategies align businesses that serve the same target market, but do not directly compete with each other. Cross-promotional marketing helps you reach a larger audience with less money and effort by pooling resources—time, money, ideas, and contacts—with others.

"The goal of cross-promotional marketing is to reach more people, more frequently, with messages that position your product or service in favorable way," says Kare Anderson, author of *Walk Your Talk: Grow Your Business Faster Through Successful Cross-Promotional Partnerships*. "You are looking for partners who will help you do that."

Cross-promotional marketing can help you to:
- Stand out in a crowded marketplace.
- Conserve cash.
- Generate more reasons for customers to buy.
- Show support for community causes.
- Reach more prospects.
- Build credibility.

Anderson cites six local businesses that joined forces one Valentine's Day for a weeklong promotion. A bookstore hosted cooking demonstrations by the author of a book on romantic meals, using cookware from the local department store and food from a nearby deli. Finished meals were displayed, with

REAL-WORLD SUCCESS STORY

Ikeda's Country Market Co-Brands Itself up the Food Chain

Developing co-branding partnerships with a variety of businesses has helped Glen and Steve Ikeda, owners of Ikeda's Country Market and Ikeda's Tasty Burgers, grow their business well beyond its local roots. Nestled in the Sierra foothills of California with a modest 6,000 square feet of space, the company has built its annual revenues from $150,000 in 1970 to more than $4 million today.

The Ikedas' involvement with co-branding began when they started buying high-end produce from farms in the surrounding area. They approached Perry's Farms in Sacramento, which had developed a strong reputation for its tomatoes, and arranged to feature Perry's Farms tomatoes by name in their store while the Perry's Farms outlet store sold Ikeda products. It was an arrangement where each brand benefits from the reputation of the other. The Ikedas have also fostered relationships with many local restaurants and a gas station, and, much further afield, the Big Island Candy Company in Hilo, Hawaii, which all sell Ikeda food products.

Glen Ikeda offers advice to anyone considering a co-branding relationship: "Pick the right co-branding partner. Make sure it's someone who shares your commitment to quality and the co-branding concept. Then monitor the relationship to ensure your brand is used appropriately, and not exploited beyond the parameters of the agreement. Remember that it is your brand, and you are its steward."

offerings from the local florist, candy store, and card shop. There was even health information from the local Heart Association!

"Cross-promotion offers the most credible, cost-effective way to attract more customers while spending less," says Anderson. "The costs go down as the number of cross-promotional partners goes up."

The trick is to spot opportunities that already exist within your business network, your neighborhood, and your community.

Evaluating Your Cross-Promotional Quotient

If the examples given above have whetted your appetite enough to make you give these techniques a try, start by taking an inventory of the intangible assets that make you an appealing cross-promotional partner—your customer lists and relationships, your standing in the community, and your business location. If these have value for you, they will be valuable to other businesses as well.

Then look for equivalent assets in potential partners. There are probably businesses in your community with assets that can be put to work for you. The key is to forge complementary relationships based on common interests.

Look at things you already do to promote yourself. Cross-promotional teams pursue joint advertising campaigns, media events, and direct mailings. They offer discounts on each other's products and services, and hang signs or post flyers in one another's places of business. Seek partners who can help you strengthen your existing efforts, share your costs, and expand your customer base.

As with any marketing, understanding your customers is essential in cross-promotions. To spot ideal cross-promotional strategies and partners, you need to know what your customers do when they are not doing business with you. The better you understand your customers, the better you will be at identifying partners who complement your business. Your best allies are organizations and businesses that:

- Serve the same customers, but do not compete with you.
- Serve people you want to attract.
- Have a name that lends prestige, credibility, or other value for you.
- Have buying cycles that complement yours.
- Are involved in the same kinds of community activities or events.

Don't underestimate your value. If you've been in business for a while, you have probably developed solid relationships with your customers that can be of great value to other businesses. Take stock of everything about your business that can be leveraged to attract and forge cross-promotional partnerships. Also, learn to spot these qualities in potential partners. There are many businesses in your community that have similarly accrued value that can be put to work for you.

Here's a grab bag of cross-promotional possibilities for you and your partners to consider:

EXECUTIVE BRANDING

Solomon McCown Builds a Reputation through Organizing Panel Discussion

Helene Solomon, a principal in the Boston-based strategic communications firm Solomon McCown & Co., organizes an educational panel discussion series with the title, SM& Presents. Since 2003, the firm has organized seven panel events comprised of Solomon principals alongside guest experts, showcasing topics that align with the firm's expertise in strategic communications.

Solomon chose the panel discussion model because she saw an opportunity to establish relationships with prospects, referral partners, and influencers in targeted industries. "We cover a range of issues that position our principals as strategic thinkers to influential audiences," says Solomon. "We invite panelists with existing name recognition and an existing sphere of influence, which boosts the value of our events, enhances our own credibility, and creates audience and media appeal."

Each event reflects the firm's core focus area with a topic likely to resonate with potential clients. "As we conceive events, we apply a three-question test: What are our business objectives? What potential partners will lend credibility and a mailing list? Can we do something that no one else has done?" Solomon finds allies by researching business publications, trade associations and charitable organizations.

A recent SM& Presents panel titled, "Good Business Means Sometimes Having to Say I'm Sorry," featured Ashley McCown, SM& executive vice president, a partner from a Boston law firm, the vice president of an insurance firm, and a

---

- Print joint promotional messages on your cash-register receipts.
- Offer a reduced price, special service, or convenience if customers buy from both you and your partner.
- Hang signs or posters promoting one another on your walls, windows, or products.
- Drop one another's flyers in shopping bags.
- Pool mailing lists and send a joint promotional postcard.

principal of the American Red Cross. The publisher of *Massachusetts Lawyers Weekly* moderated the discussion.

"This event helped us reach a broad range of industries, from corporate CEOs, to health care, to attorneys who, when faced with a client crisis, recommend strategic communications firms," says Solomon. "Our partnership with Massachusetts Lawyers Weekly gave us access to their mailing list, which helped us reach the Boston legal community better and more cost-effectively than we could have on our own."

The event attracted 150 participants, a perfect number to facilitate networking, and was covered in the *Boston Globe* and the *Christian Science Monitor*. The event was so well received that it was repeated for the Health Care Section of the Massachusetts Bar Association and the Newton-Wellesley Hospital Leadership Forum.

Another event, "Standing Out in a Crowded Field: Attracting Resources to Meet the Ambitions of Today's Social Entrepreneurs," targeted Boston's local nonprofit community. Co-sponsored by the Association of Small Foundations, Root Cause Institute, Social Innovation Forum and United Way of Massachusetts Bay, the discussion focused on the current state of philanthropy and the pros and cons of applying business models to nonprofits.

"This one-hour program attracted 200 attendees and established our firm as thought leaders before targeted audiences," says Solomon. "I developed high-level connections with great partners and referral sources, and was invited to take part in another panel featuring a former Massachusetts gubernatorial candidate. We're now planning subsequent panels that leverage Web 2.0 technologies to create a blog or series of podcasts on social entrepreneurship."

- Promote partners' products during their slow times, and ask them to do the same for you.
- Share inexpensive ads in local shopping papers or a nonprofit event program.
- Give a joint interview to local media.
- Put one another's promotional messages on counter stands or floor stands in waiting areas.

REAL-WORLD SUCCESS STORY

How a Travel Agent Cross-Promoted Her Way to Radio Stardom

Fanny Pettijohn, owner of Malachi Travel Group in South Field, Michigan, learned how creative thinking can lead to huge rewards when she orchestrated a very successful cross-promotion with a local radio station. "I worked for 20 years at the Bahamas Tourist Office. But when I went into business for myself, selling leisure and incentive travel, I quickly learned I'd have to create my own opportunities—that I'd literally have to go out and make things happen."

In the dead of the Detroit winter, Pettijohn seized the moment. She contacted the sales manager of a local radio station, and pitched a jointly sponsored listener-appreciation contest offering free trips to Jamaica.

"I needed to get my name out to my community, and radio seemed to be the best way to do that," says Pettijohn. "I told the station manager I would assemble a team that included the radio station (who would give free advertising), a Jamaican tour company (who covered airfare), the Jamaica Tourist Board, and a hotel that provided accommodations."

The results were phenomenal. The highly publicized event was promoted on the radio every morning for a full month. The station gained listeners, and the tour operator and the tourist office got tons of valuable exposure and thousands of dollars worth of advertising they could not have afforded on their own.

For Pettijohn, the promotion landed dozens of new customers. "At the time, it was really cold here in Detroit," recalls Pettijohn. "Listeners would call in and say, 'I don't mind that I didn't win, I just want to go to Jamaica.' I got dozens of leads. Even employees at the radio station wanted to go. I got that business as well. And because the promotion was so successful, the radio station became a client. I now get all their incentive business."

• Train your staff to mention how your partner's products can be used with yours.

• Give a sample of your partner's product to your customers when they buy a large quantity of your product, and have your partner do the same with yours.

• Use door hangers, posters, flyers, or postcards to promote special offers for one another's products.

- Co-produce an in-store or office event—a demonstration, celebrity appearance, free service, or lecture.

Action Groups

One by one, twelve people connect to a conference call led by Terri Levine, founder of Comprehensive Coaching U in Philadelphia, Pennsylvania. Each then takes a turn reading a personal marketing scorecard, ranking progress on goals and acknowledging shortcomings. When somebody exceeds a goal such as an income projection, participants applaud and celebrate. If somebody has a problem, everyone offers advice.

What's going on here? It's a small-business marketing action group based on author C.J. Hayden's popular *Get Clients Now!™: A 28-Day Marketing Program for Professionals and Consultants*.

Two national bestselling books, *Your Money or Your Life* and *The Artist's Way*, helped launch goal-oriented groups that combine elements of book circles, support groups, and 12-step programs, but focusing on goals originally presented in these books. Taking a cue from the popularity of book study groups, business marketing action groups endeavor to organize people with common interests for their mutual benefit.

Groups such as these are a natural in the small business arena. Helping participants stay motivated with what could be called "benevolent peer pressure," they provide the motivation to establish and follow through on marketing and sales goals.

"I started my first action group a year and a half ago," says Levine. "But four months into the first program, I ran into Get Clients Now!, and saw the value of using a programmatic marketing book as a blueprint for the group. Now, the book is our common ground. Using a book has given the group more structure, and provided everyone the same common denominator."

Levine's action groups are now six months in duration, and meet each month for three 30-minute teleconference sessions. They're geared to service professionals dependent on self-promotion—financial planners, consultants, and freelance writers and designers—and focus on setting goals and achieving results based on specific steps.

"Every participant has their own agenda. Some are concentrating on getting prospects by making more cold calls; others are researching the Internet to develop an e-commerce strategy. When we get together, we review the actions participants committed to at the last meeting, as well as the results or where they got stuck. Participants then commit to new actions based on progress up to that point."

Action groups keep participants focused. "Many psychologists see affiliation as a primary motivational factor for human beings," says Hayden. "Through the act of associating with others on the same path, you can stay motivated to do what it takes to be successful."

Accountability is also at the heart of successful action groups. Members make commitments and share them with the group. At each session, members ask one another about the commitments, what they have accomplished since the last meeting, and what will come next.

"Your fellow team members expect you to follow through on goals you established. If you get stuck, they'll help you. But, if you keep showing up with excuses, they'll call you on it," she says.

Another bonus is support. "Having someone else to complain to or celebrate with delivers psychological and emotional rewards," says Hayden. "It's great to know others care about your progress. When you hit a roadblock, talking about it for a few minutes may be all you need to get back into action. And having people to share your success with makes it so much sweeter."

Annie Hammond, a professional business coach in Santa Cruz, California, says an action group made her feel that she was part of a greater effort. "It was helpful in terms of hearing the challenges people were having and also their breakthroughs," says Hammond. "If somebody else in the group is struggling and suddenly lands a client, it's very encouraging. And when you hear about the successes and failures of others, it helps you stay motivated, focused, and inspired."

Others feel being exposed to different points of view within a group breaks the isolation that often overcomes sole practitioners. "Just hearing your problem restated by another person gives you new insight," says Susan Schwartz, an image consultant in San Mateo, California. "A group lets you share ideas and test your assumptions. Bouncing ideas off others is a great way to brainstorm solutions."

Nancy Albu, a financial advisor in St. Catharine's, Canada, decided to form an action group after her office was directed to develop a sales plan, build prospect lists, design marketing materials, and establish better telephone techniques and a referral-generating process. "Frankly, none of us were marketers," she explains. "We were daunted by the enormity of the challenge and didn't know where to begin."

Based on her previous experiences in networking groups, Albu proposed an intra-office action group. "I said to everyone, 'Let's put our expertise together!' So we created a marketing action group comprising all twelve people in our office. Having this type of structure in place helped us chart our course, stay on track, and achieve our goals without having to reinvent the wheel."

A successful action group is built on the goals and commitments of those involved. Any group of people with similar goals can create a structure for working together. Members don't have to be in the same industry, and sometimes it's better if they aren't. It's amazing how much a freelance technical writer, for example, can contribute to a financial advisor, and vice versa.

A group can have as few as three people, but five to ten is better. Ideally, your group is small enough so that everyone has a chance to report at each meeting, but not so small that the group founders if some members drop out along the way, as often happens.

Some groups benefit from a professional leader. In others, members can take turns leading. In a peer-led group, the meeting leader has to be as strict as a professional would be; he or she has to begin and end sessions on time, and give everyone a chance to report. Leaders must not let members slide on commitments, and must allow time for all members to share successes and failures before focusing on particular issues or challenges chosen by members.

Group meetings can be structured as mini-workshops, focusing, for instance, on a subject as specific as how to market professional services to corporations. Alternatively, a group can spend time brainstorming solutions to challenges facing individual members. The key is that before the meeting ends, members need to commit to something specific they will accomplish before the next meeting.

14 Reach Out and Connect

A s a small business owner, you have to be personally involved in your marketing. You need to make human contacts that generate cooperation and referrals, and you must form a network of people who know you, trust you, and respect your business enough to recommend you to prospects when opportunities arise.

Why You Need to Network

Networking is an ongoing strategy, not something to do only when you need business. Networking keeps you visible. It cements your existing relationships with those who know you. Networking ensures that you come immediately to prospects' minds when they, or people they know, need the products or services you offer.

There is no substitute for human contact. The more you network, and the more distinctive you make yourself, the more you will be remembered and

REAL-WORLD SUCCESS STORY

Networking Reels In the Big Fish

R.A. Miller & Company, Inc., a consulting firm that works with food, beverage, chemical, and lubricant packagers, recently landed their first big contract: to modernize the packaging facilities of a multinational company. It was an entrepreneur's dream.

How did Roger Miller, the company president, reel in this big catch? Miller joined a high-profile trade association in his target market, the packaging industry, where he could meet the "movers and shakers" of that industry.

He didn't just join it; he got actively involved in the association. He volunteered to become a member of a high-profile committee, and worked on behalf of association members. This raised his visibility among key association executives, and helped Miller get to know his prospects personally. His involvement also helped him establish trust, while demonstrating his knowledge, expertise, and competence.

When a committee member heard of a large project where Roger's specific talents, industry experience, and knowledge were required, he recommended Roger to the ultimate decision-maker for the large project. This opened the door for Roger to meet with the client, make a presentation, present a quotation, and eventually get the project.

"For small businesses, rubbing shoulders with key decision-makers and developing a stream of high quality leads is one of the most effective ways to grow a business," says Miller.

recommended. Networking ensures that those who know you continue to connect with the person behind your *slightly famous* reputation.

Establish a Reputation

Though discussed under different headings, the importance of networking in building a reputation is addressed throughout this book. When you're speaking at a networking venue, discussing your business in a leads-exchange group, or working on a committee in a trade or service organization, you're establishing your reputation.

REAL-WORLD SUCCESS STORY

Susan RoAne on Networking as a Lifestyle

Susan RoAne, author of the bestselling book *How to Work a Room*, defines networking as a reciprocal process where people share ideas, leads, information, and support with each other, enhancing the personal and professional lives of everyone who participates.

"If your goal is to reach the most people who can genuinely make a difference to your business, you need to network," says RoAne. "Networking should be an ongoing strategy, not just something to do when you need the business. It should become a natural part of your life that's rooted in the idea of 'being neighborly' and helping others.

"Because this is a global economy, nobody is truly independent anymore," says RoAne. "If you only stay in your own cubicle, you're missing the opportunity to be part of the great word-of-mouth people can give you because they know you, like you, and trust you."

In researching *The Secrets of Savvy Networking and Networking: Beyond the Buzzword*, RoAne found traits common to great networkers, including:

• They treat people as people, not as prospects. Those who treat people as prospects are usually transparent and have a presence that screams, "I have an agenda!"

• They "goodmouth" people. Great networkers go out of their way to pass on nice things said by a third parties, such as, "Oh, I just talked to Joe Jones who said you are a gifted Web designer."

• They help others unconditionally. Great networkers give and they get, but they do not "give to get," which is manipulative.

• They don't view networking as an entitlement program. Great networkers know they're not entitled to the connections and contacts of others. They know they must earn access to relationships through their deeds.

According to RoAne, the best networkers are so natural in their approach that others don't even realize they're doing it. "Networking is not a numbers game," says RoAne. "It's not a spreadsheet activity you add to your to-do list. Networking is about taking down contrived barriers between business and life, and seeing opportunity everywhere."

Jose Mata of Adcom Worldwide, an international freight-forwarding service, built a reputation by giving seminars on international shipping and trade at local Small Business Administration offices, banks, and chambers of commerce. Mata's seminars have made him a resource for people thinking about starting import/ export companies.

"I always realized that the best way to find new prospects was to approach places where they congregate, and give away my expertise," says Mata. "This way, I position our business as a partner in the minds of seminar attendees. As a result, I enjoy a lot of referrals from businesses that have come to know and trust me."

The more Mata helps prospects understand his industry, the more people seek him out and refer prospects to him. Moreover, he's made many friends among conference organizers who know he has the participants' best interests in mind.

Get More Referrals

The most compelling reason to network is that you'll get more business through referrals. Networking inspires trust, and trust inspires people to refer business to you. The more people who meet you, like you, and trust you, the more relationships you'll develop among people inclined to refer business to you.

Even more important, referred customers come to you ready to do business. In most cases you don't need to educate them about the benefits of your products and services.

Even more important, a referral-based business is a stable business. A steady stream of word-of-mouth referrals means you never have to worry about where your next client or customer will come from. A business built on referrals has tremendous growth potential, as referrals in turn generate further referrals.

Bypass Competition

A loyal network of business contacts can put you in touch with business opportunities and introduce you to decision-makers.

Danna Yuhas, founder and president of the technology marketing and communications firm Market Impact, learned that a prospective client was

REAL-WORLD SUCCESS STORY

Networking Is Not a Dirty Word

Stephanie West Allen's business, Allen & Nichols Productions, offers humorous keynote addresses and training programs for corporations. Though informal networking has always come easy to her, networking specifically to grow made her uncomfortable. She particularly disliked the idea of being a salesperson.

"I've always been good at networking for non-business activities," says West Allen. "I enjoy meeting people and helping others when I can. But I just couldn't get over the uncomfortable feeling I had when I tried to network at business events."

The problem, she realized, was that she was approaching business networking in the wrong way, which led to negative connotations. "In the early days, I attended networking events trying to find as many people as possible to drown with information about my company," she recalls. "I did not feel all that comfortable networking, because I felt being pushy was a necessary evil of being in business."

At the same time, she began to notice that most of her business was coming from what she had considered non-business sources, including friends, colleagues, and former co-workers. These were people in her immediate circle who knew and trusted her. These were people with whom she had a relationship first, and from whom referrals followed only as a result.

"One of my friends was the director of the National Kidney Foundation," says West Allen. "Because we were friends and she knew my business, she invited me to speak at her association. Another friend referred me to speak on an educational cruise, and my ex-boss, a lawyer, hired us to come do a program."

Once she realized that networking was about making human contacts, not pushing her business aggressively, she became more comfortable with business networking and found it less of a chore. "This simple realization showed me that networking is not about going into a room full of strangers and pushing yourself on them. Now, I try to learn more about others, looking for ways to help them succeed."

And because she's seen as a genuinely helpful person, referrals come her way. "I initially thought networking meant you had to hard-sell strangers. Now my goal is to connect with others and form mutually supportive relationships, rather than trying to convince everyone I meet that they need me. I've found this to be more comfortable and also more effective."

looking for telemarketers. She referred one of her networking contacts, providing a vivid description of this person's eagerness and ability to sell.

Based on her referral, the company called her contact for an interview. "What is so amazing is that, with the exception of her exceptional selling abilities, this telemarketer did not have any of the other qualifications that were specified in the advertisement," recalls Yuhas. "The referral had allowed her to bypass the entire screening process, based on word-of-mouth and trust."

Targeted Networking

Before you try to meet as many people as possible, do your homework: devise a networking strategy likely to advance your business goals by putting you in touch with the best members of your target market.

Scott Testa, chief operating officer of Mindbridge.com, focused his company's networking efforts on profitable industries where they had an established track record. He drew from his experience in the financial services sector, and targeted credit unions through their trade organizations and other centers of influence within the credit union industry.

"We'd spend time at these association meetings; we'd meet prominent people within the industry, introduce ourselves, and demonstrate our track record with credit unions," says Testa. "Once we'd earned their trust, which was easy because we could point to relevant clients and press coverage, we'd ask for names of anyone that might want to learn more about our services."

Testa has successfully networked his way into several industries, including credit unions, financial services, non-profits, payroll companies, and banking. "When you become an industry insider and do a good job, word travels fast, and you become the preferred provider to that industry," says Testa. "We tapped into a sense of camaraderie that exists among members of our target markets."

Like Testa, spend your time networking in groups that will put you in touch with the right people. Here are some different venues to consider:

General Business Organizations General business organizations are as eager to find you as you are to find them. To identify the right organizations, check your library; search the Internet; talk to your peers, clients, and customers; and read the business pages of your newspaper.

Once you've identified a few likely sounding organizations, do some investigative homework before you join. Attend a couple of meetings. Talk to members and read issues of the organization's newsletter. Look for opportunities to get involved that match your goals and expertise, and that will show off your talents and abilities. Only when you're sure the organization will promote your business interests with key contacts in your industry should you become a member.

Associations There are associations for just about every interest, industry, and profession in existence. These groups provide some of your best networking opportunities because they are tightly focused on a specific set of interests or problems, and if your business serves those interests or solves those problems, you've hit paydirt—in fact, the mother lode.

Networking at associations for members of your target market gives you the opportunity to become a preferred vendor among members. For instance, a professional editor might frequent speaking-industry gatherings, and become known within that industry. This strategy works well because you have few or no competitors within the group.

Chambers of Commerce Your local chamber of commerce can be an excellent networking source. Chambers usually have several types of networking opportunities and leads groups, representing different industries.

As with other such groups, membership can be beneficial, but only when you get really involved. Go beyond the popular networking "mixers," where you'll have a hard time targeting your market, and attend special-interest roundtable sessions, or volunteer to lead a committee, or take on important tasks. This not only helps you stand out, but also makes it easier to meet others with common interests.

Leads Groups There are many established business organizations whose sole purpose is to promote networking, such as Le Tip and Women's Business Net-

TIPS FROM THE GURU

Bob Burg on the Secrets of Endless Referrals

The larger your network, the more opportunity you have. "There's an old expression about digging a well before you need the water," says Bob Burg, author of *Endless Referrals*. "One of the best ways to build a self-sustaining business is establishing and maintaining a network of people who know you, like you, and trust you. You establish your network before you need it. That's the key."

The problem is that many people think networking is an exercise in passing out as many business cards as possible. They talk everyone's ear off. They only think they are networking and are disappointed when the process doesn't work.

You've Got to Give to Get The problem with this style of networking is that it does not focus on cultivating mutually beneficial relationships. "Successful networkers get referrals by continually putting other people's needs ahead of their own," says Burg.

Networking with only your own interests in mind will not work. Aggressive networking turns people off because it fails to establish trust. Networking is not just about getting ahead in your own life, but helping others get ahead in their lives as well.

A financial planner who attends networking meetings with the ice-breaking question, "Do you need any help with your investments?" will not get much out of networking, because he seeks only personal gain without bothering to discover what he can do to help the other person.

"Let's say you're an accountant, and you introduce a doctor to a colleague who specializes in working with physicians. It takes nothing to connect these two people, but you'll be seen as a person who goes out of their way to be helpful.

work. Most leads groups try to reduce industry overlap within the group by limiting the number of members from any one profession. Before joining, visit these groups, and talk to members to evaluate their tone and attitude. Do the members seem supportive of one another? Does the leadership appear competent?

Special Interest Groups There are networking opportunities to be found at any number of special interest groups that are not specifically related to any particular business. These include groups based on hobbies (garden-

People appreciate these types of gestures, which puts you in a position to get their referrals down the road," says Burg.

Listening Great networkers are great listeners. They invest most of their conversation time getting others to talk about themselves and their businesses. They ask a lot of friendly questions that are fun to answer.

"The 'listen more' principle is ideal for people who don't like a crowd," says Burg. "After all, it's a lot easier to be a good listener than a good talker. Once you've established some sort of genuine rapport, you should then ask for that person's business card."

Burg disputes the notion that networking is primarily about handing out your own business cards. "You should use your business card as a means to get the other person's business card," says Burg. "As far as I'm concerned, this is one of the few truly legitimate benefits of business cards in the networking process."

If you see that person later in an event, make it a point to stop by and call your networking prospect by name. This is impressive, because so few people do it, and because the prospect has by then most likely forgotten your name. This gesture will ensure that he or she remembers you.

Send a Note Immediately after the event, take a moment to write a brief, handwritten note to each person you met whom you'd like to cultivate. Do this as soon as you've left the event.

"The impression you will make is truly outstanding," says Burg. "Very few people do this. This simple gesture has a lot of class, and shows that you are conscientious. It will impress your prospects to no end, and ensure that you are remembered."

ing, cooking, sports), alumni groups at colleges and universities, civic groups like the Lion's Club and Rotary International, and religious organizations.

Getting the Most from Memberships

Joining networking organizations puts you in touch with many people; it is an invaluable way to build your professional network. To get the greatest benefit, you need to work at it consistently. Here are some points to keep in mind.

Show Up!

The degree to which you are successful at networking is determined by the amount of time you invest; it's not enough to pay your membership dues and attend a networking event from time to time. Effective networkers see their efforts as investments that pay tremendous dividends as they expand and maintain their network.

By regularly attending networking events, you maximize your chances of being in the right place at the right time. Since you aren't trying to rush into a business relationship at any one meeting, you will become an accepted part of the scene, and fellow members will feel more comfortable interacting with you when you've become a familiar face.

Get Involved!

The more you assume an active and—even better—a leadership role in an organization, the more likely it is that you'll connect with the people who will bring you business.

"I've been on the board of a professional organization called The Association of Women in Communications (AWC) for five years," says Marika Flatt, National Media Director for Phenix & Phenix Literary Publicists. "The first year I joined the organization I was asked to fill a board position that really opened up networking opportunities. I found that just by being involved in AWC I have people contacting me that I might not have known directly. A lot of times I'm not actively out there trying to network. But because I am so involved in the organization—I've taken a leadership role—I'm very visible."

Follow Up!

Start thinking about follow-up the moment you establish contact with someone. When you discover something unique or interesting about their business, write it down immediately.

A follow-up can range from a phone call or meeting (when appropriate)

REAL-WORLD SUCCESS STORY

Niche Networking Creates a Buzz for Mannequin Madness

When Judi Henderson launched Mannequin Madness, a business that buys, rents, and sells used mannequins, she knew the unique nature of her business meant she'd need to think carefully about targeting prospects. But her first call wasn't to a prospect; it was to potential referral sources likely to bring her business.

"I approached major department stores, figuring that people who needed mannequins might begin their search there," says Henderson. "I approached retail managers, letting them know about my business. I kept fanning out to new niche markets of likely prospects, and found a lot of opportunities to establish referral relationships. "

Soon, major department stores were sending her referrals, and even became sources for used mannequins. She approached lawyers (who often need mannequins for display in trials), meeting and convention planners, theater stage designers, and photographers. All became new markets for mannequins.

"All of these groups turned out to be great ongoing referral sources," says Henderson. "Things really kicked in when I joined their trade organizations and started networking at their meetings and trade shows. Word-of-mouth spread fast, because I stood out and everyone in these niches knew one another. Now, people think of me when anyone they know needs a mannequin."

The unique nature of her business and strong word-of-mouth have created

a buzz that encourages referrals and attracts media attention. "I've been in local newspapers and television, and was interviewed for a special event magazine," says Henderson. "My constant networking and outreach strategies attract a lot of attention, to the point that people now call me 'the mannequin lady.'"

to a handwritten note, article, or other information related to your business. Be ready to supply a reminder of who you are and what you do. Make sure to offer something—an idea, information, referral, or resource—of interest to the other person.

A contact-management system—paper-based, computer-based, or a combination of the two—is an essential networking tool that will help you follow up effectively.

Centers of Influence

Centers of influence are easy to spot. They are well established within a networking community. People know and trust them. At networking events, people tend to revolve around them. They stand out as the most sociable people, the "hubs" that link others together within the group. When somebody makes a point, all heads turn to them for a response. When they speak, people pay attention.

If you approach these people, they are usually quite willing to work you into their existing network. The more you connect with centers of influence, the faster you'll become a center of influence yourself.

The most powerful centers of influence are industry pundits, industry website proprietors, writers, speakers, and publication editors. Look for those who interpret and shape your market, and start the trends followed by your industry. If you gain their trust, they can spread the word about you within their network and give you credibility.

Online Networking

Tucked into a space no bigger than a computer monitor is a cyber community of individuals willing to do favors for others—more than 11,000 people in all, living in 133 countries. They are members of a group called Friendly Favors, and they are on tap to help out a friend or a friend-of-a-friend—even a friend six times removed—no matter where on the globe they reside.

The creation of Sergio Lub, a master networker and entrepreneur active in over a dozen organizations, Friendly Favors is a website that acts as a cyber Rolodex. "The site contains more information than a collection of business cards, and is highly interactive because members are responsible for updating their entries," says Lub. "Friendly Favors harnesses the real value of the Inter-

TIPS FROM THE GURU

Ivan Misner on Developing a Networking Contact Sphere

Dr. Ivan Misner, co-author of *Masters of Networking*, and founder of BNI (Business Network International), the largest networking organization in the world, believes that every goal is attainable if you cultivate "human" resources. "Networking is a natural part of life. Each of us relies on a network of people we know and trust," says Misner.

A network starts with any group (formal or informal), organization, institution, company, or individual you associate with for either business or personal reasons. We all have many networks, both formal and informal, to which we belong—groups some call "contact spheres," in which you can develop and benefit from symbiotic relationships.

"My favorite example of a contact sphere is the caterer, the florist, the photographer, and the travel agent. I call this the 'wedding mafia,'" says Misner. "If one gets a referral to a wedding, then they all get a referral to the wedding. These professions, more than most, have truly learned how to work their contact sphere." Here are a few basic principles Misner recommends for focusing your efforts:

• Identify as many professions as possible that fit within your company's contact sphere. Take a look at the professions your industry tends to work with, so as to get an idea of the natural sources of repeat and reciprocal referrals. Create a list of these professions.

• Identify specific individuals who could fit into your contact sphere. Go to various networking groups, and build your business-card file and database.

• Invite these people to participate in networking groups with you, so that you can formalize your relationship and have a way to stay in regular contact. Maintaining the relationship is key. A good way to do that is to participate in groups that bring you together on a regular basis.

• Evaluate those professionals in your contact sphere to whom you refer clients. If they are not reciprocating, you may have to replace them with others who are willing and able to reciprocate.

net, and that's its ability to help people with common interests and concerns to connect with one another."

Cyber, or online networking, enables you to escape the limitations of face-to-face interactions. Online communities have been growing at a phenom-

EXECUTIVE BRANDING

Education Brings Craft Beer to the Masses

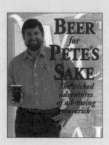

Pete Slosberg's career in beer began by accident. In 1979, as an executive with IBM, he attempted to make wine in his kitchen, but grew impatient with the long wait for wine to mature. He turned to beer instead, brewing a variety of exotic beers and enlisting friends as tasters. His prize creation was Pete's Wicked Ale, a brown ale that carried an image of Pete Slosberg himself emblazoned on each bottle.

When Pete's Brewing Company was founded in 1986, Slosberg was determined to make Pete's Wicked Ale a respected national brand, but he faced entrenched national brands and a public with limited knowledge about craft beers. Rather than mimic larger brewers' gimmicky advertising campaigns, Pete positioned himself as the spokesperson, educator, and ambassador for the fledgling microbrew industry.

Don't just push your product, push your category. As one of only 33 craft brewers in America in 1986, Pete knew that beer consumers had little knowledge about craft beers. "We promoted our product by raising awareness for the entire craft beer category," recalls Pete. "I did extensive missionary work for my industry, operating equally as company spokesperson and as the voice of craft beer education."

Pete's branding strategy centered on craft beer education. He targeted consumers, distributors, waitstaff and anyone with a stake in promoting his product. A centerpiece of this effort was Pete's Landscape of Beers™, a simple reference

enal rate, because they allow you to connect with like-minded people all over the world without the expense of attending real-world networking events. Online networking venues tend to fall into three categories:

E-mail Discussion Groups

E-mail discussion groups, also known as listservs, allow participants to join an e-mail network composed of those with a strong interest in the group's topic. Members post messages, which are sent to the group on a daily, weekly, or monthly tool that could make anybody a beer expert in 10 minutes.

"We used this simple chart as a consumer brand awareness tool in bars that carried our product," says Pete. "Moreover, the beer chart would show retailers, carrying mostly middle-of-the-road, mass production beers, that they weren't offering their customers enough beer choices."

Develop a personal connection. Pete got personally involved in the branding process, spending 100 days a year on the road promoting Pete's Wicked Ale. He educated his marketplace about craft brews, connecting with wholesalers, retailers, and consumers through numerous public appearances, while linking his persona and passion for beer with public perception of his product.

Pete courted beer wholesalers by organizing "brew on premises" events, inviting wholesale employees and salespeople to learn how to brew their own beer. "These events established a personal connection between our company and key salespeople and differentiated us from the big guys," says Pete. "I got to know our wholesalers and their people on a personal level, and the events were a lot of fun. Each person left with a personalized six pack of beer they made themselves, and many left a bottle on their desk as a memento. This created great mindshare and a personal connect to our company."

Pete's Brewing Company's sales grew from $130,000 in 1988 to $5.5 million in 1992, a 3,967 percent increase. *Inc.* magazine later ranked Pete's among its 500 fastest growing privately held companies in the United States. "You can enter a crowded market by demonstrating a compelling point of difference," says Slosberg, who wrote about his beer adventures in his book, Beer for Pete's Sake. "When companies connect personally with their marketplace, they form deep, loyal connections with consumers that you can't buy through advertising."

basis, depending on the group, and participate in ongoing online discussions.

There are e-mail discussion lists devoted to just about every topic imaginable, from knitting to human resources. You can find lists that relate to your target market at Topica (www.topica.com).

Web Forums

Also known as "bulletin boards," Web forums are hosted at specialized Web sites, and are often moderated by a host or site owner. They allow participants

TIPS FROM THE GURU

Nancy Roebke on Networking in Online Communities

Nancy Roebke, executive director of Profnet, Inc., a professional business-leads generation corporation, is a champion of online networking, believing that online forums, newsgroups, and e-mail lists provide some of the best ways to "meet" prospects and exchange information. Here are her suggestions for making the most of these opportunities.

Share Information   Nancy posts information to such sites regularly to develop name recognition, and also to position herself as an expert in her field. "I currently write for several online and offline publications," says Roebke. "These articles generate a lot of interest in my firm. I get calls on my toll-free line almost every day from people who've read one of my articles."

Connect with Like-Minded People   "I read posts from other members, and when their opinions or presentations mirror my own," says Nancy, "I send a private response of encouragement, seeking to build a circle of like-minded individuals." Because she had gone out of her way to connect with certain people, Nancy was invited to join the board of a significant project being undertaken by members of this list. "This was a direct result of the responses I made to the like-minded members of the group."

Be Helpful   As with all networking, the philosophy of giving before receiving works best. Read the interactions and contribute positive, helpful information. You will be amazed at the people who contact you saying, "I saw your post on the list. How can your services help my firm?" And your post wasn't even about your firm. It was just a helping hand to someone.

Applaud the Efforts of Others   Nancy sends private messages to members

to post messages in common areas that members can read and reply to at any time. Web forums are like ongoing group conversations. One of the largest directories of forums can be found at Delphi Forums (www.delphiforums.com).

Newsgroups

These are similar to Web forums, but usually not moderated. There are tens of thousands of newsgroups around the world, on as many subjects. To read in response to useful posts. "The community is stronger when people feel comfortable and develop personal relationships," she says. "Accolades are always appreciated, and can be great marketing tools if used properly."

Nancy sends virtual postcards to everyone who introduces himself or herself, welcoming them to the group and offering a friendly ear. "In these postcards, I also asked for info about their businesses. This was one of the best relationship-building tools I used."

Use Your Signature File The right signature, or "sig," can generate more leads than you can handle. "My current sig offers a free report on how to stop cold calling," she says. "This report is set up on an autoresponder that is available 24 hours a day, 7 days a week. When someone requests the report, I am notified of that request." Her current "sig" reads:

Nancy Roebke

mailto:execdirector@profnet.org

Executive Director, ProfNet

http://www.profnet.org

How To Stop Cold Calling—And Get MORE Business!

Free report tells you 10 secrets of getting referrals.

Get your copy by e-mailing mailto:secrets@profnet.org today!

Expect It to Take Time There is no way to shorten the relationship-building process, but the time you have to spend to build mutually beneficial relationships online is well worth it. "Online networking has a lot of appeal because of the volume of people you can reach," says Roebke. "But the chances of building relationships with all those people at one time are slim to none. The best online networkers build relationships one person at a time."

newsgroup messages, you need a newsreader (available in most e-mail programs). DejaNews (www.dejanews.com) provides an easy gateway to just about any newsgroup in existence.

Social Networking Websites

Social networking sites are online communities. There are hundreds of such sites, including MySpace, Friendster, and Facebook, which are directed at consumers, and business social networking websites, including Ryze, LinkedIn, and Ecademy, where members develop networks of trusted contacts through searchable member profiles.

According to Scott Allen, author of *The Virtual Handshake: Opening Doors and Closing Deals Online*, social networking websites provide several benefits, including microtargeting (you can join or create a virtual community with your best prospects) and market research (you can take the pulse of your target market with a candor rarely found in focus groups and surveys).

Moreover, social networking websites can serve as vehicles to demonstrate expertise and thought leadership. "Social networks are accessible outlets to establish your expertise," says Allen. "When you speak up in a mailing list, discussion forum, blog, or online community, you can reach hundreds of thousands of people. Because word-of-mouth flows through online social networks, you can reach prospects and referral sources."

Most of the rules of successful face-to-face networking also carry over to online networking. Don't approach online networking with the intent of aggressively pitching your products and services. In online as in other kinds of networks, that approach will do more harm than good. Online networking is about creating visibility and familiarity, and helping others in a way that results in trust and relationships.

Cultivating Referrals

When prospects come to you by referral, they are predisposed to doing business with you. And most people are happy to refer business to those who deserve it. Why? It makes them look and feel good.

"Do you ever remember sitting around a table with some friends and someone says they're looking for, say, a good house cleaner?" says Robert Middleton of Action Plan Marketing. "All of a sudden everyone at the table starts to vie for who can give the best referral. We want our friend to use our reference because we get an ego boost. We win. Someone noticed us and paid attention to us. That feels good."

Referral expert Joanne Black teaches small business owners and corporations the art of "referral selling," something that she has designed to help businesses attract the type of customers they want. "In over thirty years of working in selling professions, I appreciate that the best way to build any business is through referrals," says Black. "Referral prospects are pre-qualified. And because someone they trust has recommended you, you have immediate credibility and don't have to sell them as much. Best of all, referral business comes to you!"

Although referrals are the best way to get new business, most businesses do not employ a strategy that encourages and rewards referrals. The trick is seeing your *slightly famous* universe as a breeding ground for referrals. Where do referrals come from? From satisfied clients (both active and inactive); business associates who know you personally; and anyone who trusts your firm and the quality of your work enough to recommend you to others.

Black suggests the following strategy for easily increasing your referrals:

Cultivate Trust People will only refer business to those they trust. Attending networking functions to see how many business cards you can get, or pass out, will not amount to much. That's why implementing a long-term referral strategy takes time, patience, and personal integrity.

Businesses that get the most referrals are those that go out of their way to connect with people. They don't meet someone for three minutes at a networking event, and immediately ask for a referral. Instead, they establish a relationship, gain trust, and ask for referrals only once the "human connection" has been established.

Ask Getting referrals from your clients, customers, vendors, or anyone else with a relationship to your business can be as easy as letting them know you want them. Often, people in the best position to refer business to you don't realize they are sources for business leads. Or, like many of us, they may be just too busy to think about referring customers to your business, so they need a boost or reminder.

"Before asking for referrals, be absolutely clear on what you are asking for," says Black. "Do not be overly broad. The more specific you are about what you are looking for, the easier it is for someone to think of someone to refer."

Asking clients and customers for referrals can be awkward. A way around this is sending clients a form letter upon the completion of some work you've done for them. Tell them that you would appreciate being allowed to use them as a reference, and that you appreciate referrals, if they know of people who might need your services.

Educate Your potential referral sources may not recognize the referral opportunities that are right for you. If you make use of the advice in previous chapters on how to clearly identify your market niche through positioning and branding strategies, this will be less of a problem.

Reward Referrals Always acknowledge referrals. Eva Patel, a *slightly famous* skin care specialist in San Francisco, developed a "referral club" to reward current clients who refer others to her Skin Rejuvenation Clinic. She offers free skin treatments, T-shirts, and caps, as well as items from her own line of skin care products, as rewards for referrals. She rewards "referral superstars" with gourmet lunches and jewelry.

"We've built our business on client relationships and the referrals that result from them," says Patel. "We go out of our way to thank clients who believe in us enough to recommend us to their friends. It makes them feel special, and it shows our genuine appreciation for the part they play helping us grow our business."

The biggest mistake regarding referrals is that too many people take others' generosity for granted, forgetting to acknowledge the favor someone has done them in referring business—and reciprocating, if possible. For small referrals, a thank-you note or phone call will suffice. But if a colleague refers a major piece of business to you, send a gift that is appropriate to the size and scope of the referral.

15 Keeping in Touch with Newsletters

lise Benun began publishing her newsletter, *The Art of Self Promotion*, several years ago as a promotional vehicle for her business. A well-known marketing consultant, she filled her newsletter with information drawn from her experience. She used her newsletter to provide solutions to her prospects' most pressing marketing challenges, and chose topics that demonstrated her abilities and credentials.

"I used my newsletter as a brochure when someone wanted to know more about my work. It gave me tremendous credibility, and helped me keep in touch without being seen as a pest," says Benun. "The best keep-in-touch methods provide useful information while reminding people that you have something valuable to offer."

Building long-term business relationships isn't a hit-and-run proposition. If clients, customers, or prospects haven't heard from you lately, it's unlikely your name will come to mind when they need your products and services.

To make the most of your business relationships, you need to keep in touch regularly with everyone who's part of your business world—your clients, customers, vendors, associates, and prospects.

Newsletters provide one of the best ways to keep in touch and maintain their awareness of your brand. A newsletter can increase customer loyalty and make those who've never met you feel like they've known you for years. The best newsletters provide useful information that positions you as a source of information, which builds your credibility and establishes top-of-mind awareness that results in sales and referrals. If your newsletter is done correctly, people will eagerly look forward to receiving it.

Print Newsletters

A simple newsletter can be created using a single 8½″ × 11″ sheet that is printed and folded to become a self-mailer. More elaborate presentations usually involve larger sheets that are folded to become envelope inserts. Printing costs will naturally vary widely, depending on the format, quantity, complexity, and use of color. In addition, you will have expenses for graphic design, editorial help, mailing list management, and postage.

Whatever your budget, you need to make some basic decisions about your newsletter's layout and develop a design that supports your brand identity. Because most people do not have the design skills to produce a quality newsletter themselves, a smart strategy is to develop the copy in-house, and hire a designer for layout and production. Consider hiring a good designer to develop a template for your newsletter. This involves an initial investment, but saves money in the long run since you can use the template for all future issues.

A money-saving shortcut is to use newsletter templates that come with popular word-processing programs like Microsoft Word, and print your newsletters on a laser printer. Although these templates are somewhat bland, they can be personalized with company photos and graphics to present a distinctive appearance.

TIPS FROM THE GURU

Jeff Rubin Shows Off His Skills in a Newsletter for Newsletter Clients

Jeff Rubin has become known for his expertise in writing, designing, and producing company newsletters through his company, Put-It-In-Writing. Jeff advises clients to use newsletters to build the person-to-person connections that are, ultimately, the foundation of any successful business.

"The best businesses provide their clients and customers with exceptional service and value," says Rubin. "A newsletter is a way to connect with people while giving them information they can use. A regularly distributed newsletter can help you spend less time chasing work, and more time building relationships that attract new business."

Jeff's own newsletter, *The Write Stuff*, helps him regularly connect with prospects, vendors, and colleagues. He also uses his newsletter as a cross-promotional tool by profiling his vendors, who also promote his newsletter at their businesses. Jeff sends his newsletter to professional speakers—one of his target markets—and also features articles written by colleagues in the National Speakers Association.

The newsletter brings him most of his new clients; it "is an extension of my overall relationship-building strategy because of its reader-valued articles and dependable presence," says Rubin. "It's been the best way for me to stay visible and maintain a competitive edge. By maintaining personal relationships with customers and referral sources, they see me as a person always looking for ways to help them succeed and prosper. And because I mail my newsletter once a quarter to everyone in my network, people remember me."

E-Mail Newsletters

Due in large part to their cost-effectiveness, e-mail newsletters are becoming the keep-in-touch tools of choice for businesses small and large. Whether you mail daily, weekly, or monthly, e-mail newsletters avoid the high cost of producing and distributing print messages, and the savings grow as your list of subscribers grows. E-mail newsletters can be used to:

- distribute articles, tip sheets, and anything else you've written.
- express your opinion about topics related to your business.
- direct recipients to your website and sell more products and services

- help the media and other centers of influence stay attuned to your business.
- increase income by selling products and services through affiliate arangements.
- encourage feedback from clients and customers.

If you create a really valuable newsletter, it will be passed along to friends and colleagues, creating virtual word-of-mouth and attracting new subscribers.

Janine Giorgenti, a New York-based image consultant and custom clothing designer, saw her daily e-mail newsletter, Dressing Tips, increase sales by 20 percent in the first six weeks after she started it. In separate daily e-mails to men and women, Giorgenti answers one simple fashion question a day. For instance, "Can what I wear make me look taller?" (Yes, wear vertical stripes in your suits. This will add an inch to your apparent height.) Or, "Can I wear a button-down-collar shirt with a suit?" (No! A button down collar is sporty, and should be worn with a sport coat and slacks.)

As a testament to the success of the newsletter strategy, Giorgenti has attracted more than 6,000 subscribers since her campaign began. New customers generated by Dressing Tips have driven as far as 200 miles to meet with Giorgenti, and one new customer gave her a $6,000 order at their first meeting.

Provide Useful Information

People subscribe to newsletters because they believe they will receive something valuable that's not readily available elsewhere. The more relevant the information, the more readers will look forward to receiving your e-mail newsletter.

Even though your newsletter may be built around your products or services, your message must be that you are an impartial source of useful information. You can do this by offering material drawn from a variety of sources. Scan publications in your field for topics that relate to your business, and use them as starting points for your own articles. This not only supports your expertise, but also demonstrates that you have a broad understanding of your industry.

REAL-WORLD SUCCESS STORY

International Living Uses E-mail Newsletter to Reach a Global Audience

International Living, a resource for people planning to buy foreign real estate or live abroad, was launched 22 years ago as a print newsletter. Today, the company still mails its monthly print newsletter to 30,000 subscribers but has established an even greater global presence with its e-mail newsletter, which reaches 175,000 subscribers.

"Our newsletters are at the heart of International Living, the seed from which everything else grows," says publisher Kathleen Peddicord, who credits their e-mail newsletter with taking the business to another level. "Our e-mail newsletter now provides an opportunity to communicate more often with our readers without the associated expenses of printing and mailing, and has helped us develop deeper, more personal relationships with them."

Even though the newsletters do not directly turn a profit, she explains, "they fuel other aspects of the business. Without our newsletters, we wouldn't have a business at all. They drive our consulting business, real estate business, and everything else we do."

Peddicord pays special attention to the writing that goes into each newsletter. Their e-mail newsletter is based on the personal narratives of several writers who live abroad. "We write in a very personal style, telling stories and evoking images of places around the world; our readers feel like we're part of their lives and develop an emotional attachment to us," says Peddicord. "We see this at our conferences where we meet 100 to 150 readers at a time, and they speak with us as though we're long-lost friends."

The strongest testament to their newsletters' success is their fiercely loyal following, and a long history of reader success stories. "Many of our readers have bought dream homes and started new lives overseas because they've been inspired by our newsletters," says Peddicord. "Many of them now live on beaches in Mexico, or country homes in the south of France, or own hotels in small coastal towns in places like Nicaragua. Our newsletters help readers achieve dreams of living abroad, and inspire them to take action."

Jim Davis, a financial adviser in San Francisco, sends out regular e-mail stock market and investment reports that interpret current market conditions. His articles are filled with data, calculations, and information drawn from the financial press.

Support Your Brand

Your newsletter is an extension of your brand. Make your newsletter personal. Because people build relationships with people, not faceless corporations, inject your personality into your newsletter, and write in a conversational style. Your voice and manner should become more familiar to your customers with each issue. Avoid jargon and don't be overly formal. Consider your newsletter as an ongoing conversation between friends meant to provide solutions, solve problems, and build trust.

Make It Consistent

Sending your newsletter out on a regular basis not only looks professional, it exploits the power of repetition. Remember, subscribers who haven't bought from you will form their impression of you by the quality of your newsletter and how dependably it arrives.

How frequently should you send your e-mail newsletter? Start conservatively; base your schedule on the level of effort you're sure you can maintain, increasing frequency only when you know that you can pick up the pace, and that people are interested in receiving it more often. Most businesses start with a monthly newsletter, since this is well within their power to produce, and it's frequent enough to keep them in front of their prospects. Some newsletters go out more often, sometimes on a weekly or even daily basis. But before you assume that your recipients want to hear from you that often, poll your readers about their wants and needs.

Get Permission

Before you add someone to your e-mail newsletter list, get his or her express permission. With the onslaught of unsolicited bulk commercial e-mail, commonly called "spam," most people have a low tolerance for e-mail messages that arrive uninvited. As discussed in Chapter 8, you want to try to get subscribers to "opt in" to your e-mail newsletter from your website. Most important, whenever promoting your e-mail newsletter, let people know that you will never sell or rent e-mail addresses and that they can easily "unsubscribe" at any time.

A survey commissioned by DoubleClick, an Internet advertising company, found that permission-based e-mail produces a tremendous response rate. The survey, based on a sample of 1,000 users, and with a 94 percent accuracy rate, reports that 69 percent of American e-mail users have made online purchases from companies sending them permission-based e-mails.

Coming Up with Content

While every newsletter lives or dies by the quality of its content, they are relatively doable for any small businessperson. The bottom line is to provide "news you can use" in bite-sized pieces of information related to your business. When thinking about what kind of content to offer, you can begin with real-life examples and client case studies that allow you to share insights and show readers how they can apply your solutions to their situation.

Other Content Considerations

The top of your newsletter should include, close to its title, a benefit-oriented tagline that clearly states its purpose and target audience. For example, "Feline Facts: Keeping Your Cat Healthy" or "End Clutter: Weekly Tips to Keep Your Home Organized." Also include the issue date and a link to your Web site, near the top of the newsletter.

When planning the content of your newsletter, pay close attention to the e-mail "from" and "subject" lines. Studies have shown that as many as 40 percent of e-mail recipients look at the "from" name first when deciding what to delete and what to read. Your best choices are to use your business name or your personal name, whichever has the greater brand recognition, or whichever you want to become recognized.

A standardized "subject" line brands your newsletter among recipients, and helps to ensure that it gets opened. With the rise of unsolicited e-mail, it's important that your subject line brands your newsletter, issue after issue,

EXECUTIVE BRANDING

Randall Graham Makes Wine Accessible and Fun

The wine industry in Northern California is extremely competitive, so finding ways to stand out from the crowd is essential. Yet, when it comes to branding, many wineries rush to the middle, and make safe choices, promoting their wine in a predictable, conservative style.

Randall Graham will have none of this.

For 25 years, Bonny Doon Vineyards has positioned itself as the anti-winery, and its founder Randall Graham has cultivated an industry-wide reputation for experimentation, high jinks, and building a creative (and sometimes enigmatic) brand that combines world class wine with a healthy dose of anti-snobbery humor.

Graham has challenged his industry's self-seriousness since the early 1980s, when Bonny Doon eschewed traditional grape varieties in favor of the more obscure Syrah, Grenache and Mourvedre from France's Rhone Valley. His wines have zany labels and names like Cardinal Zin and Cigar Volant (French for "flying saucer").

Graham stages show-stealing events like the Death of the Cork Wake (promoting Bonny Doon's move to screwcaps), and a wine-infused rock opera for wine industry insiders penned to the tunes of Roxanne, Stairway to Heaven, and Soul Man, loosely based on Graham's struggles against wine mediocrity and big business.

Graham's persona also infuses the Bonny Doon newsletter, produced since 1986, and mailed twice yearly to over 45,000 subscribers. Many of these subscribers have filled out a form in the wine-tasting room, but the list also includes retail and restaurant accounts, distributors, press and other members of the trade.

The newsletter itself is written in Graham's signature style of literary allusions interspersed with philosophical ramblings. In Graham's hands, the newsletter is a malleable form as well as a creative outlet for his unique take on wine and life.

In one of the more memorable examples, Graham photographed his winery team in an elaborate recreation of the Beatles' album cover for "Sgt. Pepper's Lonely Hearts Club Band," where the word "Beatles" on the original become "Bouteille" in the Bonny Doon version, with the new title "Ch. Neuf du Papers Rhonely Hearts Club Band."

"The purpose of the newsletter is utter delight and hilarity; humiliation and reprogramming of our foes; creating of a space to vent our hyperinflated sense of self importance, and propagation of the Doon mythology. In other words, to have fun!" says winery spokesperson John Locke, who attributed the success of the newsletter to its strangeness. "Randall is extremely articulate, well-read, and has a unique ability to talk about wine in a fashion where it becomes the prism through which his ideas about everything else can be illuminated."

Despite Graham's eccentricities, the articles in the newsletter always comes back to wine. The ostensible purpose of the Bonny Doon newsletter is to make sales, but its real benefit, Graham says, is communicating that Bonny Doon values good wine, but sees no reason why wine can't be fun and accessible.

"The newsletter has been incredibly central to branding the company. It gives us a lot of visibility, and connects people to the winery in a special way. Some of our customers are fanatically devoted," says Graham. "Effective newsletters are not solely focused on direct selling, but on establishing a connection with customers and creating an emotional bond that cannot be explained by satisfaction with your product alone."

until recipients remember it, feel safe with it, and don't even think of deleting it as spam. If you've chosen your newsletter name well, this is all you'll need. You can use your e-mail name, with slight variations as appropriate, to become a regular, welcome visitor in recipients' inboxes.

Write for easy reading. Post a table of contents or a concise summary at the beginning of each newsletter so readers can decide quickly whether the content is of interest to them.

Reading large blocks of text on a computer screen is more difficult than on paper. Aim for an overall word count that's 50 percent less than you would write for a print medium. Write for easy scanning, highlighting important words and phrases, and keeping paragraphs short. Set line length at 70 characters or less to avoid awkward line wrapping. Divide longer segments into smaller parts. Use caps, asterisks, dashes, and white space to set items apart.

If you have something you want to advertise, surround it with useful content, and put it somewhere in the middle. Never put an ad at the top.

Provide a "spam" disclaimer by reminding recipients how they got onto your list. Also provide clear instructions for unsubscribing: "You've received this newsletter because you subscribed to it. If you wish to unsubscribe, please follow the instructions at the end of this newsletter."

Don't forget to include full contact information, including your name, the name of your business, a phone number, an e-mail address, and your Web site address. It's also a good idea to add a copyright notice at the very end.

Getting Subscribers

Now that you've got content, start attracting subscribers. Take every opportunity to invite people to subscribe. You can do this in a variety of ways; here are some.

Announce your newsletter. A quick and easy way to get people to subscribe to your newsletter is to send a simple mailing to your existing mailing list, including current and past customers and contacts. People you know are much, much more likely to respond to your mailings than strangers. Keep it cheap and simple; a postcard mailing works fine.

Talk it up! If you give talks, ask people at the end if they'd like to be on your e-mail list. If you write articles, mention at the end that you have a newsletter. Talk about your newsletter in networking situations.

Make it easy to opt in from your website. Many subscribers from your e-mail newsletter will come from your website. Make sure you place sign-up fields on every page of your site. The easier it is to sign up, the more opt-ins you'll get. Also be sure to archive several back issues for those who will want a taste of your newsletter before subscribing.

Offer an enrollment premium. Why not give people a reward for opting onto your list? Consider premiums based on timely content, such as special reports or white papers. The trick is to offer rewards that have perceived value, but cost you little or nothing to deliver.

Find joint ventures. Contact the owners of similar lists, and propose that you swap sponsorships. This can take the form of contributing articles to one another's newsletters, or swapping promotional "plugs" for each other's newsletters on your Web sites and e-mail newsletters, or both.

Use online groups and discussion boards. Look for ones that fit your niche. The idea is not to sell something, but to give something away. Although groups are quick to crack down on sales messages, you'll be fine as long as you're giving away genuinely valuable information.

Encourage referrals. Viral, or referral, marketing is the best way to build your list. We all tell our friends about good service experiences, great stores and restaurants, something nice someone has done for you, an offer that is too good to pass up—this is what it's about. An e-mail newsletter facilitates this process by providing clients with e-mail text that can be passed along to friends and colleagues. Include an easy way for readers to forward your message to friends. And provide a "printer-friendly" alternative format, so that they can print out your message without extra screen images.

Be bold about asking subscribers to help you spread the word. Ask for referrals in the body of the newsletter. Also consider creating a campaign that rewards people who actually bring new subscribers to your list.

TIPS FROM THE GURU

Marketing Sherpa on the Elements of Great Newsletter Content

The following newsletter content tips are excerpted from *Best Practices in Marketing with E-mail Newsletters*, a report authored by MarketingSherpa, a media company that publishes case studies and best-practices data about Internet marketing.

News News is easy to find online. If you plan on featuring industry, topical, or specialty news in your newsletter, then you must have one or more of the following:

- A truly valuable perspective on the news
- News that's so up-to-the-minute or so highly specialized that the mainstream press either hasn't covered it yet, or never will
- News that has a significant impact on the lives of your readers
- The more you provide content, whether news or a news digest, that's not available elsewhere, the more value for your subscribers.

Articles or Columns You can run articles or columns written by your newsletter editor, staff members of your organization, volunteer contributors, paid writers or reporters, or syndicated columnists. Such articles can be practical, or incisive, or opinionated, or entertaining, or—best of all—have some combination of these qualities.

Fun Features Quizzes, cartoons, gossip, advice to the lovelorn, horoscopes, crossword puzzles, contests, topical jokes all have obvious appeal for consumer readers, and in many cases can benefit a newsletter as well.

Humor The former BizTravel.com tested a less serious and nonverbal approach to drawing more of its half million subscribers to its Web site by incorporating cartoons into its newsletter. In fact, the first two times a cartoon ran in the newsletter, it outperformed all the articles except one in getting people to visit the Web site.

Facts or Data Often you can obtain these at no cost, or compile them with a bit of in-house research. For instance, a pharmacy could pass along consumer safety alerts about medications. A corporate travel agency could advise its clients about both the issuing and the lifting of travel advisories and travel warnings by the U.S. State Department.

Instruction or Advice How-to advice draws tremendously on the Internet, and if well done, it gets people reading their e-mail with attention. How to disguise bags under one's eyes would work for a cosmetics company, while steps for finding and plugging e-commerce security holes would enhance the reputation and promote the services of a firm of security experts.

Reader-contributed content. Not counting columnists who are also readers, reader-generated content consists of four main varieties:

• Polls These usually involve one brief question, along with a set of short answers. Readers tell you which answer they prefer, and you soon have a fun factoid of results for the next issue.

• Surveys These generally involve more than a single question. Surveys let you know how to tailor your editorial content better to your audience.

• Questions Q&A provides very powerful content, because readers get a feeling of interactivity, see their peers actively participating in the newsletter, and see the newsletter editor demonstrating expertise.

• Letters to the Editor Letters are equally powerful because they show readers that other people read the newsletter too, establishing credibility and community.

Resources Truly useful or highly entertaining links that are relevant to the needs of your target audience can become either the main dish or the dessert of your newsletter. If you're working with a time lag between your compiling of the links and their inclusion in your newsletter, always verify the links just before finalizing that issue for distribution. Sending out dead links is a recipe for loss of customer confidence.

Year-End Best-of Revelations Instead of choosing his personal top 10 favorites for his year-end issue, Brian Livingston, editor of InfoWorld's E-Business Secrets newsletter, asked his Webmaster for a report showing the issues and the individual stories that got the greatest response from readers in the past year.

Reviews. Both consumer and business audiences can find a lot of value in your guidance on which software programs, books, restaurants, telecom vendors, and so on to patronize, and which to avoid. Reviews have the greatest value for readers when your opinions are grounded in experience and expertise, and when you offer even adverse criticism when it's due.

Case Studies If you sell complex, customized services, narrative case studies can be a good way to edify and entertain your clientele and prospects in issue after issue of your newsletter. A good plan for presenting such material is to begin with the problem or challenge faced by the individual or company, proceed to the strategy you used to address the problem, and end with the results achieved by that solution.

Distribution

There are two ways you can distribute your e-mail newsletter: do it yourself, or use an e-mail distribution service or "listserver."

If your list is relatively small, you can send your e-mail newsletter from your own computer, using popular programs like Microsoft Outlook or Eudora. Note that you must send your newsletter to recipients using the "blind carbon copy" feature, which means that no subscriber will see the e-mail addresses of any other—the ultimate Internet faux pas. The downside is that you'll have to manually add and remove subscribers, and deal with any bounce-backs, should people change e-mail addresses. You'll also find it helpful to break your list into groups of 50 names or less, so they won't be kicked out by Internet service providers as spam.

If you want to eliminate much of the administrative hassle, you can use a "listserver," an outside service that automates the process. Options include free services such as Topica (www.topica.com) and professional list hosts such as SparkList.com or BigList Inc. (www.biglist.com). Using one of these services, you send all your e-mail addresses to the company that manages it, and they handle all additions, deletions, unsubscribes, and bounce-backs. You can link your newsletter sign-up form to the listserver to automate the subscription process.

When choosing a mailing service or listserver, look for one that includes bounce management (to keep your list continually updated and free of invalid or obsolete e-mail addresses), basic management reports, a security system, and easy access to your list at all times.

A Solid Investment

Keeping in touch by means of newsletters requires a commitment. The best keep-in-touch strategies run like clockwork, put out with perfect regularity by marketers who view their newsletter as a necessary cost of doing business, like paying taxes.

A keep-in-touch newsletter program should do more than remind clients that you're still in business. It should raise your stature and enhance your credibility by sharing information and ideas that make recipients better appreciate the expertise you bring to your market niche. Don't just educate, make compelling offers to subscribers that motivate them to do business with you again and again.

While it's understandable to want visible results fairly soon after a marketing initiative, several issues of your newsletter may have to arrive before a prospect is moved to place an order or hire you. Just remember that the more you keep in touch, the greater your rewards in goodwill, an enhanced reputation, repeat business, and word-of-mouth referrals—all the benefits of becoming *slightly famous.*

16 Cause Marketing: Doing Well by Doing Good

Dancing Deer Bakery regularly receives praise for its all natural baked goods. Although customers rave about its Maple Pumpkin Cranberry Cake and Chocolate Tangerine Cookies, the Boston-based company is equally lauded for its strong commitment to social values.

Dancing Deer uses all-natural materials and green packaging, and invests in its economically challenged inner-city Boston neighborhood, paying wages well above the minimum, and providing employee stock options, profit-sharing, and language courses on company time for Spanish-speaking employees. Dancing Deer expresses philanthropic values by donating a percentage of profits to its Sweet Home Project, which helps homeless families find jobs and move into homes of their own.

From its beginnings in 1994, Dancing Deer has remained true to its principles. "People love our philosophy as much as our cookies," says Patricia Karter, CEO and co-founder of Dancing Deer. "We try to accomplish something beyond great cakes and tarts. People think Dancing Deer is special because of our business practices. They like that we stand for something more."

Karter has grown Dancing Deer from a startup to an $8 million company, and hopes to expand the company's thriving wholesale, online, and mail order business over the next five years to generate $20 to $50 million in sales.

Karter says there were times when it was tempting to take the lower road, such as when Williams Sonoma offered to carry Dancing Deer's Molasses Clove Cookies—a deal that would have doubled sales overnight. The catch: Williams Sonoma needed a six-month shelf life to put the cookies in stores nationally, which would require using preservatives.

Karter walked away from the deal, but Williams Sonoma was impressed and determined to make the relationship work. In the end, Dancing Deer created a gingerbread mix that did not require preservatives—a move that kept Dancing Deer true to its principles while beginning a profitable relationship with Williams Sonoma that continues to this day.

The Rise of Strategic Philanthropy

Nothing builds brand loyalty among today's increasingly hard-to-please consumers like a company's proven commitment to a worthy cause. Many consumers would rather do business with a company that stands for something beyond profits.

Recent studies show that consumers carefully consider a company's reputation when making purchasing decisions. The *2006 Cone Millennial Cause Study* found that 69 percent of 12 to 24-year-old Americans consider a company's social/environmental commitment when deciding where to shop, and 89 percent are likely or very likely to switch from one brand to another—price and quality being equal—if the competing brand is associated with a good cause.

The study also shows the importance younger generations place on socially oriented business practices. *The Millennial Study* shows that 61 percent of Americans born between 1979 and 2001 believe it is their responsibility to make the world a better place, and 78 percent believe that businesses have a

TIPS FROM THE GURU

Carol Cone on Choosing a Cause that Aligns with Your Business

Carol Cone, chairman and founder of Cone, Inc. and co-author of the *Cone/Roper Report*, which measures consumer attitudes about cause marketing, advises companies to actively integrate strategic philanthropy into their core business. Cone, widely regarded as the "mother" of cause marketing, calls this approach Cause Branding™ (a term her firm trademarked).

Her approach centers on aligning a business with a social cause to enhance the company brand, while at the same time making an authentic social impact. "Cause branding makes the company's commitment to a social cause central to the brand DNA," says Cone. "Cause branding programs build on a company's unique values and culture and become part of the company's soul."

"Your business goals are the starting point for identifying charitable causes," says Cone. "A company must be clear about its core values, and most importantly, how it might participate in the world in which its employees live, work, and do business. For example, LensCrafters stands for healthy vision, and cre-

responsibility to join them in this effort. Younger consumers are prepared to reward (or punish) a company based on its commitment to social causes.

In 1970, economist Milton Friedman wrote a now-famous article for the *New York Times Magazine* entitled "The Social Responsibility of Business Is to Increase Profits." Friedman argued that businesses' sole purpose is generating profit for shareholders; companies that pursued the "social good" acted irresponsibly and jeopardized profits.

Increasingly, entrepreneurs are disproving perceived wisdom that philanthropy, although virtuous, does not advance core business goals. Embracing ated a natural cause brand in its Give the Gift of Sight. PNC Financial Services supports early childhood education with PNC Grow Up Great, a cause brand that incorporates multiple partners such as Head Start, Sesame Workshop and Family Communications."

Cone suggests the following questions when considering cause branding initiatives:

- How can supporting this cause encourage greater interest in my company's products and services?
- Will supporting this cause improve the perception of my company and its products and services?
- Will this cause increase visibility for my company and strengthen our brand?
- Will the cause help us reach new customers?
- Will this cause foster relationships, partnerships, and alliances within our target market?
- Will this cause enhance employee loyalty, morale, and recruiting strategies?

Cone stresses that cause branding initiatives must be led by a company's top management. "Unfortunately, many companies create strategic cause branding programs and hand them over to less experienced executives for execution," says Cone. "A company's senior executives must actively support and champion cause branding programs, both internally and externally. This is how cause branding achieves maximum impact and credibility."

strategic philanthropy makes business sense. Whether it's called altruism, social responsibility, or corporate citizenship, strategic philanthropy provides bottom-line benefits by combining enlightened self-interest with support for social causes.

Strategic philanthropy through cause marketing helps businesses stand out in a crowded marketplace. When companies support social causes, they can boost employee recruitment, morale, and retention, and strengthen relationships with customers, clients, prospects, and vendors. Whether your business is large or small, supporting charitable causes by donating resources, exper-

TIPS FROM THE GURU

Richard Steckel on Putting Authenticity First

Richard Steckel, author of *Making Money While Making a Difference*, believes that strategic philanthropy strengthens a company's brand image by connecting with consumers' personal value systems. Steckel calls this "the halo effect."

"Consumers have a wealth of new products and services to choose from, and it's tougher than ever keeping them loyal," says Steckel. "Consumers are starved for evidence that businesses stand for something meaningful, and look for behavior that reflects those values."

As an example, Steckel notes Big Bill's New York Pizza, a business he has patronized for years, in part because of its strong ties to the local community of Centennial, Colorado. "Bill is a local icon, foremost for his New York style pizza, but equally as a homegrown hero with commitment to the local community, including sponsoring a local baseball team."

"When you go to Big Bill's any time during the year, there's a group of kids having a celebration," says Steckel. "They are connected to Big Bill because he's involved with their team. Their parents are loyal to Big Bill's because they know that he genuinely cares about kids, and the values that sports teach young people."

To be effective, cause marketing must come from the heart in a way that is genuine and creates an emotional bond with others. You have to be sincere. You have to be honest. You have to actually do good, not just do things that make it look like you're doing good.

"Though it's Bill's excellent pizza that gets them in the door, it's his ongoing community involvement that keeps them coming back as lifelong customer evangelists," says Steckel. "Little kids look up to Bill. Parents look up to him and think, 'You're somebody I want my child to emulate.' What businessperson doesn't want to be like that?"

tise, or service is of mutual benefit. Moreover, by embracing a social cause as a central part of your brand identity, you humanize your brand, thus speaking to consumers' desires to do business with ethical companies that care about and invest in issues that make the world a better place.

"Companies face increased competition and commoditization," says Philip Kotler, author of *Corporate Social Responsibility*. "By actively supporting social causes, a company can develop a social track record that distinguishes it from competitors in a crowed marketplace where consumers consider social principles when choosing one company over another."

Cultivating Loyal Customers

Strategic philanthropy attracts customers who share your values, and consumers reward such socially engaged companies with their loyalty. People feel good knowing that some of their money will support social causes. Over the past decade, socially responsible investing has risen more than 258 percent, from $639 billion in 1995 to $2.29 trillion in 2005, according to the Social Investment Forum.

Consumers will pay top dollar for products and services of socially engaged companies. Starbucks, for example, makes contributing to communities and the environment a guiding principle of its mission statement. It practices socially responsible investing and supports youth literacy through its Starbucks Foundation. These social practices build invaluable good will.

Attracting and Retaining Employees

Employees increasingly seek meaning on the job. Cause marketing creates a culture of shared values, contributing to increased retention and high morale, as well as attracting like-minded prospective employees.

According to Business for Social Responsibility, a global resource for the socially responsible business community, a company's commitment to social principles serves as an "organizational touchstone" and a central frame of reference for organization decisions. This strengthens cultural cohesion and social solidarity, even in companies with thousands of employees dispersed across the globe.

Alan E. Lewis is the founder of Grand Circle Corporation, a provider of overseas vacations for Americans over 50. Grand Circle's business model includes a strong commitment to philanthropy, including Grand Circle Foundation, a charitable fund that has donated $25 million to date, equivalent to $10 from every vacation booked.

"Philanthropy should become part of a company's corporate culture," says Lewis, who encourages employees at Grand Circle's 45 international bureaus to volunteer time and participate in philanthropic activities during work hours. The company welcomes feedback about causes employees want the company to support. "This kind of philanthropic commitment helps attract and retain good people."

Cause-Related Partnerships

Cause-related partnerships can involve joint fundraising events, or longer, more complex arrangements. Both partners benefit. The nonprofit acquires needed resources such as donations, volunteers, and heightened visibility; the business partner achieves strategic marketing objectives, such as increased sales and goodwill.

Cause marketing had its beginnings in 1984, when American Express launched its Statue of Liberty Restoration Project, a campaign that raised $2 million to restore the national landmark while garnering considerable exposure and goodwill for American Express. In the wake of this project, sales using the AmEx card rose 28 percent and new AmEx card applications grew 17 percent.

Choosing a Nonprofit Partner

David Hessekiel, founder and president of Cause Marketing Forum, insists that companies must never lose the "marketing focus" of community partnership efforts. "Even though the basis of the relationship is to advance philanthropy, your cause should generate interest in your company and encourage people to buy from you," says Hessekiel. Here are some general principles to follow when applying this advice:

Take Stock What about your business would appeal to a nonprofit partner? If you have a publishing company, consider supporting the public library. If your clients are primarily middle-aged women, think about supporting a relevant cause, like breast cancer research.

Fireman's Fund Insurance Company Offers Help on the Local Level

Fireman's Fund Insurance Company launched Fireman's Fund Heritage in 2004. It provides grants to help pay for needed training and equipment. The program not only helps local fire departments struggling with shrinking budgets and rising equipment costs, it also enhances the company's relationship with its independent agents.

When doing business with Fireman's Fund®, agents build an account that they can allocate to fire departments in their local communities. The grants raise the awareness of Fireman's Fund. They also build exposure for local agents through grant awards ceremonies that are usually held at the local fire station and often attended by prominent members of the community.

The this program, Bolton & Company Insurance, an agency with locations in Pasadena and Oxnard, California, awarded a $25,569 grant to the Pasadena Fire Department. This money bought two new thermal imaging cameras that help firefighters and rescue workers find victims despite smoke and darkness and be able to locate the source of the fire quickly.

Fireman's Fund promotes the program through its website, monthly e-newsletter, and by sponsoring booths at fire-related trade shows across the country, where the company encourages fire departments to complete a survey about their specific funding needs. The company uses the information to connect agents to resource-strapped departments in their communities.

Since the program's inception, Fireman's Fund Heritage has donated more than $12 million to over 450 different departments and organizations nationwide.

Cadence Network is an expense management firm serving the banking, restaurant, retail, and grocery industries. For years, the company has led an energy consumption initiative to preserve finite natural resources such as water and recyclable waste. In these efforts, it partners with The Arbor Day Foundation. "We chose to work with The Arbor Day Foundation because it aligns with our business, including natural resource conservation and paper reduction," says Jeffrey Hart, Cadence Network CEO.

Think Local "Supporting local schools when your business serves young parents is more likely to boost enthusiasm within your target market," says Hessekiel. "The more you localize your initiatives, the more relevant they become, and the more impact they'll have on members of your target market."

Johnny "Love" Metheny is a Slightly famous nightclub owner in San Francisco with a string of local ventures to his name. Whenever he opens a new club, he shares the limelight with a local charity. "I have a history of including the Leukemia and Lymphoma Society in my grand openings," notes Metheny. Beyond these events, Metheny volunteers time to the cause, serves on its board, and was voted Man of the Year by the Leukemia and Lymphoma Society in 1991. So, while it is beneficial to his business, his association with the organization is more than just a marketing ploy, and is rooted in the local community he serves.

Pick Wisely and Realistically Before partnering with a charity, get to know the people you'll work with, and get a feel for what they can deliver. "Just as most business executives are not expert at solving societal problems, most nonprofit executives are not world-class marketers. Don't expect them to run your program," says Hessekiel.

Establish Measurable Goals Up Front Establish agreed-upon, realistic goals at the outset and measure how well you achieve them. Put them down on paper and refer to them as you implement and evaluate the program.

Get the Word Out Your cause-related promotion campaign needs just as much promotional support as any other marketing initiative, and you must take steps to ensure that your target market knows about your efforts. As your partnership takes shape, become ambassadors for one another. Talk about your charitable partner, have flyers available, promote the organization (and your partnership) on your website. Ask your partner to do the same.

Donating Cash, Products and Services

Donating money to nonprofits is a common way of supporting a social cause while helping nonprofits generate required resources. Shorewood Realtors, the largest independent realtor in Los Angeles County, has pledged a percentage of its profits in perpetuity to the Manhattan Beach Unified School District, a highly rated school district and one of the top reasons families want to buy houses and live in that community.

If you're short on cash, consider in-kind donations of products, services, and inventory. You may be able to put unsold or excess inventory to productive use, and in-kind goods donations are tax-deductible at the fair market value of the donated items. Each year, for instance, McSwain Carpet & Floors donates inventory items to a range of organizations that offer pre–school education, job training, and housing in the inner cities of Ohio and Northern Kentucky.

Organizing Charitable Events

Charitable fundraisers, such as food drives, auctions, and holiday parties generate an immense amount of goodwill and publicity for their business sponsors while raising money for a good cause.

New Belgium Brewing, makers of the acclaimed Fat Tire Ale, hosts the Tour de Fat, which it deems a "philanthropic cycling circus" that marries sustainability, playfulness, and beer. A signature event that takes place each year in select cities where New Belgium products are sold, the Tour de Fat is part bike rodeo and part circus, where participants enjoy fire-jumping bike acts, cycling games, a bike parade, and live music. Costumes and decorated bikes reign supreme. Admission to the event is free, with all profits from beer sales going to local nonprofit organizations. New Belgium has held this "whimsical ballyhoo of the bike and beer" over 70 times across the Western U.S. and raised over a half million dollars for bike-related activism.

"We created this event in 1999 because it aligns with our company-wide commitment to environmental sustainability," says event evangelist Chris Winn. "We believe the bike is truly one of the mankind's most sustainable inventions. Our belief, which goes to the core of our brand identity, is that sustainable living should be a celebration, not a compromise. Tour de Fat has reached a lot of people about the simple joy of riding a bike, all the while sharing our message."

REAL-WORLD SUCCESS STORY

Mark McMahon Becomes Famous for Charitable Work

Cosmetic dentist Mark McMahon made himself a media mini-celebrity with a thriving practice due in part to his high-profile pro bono work in his community, a strategy that landed him radio and TV appearances in areas where he worked.

McMahon established partnerships with local charities, including a homeless shelter and a shelter for battered women, and offered free dental services to their members. Before each event, he contacted local media and let them know what he was up to. Several TV crews showed up, filmed him treating patients, and later aired the segments on the evening news.

"These events were surprisingly easy to arrange, and every year, they'd help us get press simply by doing these charitable promotions," McMahon says. "Local television news stations loved the emotional element. And it was obviously rewarding to see patients after we'd treated them who'd been in pain for months talking about how glad they were to be relieved of their toothaches."

Another project involved the Delancey Street Foundation, a residential educa-

Pro Bono Work

When Eunice Azzani, an executive recruiter, volunteered to serve on the board of the San Francisco AIDS Foundation, she didn't anticipate that it would connect her with executives from Mervyn's, Bank of America, and Wells Fargo Bank, all of whom eventually hired her to work for them.

tion center for former substance abusers and ex-convicts. "I agreed to treat some of their members' acute dental needs," McMahon says. "I quickly appreciated the media appeal of transforming the appearance of these rough-looking guys."

McMahon captured the event with before and after photos. "These guys had missing teeth and terrible smiles," he says. "So I had a professional photographer capture before pictures of these guys in street clothes with their snarling faces. After I fixed their teeth, we took more pictures, but this time dressed the guys in suits and ties, now looking like lawyers and accountants, with me sitting right in the middle. The media loved it, and it was great seeing these men looking like new."

McMahon's TV appearances created name recognition. "After I did the story on a local television show, I was recognized in my gym by a masseuse who had seen the show," McMahon recalls. "She said, 'I was thinking about you this morning while I was flossing my teeth.' She became a great source of referrals."

"People don't hire a piece of paper or a process. They hire people they trust," Azzani says. "Volunteering for a position at a local organization makes you very trustworthy." She advises business owners to target causes they believe in. "If you're helping with a cause you believe in, people will see that you care. And they'll realize you will probably care as much about your work."

TIPS FROM THE GURU

Chip Conley and Eric Friedenwald-Fishman on Putting Your Influence to Good Use

The following tips have been adapted from *Marketing That Matters: 10 Practices to Profit Your Business and Change the World* by Chip Conley and Eric Frieden-wald-Fishman (Berrett-Koehler Publishers).

Look for opportunities to advance social causes by leveraging direct relationships with employees, customers, strategic partners, and suppliers. By using your company's access to the mind/time share of your target market, your marketing can be harnessed to express a social cause through your online presence, advertising, public relations, and direct mail. Consider your billing, in-store signs, and other communications as vehicles to provide your customers with opportunities to directly impact issues.

Stoneyfield Farms looked at its yogurt container lids as an untapped opportunity for empowering its customers to help advance a more sustainable environment. Through Stoneyfield's Lid Program, the company puts messages about environmental and sustainable agriculture on every yogurt container lid, educating its customers and often giving them the opportunity to impact the issue via the Web.

Design your core product or service as a social change tool. For example, when Shorebank makes a loan or accepts a mission-based deposit, it uses traditional financing services to advance its customer's community vision to reinvigorate neighborhoods and improve the environment. Customers who buy certificates of deposit direct their deposits to the improvement of urban neighborhoods and resource-dependent rural communities.

Take a stand. Whether communicating with your customers and employees, demanding responsible practices from your suppliers, or using your influence within your industry or trade associations—your company can take advantage of many platforms to lead your business and industry in support of a social cause.

Clif Bar challenged the industry norm of not using recycled content in catalogues by testing batches of catalogues with various percentages of recycled content, then shared the results with executives by presenting the company's proprietary findings at catalogue industry conferences. Other companies were encouraged to follow its lead.

REAL-WORLD SUCCESS STORY

Michael W. Peterson Reaps the Joy of Helping

Michael W. Peterson, a financial planner in Chambersburg, Pennsylvania, donates pro-bono work two to three hours a month to give something back to the community where he grew up. "I've taught college planning seminars, and offered sessions on financial planning at our local library," says Peterson. "Does it help my image? Absolutely! Pro-bono work has been a great source of networking in my community, connecting me with great people, such as nonprofit board members who are prospective clients."

Pro-bono work also delivers emotional rewards, says Peterson, who recalls a free seminar where a single parent approached him to talk about her daughter's college financing challenges. "Although this woman's daughter had very good grades, the parents had limited her college choices to a local state school because of their low family income," says Peterson. "I saw this as huge mistake, sat them down, and showed the mother how her daughter was eligible for a ton of financial aid."

Peterson's advice helped the family get their daughter into American University in Washington, D.C. "Their daughter wanted to major in international business, but they'd scratched one of the top schools off their list because of the cost. It felt great helping them find a way to put that school on their list, and her daughter got her dream back."

The Socially Responsible CEO

According to Chuck Ames, a former partner at consulting firm McKinsey & Company, it is every CEO's "number one" responsibility to set a company's ethical practices.

A recent *Business Week* story titled "Beyond The Green Corporation" profiled several companies now embracing socially oriented business practices. These included giants such as General Electric, which has invested billions in wind power and hybrid engines, and Wal-Mart Stores Inc., which has pledged to slash energy use and purchase electricity derived from renewable sources.

EXECUTIVE BRANDING

Marc Benioff Weaves Philanthropy into Salesforce.com

The following account is drawn from *The Business of the Changing World: Twenty Great Leaders on Strategic Corporate Philanthropy*, by Marc Benioff and Carlye Adler (McGraw-Hill) and other sources.

From the start, philanthropy was woven into the DNA of my company, salesforce.com. It was 1997, and I realized that American companies weren't doing enough for their communities; I was spending about $100 million on corporate philanthropic programs.

At the time, I was an executive at Oracle when CEO Larry Ellison tapped me to start the company's first major philanthropic initiative. We donated thousands of computers to underserved schools, but our small team felt like the effort fell short of leveraging Oracle's full philanthropic potential.

I realized that philanthropy was about more than writing a check; if we had been able to draw on Oracle's full assets—its employees, its customers, its partner—we could have made a much bigger contribution. That was a defining moment that helped inspire my belief in "integrated philanthropy." To be truly successful, corporate philanthropic programs must be woven into the fabric of the organization. The easiest way to do that? Start from the beginning.

The concept that I like the most, and the one that I've taken most to heart, is the belief that people can't be united or focused unless they share a common philosophy—a philosophy that gives their effort a greater meaning. I've seen how important this concept is in business. Shortly after we started Salesforce.com in 1999, we launched the Salesforce Foundation with 1 percent of the company's

Patrick Cescau, CEO of Unilever, a company that owns many global consumer product brands, exemplifies the new socially engaged executive. In Brazil, Unilever operates a free community laundry in a São Paulo slum, provides financing to help tomato growers convert to eco-friendly drip irrigation, stock. As chief executive, I made a commitment to donate 1 percent of company profits to the community (through product donations) and 1 percent of employee working hours to community service.

The 1-1-1 model—equity, profits, and employee time—ensured that as our business grew, so would our contribution to the community. By leveraging the energy of our entire ecosystem, we have been able to make contributions that have exceeded expectations. A great deal can be achieved through product donations. More than 1,000 nonprofits--including United Way, the Red Cross, and the Elizabeth Glaser Pediatric AIDS Foundation—use us to manage their nonprofit programs. We have created more than 60 technology centers and media programs with schools and non-government organizations in 12 countries, including Kenya, Israel, Japan, Ireland, and Singapore.

To be truly successful, companies need to have a corporate mission that is bigger than making a profit. By integrating philanthropy into our business model, our employees feel that they do much more than just work at our company. People are here to do more than just make money--they want to make the world a better place. This explains why our biggest contributor is our workforce. About 85 percent of Salesforce.com's employees are active in philanthropy, so far contributing over 30,000 hours volunteering in the community; our success would not be possible without their desire to contribute and their generous spirit.

Google recently followed Salesforce.com's lead and put 1 percent of its equity aside. What if this were done on an even more massive scale? If embraced by others, this could lead to what *Fortune's* David Kirkpatrick called "the end of philanthropy" and prove the power of the integrated model. By sharing a common and important mission, we are united and focused, and have found a secret weapon that ensures we always win. It's my hope that integrating philanthropy into business isn't a lofty idea, but the secret weapon for twenty-first century companies to achieve success.

and recycles 17 tons of waste annually at a toothpaste factory. In Bangladesh, a nation with just 20 doctors for every 10,000 people, the company funds a floating hospital that offers free medical care. In India, the Unilever staff has helped thousands of women in remote villages start micro-enterprises.

REAL-WORLD SUCCESS STORY

Gilden Tree Discovers That People Want to Hear About the Good They Are Doing

Gilden Tree produces a line of spa products that are carried by up-scale retailers and salons. Though headquartered in the American heartland of Omaha, Nebraska, the company has brought big changes to a small village in rural Pakistan and offers hope to local women mired in poverty.

While shopping in a local market in her husband Kumy's native Pakistan, Ann Thariani discovered jahwaan, a handcrafted terracotta tool, like a pumice stone, that was used to remove dry skin and calluses from feet. When the Tharianis returned to the U.S. and founded Gilden Tree, they started their business with the Footscrubber®, their branded version of the jahwaan.

Seventeen years later, they are selling 100,000 units per year. Gilden Tree employs a group of village women who hand-produce the product. The Tharianis explain, "Within a couple of years, it became clear to us that the Footscrubber had struck a chord here in the U.S., and we wanted to give something back to thank these women for their amazing work. We began to pay for the education of their children, and later for the women themselves.

As Cescau sees it, helping such nations overcome poverty, water scarcity, and the effects of climate change is vital to staying competitive in coming decades. "You can't ignore the impact your company has on the community and environment," Cescau says. CEOs used to frame thoughts like these in the context of moral responsibility, he adds. But now, "It's also about growth and innovation. In the future, this will be the only way to do business." As with any important company initiative, executives act as chief spokespeople

"The impact on the women's lives has been dramatic," says Ann Thariani. "There's a real change in the power of families once a woman can earn money. Our business gave them disposable income for the first time."

Although the company kept a low profile about their social efforts, they decided to incorporate their social mission into their marketing in 2003. "The response has been pretty extraordinary," says Ann. "We were featured in TIME magazine as well as other national publications because of our focus on giving something back."

Today, Gilden Tree pays the education costs for their Pakistani employees' children and arranges tutoring for the women. During a subsequent visit of the Tharianis to Pakistan, a worker commented with a smile, "Oh, that daughter of mine –she's always got her nose in a book!" It was a defining moment, one of which the Tharianis are very proud. The seemingly impossible had become possible.

"Our social commitment is very emotionally rewarding. By building educated families among our workforce, we are not only doing performing a social good, but we are also gaining dividends for our company— we cultivate happy employees, which has virtually eliminated quality control problems because we have such loyal employees."

and educators to send the message that their company is serious about its philanthropy projects.

Social Entrepreneurship

Founded with the aim of helping individuals on the margins of society—the homeless, ex-offenders, and people recovering from chemical dependencies—Pioneer Human Services in Seattle, Washington, has provided hous-

EXECUTIVE BRANDING

Ray Anderson Calls Himself "The Greenest CEO in America"

Ray Anderson wants to inspire the business world to see that doing the right thing is a smart thing. As founder and chairman of Interface Inc., a Georgia-based manufacturer of free-lay carpeting, which he founded in 1973, Anderson is a widely acknowledged thought leader in the green business movement.

It wasn't always so. Anderson is a reformed "plunderer of the earth" (his words) who for the past decade has been trying to make amends for the environmental damage wrought by his earlier company. Anderson once said of his former, environmentally insensitive self, "Some day, people like me may be put in jail."

Anderson's environmental epiphany came after reading the 1993 book, *The Ecology of Commerce*, written by entrepreneur Paul Hawken. It chronicles the decline of the natural world, and posits that business and industry are the only entities pervasive and powerful enough to reverse that decline. Anderson made a commitment to make Interface 100 percent environmentally sustainable, with a lifetime goal of becoming the most successful carpet maker that never takes another drop of oil from the earth.

Interface is more than one-third of the way toward achieving its goal of 100 percent sustainability by 2020—a mountainous challenge, because the carpet making industry is so petroleum-intensive. One innovation involves using 100

ing, employment training, treatment, and counseling to more than 100,000 people since 1963.

The unique feature of this "social enterprise" is that it earns 99 percent of its income through business ventures, including retail cafés, institutional food services, aerospace precision machining, and contract packaging and fulfillment.

Pioneer is part of the growing trend of social entrepreneurship that combines the pragmatic, results-oriented methods of entrepreneurial business

percent post-consumer plastic soda bottles as raw material for Interface's petro-
leum-based polyester commercial fabric products. Similarly, Interface sources
renewable materials for many of its products, for example using a fiber derived
from corn to make carpet tiles.

The Center for Ethics estimated that the cumulative savings derived from
Interface's sustainability efforts since 1995 are in excess of $335 million. At the
same time, Anderson is convinced that his company's environmental efforts
have made Interface stronger financially.

Anderson now evangelizes sustainability to other business leaders, hoping
to convince corporate executives to give environmental stewardship the same
priority as the share price. He articulated his views on sustainable capitalism in
his 1998 book, *Mid-Course Correction: Toward a Sustainable Enterprise: The
Interface Model*.

Anderson gets his message out through a wide range of charitable and foundation activities, including the Alliance to Save Energy, which he funded. He has
also served on the President's Council on Sustainable Development. Anderson is
always available for interviews and public speaking engagements, and has given
over 1,000 talks on environmental topics since 1994.

"Business and industry...have to change, or we will take the world down
with us," Anderson once told an interviewer from *U.S. News & World Report*. He
believes that his evangelism, combined with Interface's visible examples of successful sustainability, are part of a growing effort to gradually change the minds
of American leaders. The idea is that they will see that sustainability is consistent
with achieving profits.

with the goals of social reform. Social enterprises seek financial self-suffi-
ciency through commercial activities that cover operating costs and generate
profits that are reinvested back into the organization.

Tom White, publisher of *Social Enterprise Reporter*, describes the social
enterprise landscape. "Most businesses already spend money on janitors,
document shredding and imaging, landscaping, catering, shipping services,
or fresh coffee beans, so why not work with social enterprises to meet those

needs? Nonprofit social entrepreneurs can make great partners. As a business, you get a competitively priced product or service that also helps solve social and economic problems in your community." Nevertheless, he advises businesses to "evaluate potential social entrepreneur vendors on their business capabilities." He concludes, "The fact that they address social problems is an added benefit, but not the main reason you should choose them as a vendor."

Cause Marketing Goes Global

We live in a global economy. As consumers increasingly buy products from all over the world and travel to other countries, and as more companies employ a global workforce and serve a global customer base, global philanthropy helps companies earn a positive reputation at home and abroad, while bringing less fortunate areas of the world much-needed help and resources.

Cisco Systems launched its Least Developed Countries (LDC) Initiative to bridge the digital divide by providing training for building and maintaining an Internet infrastructure. With a presence in more than 150 countries, the initiative helps developing countries integrate into the world economy, and helps Cisco gain contracts with governments in third-world countries.

INDEX

ABOUT THE AUTHOR

Steven Van Yoder is a recognized expert on public relations, executive branding, and thought leadership marketing. His work has appeared in more than 200 publications, including *Entrepreneur, Inc, American Executive,* the *Washington Post, PR Week, Financial Executive, Home Office Computing, Costco Connection, Industry Week, Brand Marketing,* and dozens of trade, business, and consumer publications. He speaks regularly to business groups, and his insights about marketing, branding, and thought leadership marketing appear on hundreds of websites.

Get the Word Out Communications, his San Francisco-based marketing, branding, and public relations firm, has helped hundreds of companies become recognized authorities in their industries, reach their best customers, and develop a unique brand identity to attract more business with less effort. Drawing from years of experience as a working journalist, Yoder harnesses both traditional and online media to help companies become recognized leaders in their industries.

He is a graduate of Miami University. A former co-chair of the San Francisco Chamber of Commerce's Market Success Series, he is also a graduate of the San Francisco Renaissance Entrepreneurship Program. He is a member of the Institute of Management Consultants, The American Society of Journalists and Authors, and president of Rotary Club of San Francisco Golden Gate.

Van Yoder is a dedicated social entrepreneur, and is founder and director of Global Initiative to Advance Entrepreneurship (www.givefoundationonline.com). Steven is using his expertise in cause-related marketing to assemble an alliance of business and nonprofit partners around the goal of alleviating poverty in the U.S. and abroad. He plans to spend the coming years forging alliances within the social and business sectors for initiating and promoting global poverty projects and teaching global entrepreneurship.

Steven Van Yoder is based in San Francisco, and can be reached at steven@getslightlyfamous.com.